BRADY VS MANNING

Also by Gary Myers

Coaching Confidential
The Catch

BRADY vs MANNING

THE UNTOLD STORY OF THE RIVALRY THAT
TRANSFORMED THE NFL

GARY MYERS

CROWN
ARCHETYPE
NEW YORK

Published in the United States by Crown Archetype, an imprint of the Crown Publishing Group,
a division of Penguin Random House LLC, New York.
www.crownpublishing.com

Crown Archetype and colophon is a registered trademark of Penguin Random House LLC.

Library of Congress Cataloging-in-Publication data is available upon request.

ISBN 978-0-8041-3937-3
eBook ISBN 978-0-8041-3938-0

Printed in the United States of America

Book design: Patrice Sheridan
Jacket design: Christopher Brand
Jacket/frontispiece photograph: Winslow Townson / Getty Images

9 10 8

First Edition

To Allison, Michelle, Emily, and Andrew

CONTENTS

INTRODUCTION

Tom Brady was warming up at the old Foxboro Stadium prior to the first start of his career. It was the third game of the 2001 season, and the New England Patriots were already desperate. They had lost their first two games to the Cincinnati Bengals and New York Jets, they had just lost starting quarterback Drew Bledsoe with a sheared blood vessel in his chest that nearly killed him, and head coach Bill Belichick feared owner Robert Kraft was going to fire him even though it was only his second year in New England.

The Patriots were playing the Indianapolis Colts and their young superstar Peyton Manning, who was in his fourth season and already established as one of the best quarterbacks in the NFL.

Brady was a forgotten sixth-round pick in 2000. He'd thrown just three passes as a rookie but had played the final series after Bledsoe was hurt against the Jets and threw ten passes in the loss. Now all the pressure of the season was on him. If it had been put to a vote right then whether, thirteen years later, either Manning or Brady would have won four Super Bowls and three Super Bowl MVPs, Manning would have been a landslide winner, carrying all six New England states, especially the great state of Massachusetts.

Brady had fought for every snap he received at the University of Michigan and had overcome the indignity of having 198 players, including 6 quarterbacks, taken ahead of him before the Patriots wrote his name on the draft card that is displayed in the

Pro Football Hall of Fame in Canton, Ohio. Now, however, with Bledsoe out indefinitely, the Patriots starting job belonged to him.

The greatest rivalry in National Football League history began with a pregame introduction that was hardly necessary.

"Hey, Tom," a player wearing the Colts white jersey number 18 said, extending his hand.

Brady looked up. The player introduced himself.

"Peyton," he said to Brady.

Of course, Brady knew who he was. Everybody knew Peyton Manning. He was the number-one overall pick in the 1998 draft. He was the new fresh face of the league, with Dan Marino and John Elway nearing the end of their careers. Brady was impressed that Manning knew his name.

Brady smiled, but resisted saying what was going through his mind: *No shit. I know who you are.*

"That's funny," Manning said when the story was relayed to him years later.

"It was a very polite thing for him to do, especially being on our field," Brady said. "That really speaks to his character. He always does the right thing, says the right thing, acts the right way."

Manning learned from his father, Archie, to introduce himself even when he thinks the person knows who he is. "It's a Southern thing," Archie said. That's how he does it. That's what he taught his three sons.

"I like when people introduce themselves to me, because I meet a lot of people. So it helps," Peyton Manning said. "I don't assume anybody knows who I am automatically."

That was the start of an intense rivalry and a terrific friendship. Brady vs. Manning. Manning vs. Brady. Regardless of who comes first, they have been magic—like Magic vs. Bird.

Brady won that first meeting by 31 points over a Colts team that Manning, who had two interceptions returned for touchdowns in the game, said was "pretty terrible." Since then, Brady vs. Manning has been the most compelling matchup in the NFL. Through the 2014 season, they faced each other 16 times. It's Brady 11–5, including 2–2 in the playoffs. Brady won the first two postseason matchups, including one AFC championship game when Manning played for the Colts. Manning won the next two, an AFC championship game with the Colts and another one in his second season with the Broncos in 2013.

The argument has been going on for more than a decade in stadiums, living rooms, luxury boxes, sports bars, fantasy leagues, and wherever they have high-definition televisions: Who is better, Brady or Manning?

The red, white, and blue confetti, the Patriots colors, coming down on Brady for the fourth time in his illustrious career after the Patriots beat the Seahawks in Super Bowl XLIX in Phoenix provides one answer. Brady leads Manning in Super Bowl victories 4–1. He leads him in Super Bowl appearances, 6–3. But he's also had the benefit of playing his entire career for Belichick, arguably the greatest coach since Vince Lombardi. Manning played for Jim Mora, Tony Dungy, and Jim Caldwell in Indianapolis, then three years for John Fox in Denver, and then for Gary Kubiak, who took over the Broncos in 2015. None of Manning's coaches approach Belichick in stature.

Who has been the better quarterback? Manning is the greatest regular-season player, not just quarterback, in the history of the NFL. You want Manning in the regular season. You don't lose much by taking Brady, but you definitely want Brady in January and on the first Sunday in February. By the time Brady picked up his fourth ring, he was 21–8 in the playoffs with the best postseason winning percentage in league history. Manning was just 11–13.

When Brady won his first Super Bowl, he was the youngest quarterback to hold the trophy. When he won his fourth Super

Bowl, he was the fourth-oldest quarterback to win it all. He has stood the test of time. The thirteen-year period between his first and latest Super Bowl victories is the longest sustained run of excellence of any quarterback in NFL history. The ten-year gap between his third and fourth titles is also the longest for any quarterback. Brady won the first nine playoff games of his career, resulting in three Super Bowl titles.

Manning holds the NFL records for touchdown passes in a season and career and for most passing yards in a season, and he'll likely finish with the most passing yards in a career and most victories by a quarterback. Manning's career numbers blow away Brady's. He has won a record five Most Valuable Player awards. Jim Brown, Johnny Unitas, and Brett Favre are next with three. Brady has two. But . . . Brady has all those rings.

Sports is all about great rivalries. The gold standards: Manning vs. Brady. Ali vs. Frazier. Magic vs. Bird. Palmer vs. Nicklaus. Wilt vs. Russell.

The Manning-Brady rivalry doesn't have the sociological implications of Magic and Bird, of course, and they are never on the field at the same time, but their greatness and popularity transcend the ultimate team sport. Manning was number two in jersey sales and Brady was number four in 2014, impressive when by now they've been around long enough that anybody who wants their jersey has already purchased it. They have played four elimination games against each other. Their rivalry defines an entire era of the NFL. Brady's most recent title tied him with Terry Bradshaw and Joe Montana for the most Super Bowl victories by a quarterback, and jumped him over Montana as the greatest quarterback in NFL history. Manning has had more heartache than happiness in the postseason. The Broncos' loss in the divisional round of the playoffs to the Colts following the 2014 season was the ninth time his team was eliminated in its first playoff game, the most one-

and-dones ever for a quarterback and the sixth time he had lost a home playoff game. Brady has been one-and-done twice in his career and lost three home playoff games.

Their battles have been epic. The television ratings are astronomical. BradyManning has morphed into one word.

"I don't think there would be Tom who he is now if there wasn't Peyton and the Colts," said Tedy Bruschi, the former Patriots linebacker. "It just goes hand in hand. Manning-Brady. What if they were in different eras and didn't have each other to push each other against their respective teams? That's the finals. That's Bird-Magic. That's what everybody wants to see. That's classic football, a matchup you remember where you were when you saw certain playoff games or when it started snowing or the three interceptions by Ty Law or Peyton Manning finally winning his. I remember all that stuff. A lot of the best memories I have playing for the Patriots involved the Colts, involve Manning."

Dan Marino and John Elway were two of the best quarterbacks to ever play at the same time. They came into the NFL together in 1983 and their careers are often compared. But Brady was shocked when told that Elway and Marino played against each other just three times before Elway retired following the 1998 season. Two of the games were played in Elway's final year, including the only time they met in the playoffs. "How is that possible?" Brady asked.

That's what has made the Brady vs. Manning rivalry so special. They faced each other at least once every season except when Brady was hurt in 2008 and Manning was hurt in 2011. They competed twice in the same season four times.

Brady is driving from Foxboro to downtown Boston on a frigid November day in his black Lexus. I am in the passenger seat. He has just finished practice and a meeting prior to a Monday night game in Carolina in 2013, which the Patriots would lose and in which Brady would trail an official coming off the field, unloading a few F-bombs about a bad noncall in the end zone that cost the Patriots the game. Brady may have the look of a choirboy, but he's a cold-blooded killer on the field. Toward the end of a 2014 loss in Green Bay, when a pass by Aaron Rodgers picked up a key first down allowing the Packers to run out the clock and deprive Brady of one last chance to win the game, America became aware of the fire and passion that drive him.

"Fuck! Fuck! Fuck!" Brady could be seen yelling as he paced the sidelines.

That was not out of character for Brady, the league's best undercover trash-talker. "I couldn't watch all of the game. I was offended by the language I saw," joked then Jets coach Rex Ryan, who himself set a modern-day television record for F-bombs when the Jets appeared on *Hard Knocks* in 2010.

I am explaining the concept of *this book* to Brady on the way into Boston as he makes the nearly hour-long drive to the apartment he's living in with his Brazilian supermodel wife Gisele Bundchen and their two children while his mansion in Brookline is under construction. I'm asking the questions, and he's answering them with a lot of thought and depth, taking his eyes off the road only at a red light or when traffic comes to a stop.

He likes the idea. He likes Manning. They are very good friends. Tom's father, Tom Brady Sr., and Archie text on Mondays during the season to ask each other about their sons and, as Tom Sr. says, "to let each other know the kids are all right." Surprisingly, after all these years, they have never met in person but feel connected through their quarterback sons.

Brady and Manning are only a year apart, the two oldest starting quarterbacks in a league that caters to the young. They have gone through many of the same experiences in the NFL. They can relate to each other. "It's been pretty cool," Brady said. "It's a pretty special rivalry."

Peyton has his younger brother Eli to share notes with, but Brady is the only other quarterback in his inner circle. At times, Brady has looked at Peyton as the older brother he never had, growing up in a house with three older sisters.

When Brady missed almost the entire 2008 season after tearing the anterior cruciate ligament (ACL) in his left knee in the first quarter of the season opener when Chiefs safety Bernard Pollard rolled into him, Manning supported him with encouraging text messages and phone calls. "I think you find out during those times who's with you," Manning said. "Everybody wants to talk to you when you're playing well, throwing touchdowns. Going through a tough time, being injured, people kind of look at you funny. You kind of reach out to Tom, tell him good luck, check in on him. When I got injured, it was the same deal. He had the same chance to do that for me. It does mean something."

When Manning missed the entire 2011 season following his fourth neck surgery, Brady was in frequent communication. "It's nice to have a peer you can really rely on and you know is completely trustworthy," Brady said. "That's the kind of relationship we have. It's nice to have people like that. I think it's been a natural thing for us."

Their absence added another layer to the argument about who was better. The Patriots still had an excellent season in 2008, an 11–5 record with backup Matt Cassel, but lost the division to the Dolphins on a tiebreaker and a wild-card spot to the Ravens on a tiebreaker. Yet when Manning was sidelined three years later, the Colts bottomed out at 2–14.

Did that prove that Manning was better or more valuable? It proved that Belichick had a better backup in Cassel and a better team around him than Caldwell had with backups Kerry Collins,

Curtis Painter, and Dan Orlovsky and the team that future Hall of Famer Bill Polian had constructed around them.

Would Brady have been Brady and Manning been Manning if they hadn't had each other?

"One isn't bigger without the other. Tom completes Peyton and Peyton completes Tom," said Dallas Clark, who played tight end for the Colts from 2003 to 2011. "It makes their legacy in the NFL that much greater by having one another and having the battles they had as individuals and with their teams. It's taken their level of recognition, taken their impact on this game, to a whole other level. What better sell is there than Manning vs. Brady? You just say that and television ratings are shooting through the roof. It was a battle. It was a grind."

Rodney Harrison, one of the hardest-hitting safeties to play in the NFL, began his career with the Chargers in 1994 and played nine years in San Diego. He joined the Patriots in 2003 and spent the final six years of his career in New England playing with Brady and against Manning.

"Let me tell you something: I'm so thankful to have played in this era," Harrison said. "Sometimes people can look and say I played at the wrong time because of the contracts and the type of money. But to be able to witness two of the greatest quarterbacks ever to play the game, to have the professionalism, the mutual respect that they have for one another, it's tremendous. I'll be able to tell my kids exactly what I witnessed. I played against Tom. I played against Peyton. I just shake my head because people don't understand the greatness and consistency over so many years and what they've been able to accomplish." Brady has often been compared to Derek Jeter, the former New York Yankees shortstop, for both his demeanor and his accomplishments. I mentioned to Brady in the midst of his ten-year drought between Super Bowl titles that Jeter won his fourth World Series in 2000 and his fifth and final in 2009, with two World Series losses in between. Brady also lost two Super Bowls between his third and fourth titles.

"It's not like you are going to win six or seven Super Bowls," he said. "Why didn't Michael Jordan win twelve championships? He won six. That's still a ton. With how good the other players are, the level playing field, especially in the NFL in the salary-cap era, it's hard to win."

I suggest to Brady that he and Peyton are the Bird and Magic of the NFL. He doesn't ask which is which. If he did, I would say Manning is Bird—he can slice up a defense with his brains, precision passes, anticipation, and instincts. Brady is Magic, just as much a student of the game as Manning and Bird and Magic, but like Magic, he is more explosive, exciting, creative, spectacular, more volatile. Bird is from Indiana. Manning played most of his career in Indianapolis. Brady is from California. Johnson played his entire career in Los Angeles.

Magic vs. Bird. Brady vs. Manning.

"I definitely think that's a flattering thing," Brady said. "I think so highly of them. So when people say you guys are comparable, that's very flattering. It's not why we play the game. It's not what motivates me. It's not about my legacy. I couldn't care less about that. I just want to win. That's what makes me feel the best. My days are committed to that."

I am meeting with Manning at the Broncos practice facility in Dove Valley outside downtown Denver after a June organized team-activity day. He is friendly and accommodating as usual, and as every reporter who has dealt with him over the years knows, he never forgets your name. I met him for the first time the day before he was drafted in 1998, when the NFL used to bring six players to New York and invite the media to join them on a cruise ship for a ride around the island of Manhattan with the opportunity to interview the players. The ride would last two hours, but the work was done in forty-five minutes. At that point, the players, media, agents, and league officials along for the ride wanted to get off the boat and go about their business, but there's not much to be done when you are in the middle of the Hudson River with the captain enthusiastically pointing out the Statue of Liberty.

Manning had been told in confidence by the Colts one day earlier they would take him over Ryan Leaf, but with the draft beginning in less than twenty-four hours, that preference was still supposed to be a secret. Even Leaf didn't know. Although San Diego, which was picking second, would be considered by most to be a more desirable city than Indianapolis, Manning was focused on the Colts.

He wanted to be the first pick in the draft. His father, Archie, had been the number-two overall pick in 1971 by the Saints, one spot after New England selected Jim Plunkett. Besides, Polian had recently been hired to run the Colts; he had helped build four Super Bowl teams in Buffalo and had put together the expansion Carolina Panthers, who made it to the NFC championship game in just their second season. San Diego's GM was Bobby Beathard, who'd done his best work when he'd had Joe Gibbs as his coach in Washington. Neither the Colts nor the Chargers were any good, but Manning would have been insulted to be selected behind Leaf. He even promised Polian, if he drafted him, "We will win a championship. And if you don't, I promise I will come back and kick your ass." Brady still had one year left to play at Michigan on the day the Colts turned their franchise around by selecting Manning.

Peyton likes Brady very much. They've played golf together. They've had dinner together. Their wives have spent time together. Manning's brother Eli has defeated Brady twice in the Super Bowl. The Manning brothers have defeated Brady four times in the playoffs.

I also outline the book project, *Brady vs Manning,* to Peyton. He's into it.

What does he think about the Magic vs. Bird comparison?

"It's hard to compare football to basketball. In basketball, you're guarding each other, playing offense and defense at the same time," he said. "I have great respect for Tom and I knew I was going to have to try to play well in order to beat the Patriots because they were going to be extremely tough to play; they were extremely well coached, and Brady was their quarterback. You always knew that was a challenge."

The NFL has been an ATM without limits for a long time now, but the emergence of the Manning-Brady rivalry coincided with a tremendous growth spurt in the league. Robert Kraft bought the Patriots for $172 million in 1994, saving the ragtag franchise from moving to Saint Louis. Twenty years later, they were valued by *Forbes* at $2.6 billion, second behind the Dallas Cowboys at $3.2 billion, and Kraft's net worth was listed at $4.3 billion by *Forbes* in 2015.

Manning vs. Brady raised the visibility and marketability of the entire NFL brand and made owners throughout the league even richer, helping revenues expand to $10 billion annually by 2014. They have been the two faces of the league during the period when its popularity exploded worldwide. "The rivalry has been great for the fans and for the game of football," NFL commissioner Roger Goodell said. "Not only are they great performers, but it's almost what they do off the field that distinguishes them as even more special. They are leaders, they're maybe the hardest-working individual players, nobody outworks them, they prepare like nobody else. They are humble in the sense that they recognize the value of the team. They want their teams to take the same approach to the game of football. They are great ambassadors of the game because they love the game. You can't ask for two better guys."

Manning is wildly popular, not only in Indianapolis and Denver but around the country. Madison Avenue has capitalized on his appeal with all his commercials, ranging from pizza to automobiles to credit cards. Brady is beloved in Boston and is a civic treasure along with Bill Russell, Larry Bird, Bobby Orr, Carl Yastrzemski, and Big Papi. Outside their home areas, Brady stirs up more negative feelings than Manning. Why? He is resented for his tremendous success, his good looks, and his supermodel wife—and his connection to Bill Belichick.

Brady steered away from any negative headlines on or off the field for nearly all of the first fifteen years of his career—until the Indianapolis Colts alerted the NFL prior to the AFC championship game on January 18, 2015, that they suspected the Patriots were deflating footballs, which would make them easier for Brady to grip, especially on days when it is cold or rainy. That gave birth to Deflategate, one of the most bizarre controversies in the league's ninety-five-year history, leading Goodell to authorize severe penalties handed down by Troy Vincent, the league's vice president of football operations: the Patriots were fined $1 million and stripped of a first-round draft pick in 2016 and a fourth-round pick in 2017, and Brady was suspended for the first four games of the 2015 season, a sanction he appealed.

Was this much ado about nothing? Did the footballs lose air pressure on their own due to atmospheric conditions, or did Brady and the Patriots cheat?

Each team prepares the footballs that its offense will use during the game. Until 2006, the home team was in charge of all the footballs, including those for the visitors, but Manning and Brady were behind a petition by quarterbacks to amend the rule and allow them to bring their own footballs on the road.

At halftime of the championship game in Foxboro, eleven of the Patriots footballs were retested. They were all under the 12.5-pounds-per-square-inch minimum, and that prompted Goodell to initiate a full-scale independent investigation by Ted Wells, a New York attorney. The Patriots tried to explain the discrepancy by citing the ideal gas law. The Wells Report, a 243-page account, was conducted over more than one hundred days and cost the NFL millions. It came to the conclusion, through mostly circumstantial evidence, that Brady was involved in a plot to have air taken out of the footballs prior to the championship game with the Colts after they were tested by referee Walt Anderson.

Wells used a connect-the-dots approach to decide that assistant equipment manager John Jastremski and clubhouse attendant Jim McNally were acting on Brady's desire to have the balls deflated. The report never accused Brady of telling Jastremski and McNally to deflate the footballs under the minimum, only that he liked them on the lower end of the 12.5-13.5 psi range. Wells cited a series of text messages between Jastremski and McNally (who referred to himself as The Deflator, which the Patriots later attributed to his desire to lose weight), and surveillance cameras catching McNally duck into a bathroom for a hundred seconds after Anderson had signed off on the twelve footballs the Patriots presented for the game. Wells wrote "that it is more probable than not that Brady was at least generally aware of the inappropriate activities of McNally and Jastremski involving the release of air from Patriots game balls."

Brady answered sixty-one questions during a thirty-minute press conference on January 22, four days after the title game and nearly four months before the release of the Wells Report. "I didn't alter the ball in any way," he said. "I feel like I have always played within the rules. I would never break any rules."

The footballs come out of the box a little slippery, and quarterbacks and equipment managers work them over until they have a comfortable feel. Then the quarterbacks choose the twelve they want in the game along with twelve backups. "When I pick those footballs out, at that point, to me, they're perfect," Brady said. "I don't want anyone touching the balls after that. I don't want anyone rubbing them, putting any air in them, taking any air out. To me, those balls are perfect, and that's what I expect when I show up on the field."

Deflategate overshadowed the Super Bowl for nearly two weeks, right up until kickoff. Brady, who never seems anxious, initially was nervous in that press conference as he was grilled with questions about air pressure, and for the first time in his career his integrity was questioned. Wells revealed in his report that Brady refused to turn over his cell phone or even allow his own attorney to pick out relevant e-mails and text messages when they interviewed him. The NFL considered that a lack of cooperation, which contributed to Brady's punishment.

The anti-Patriots faction will claim this taints Brady's legacy, even if the evidence would never get him convicted in a court of law. Patriots Nation will argue that Wells hardly proved the Patriots deflated the footballs and certainly didn't do enough to link Brady to any wrongdoing, although the consensus among quarterbacks is no equipment or clubhouse worker would make changes to the football unless directed by the quarterback. The impact on the game itself is arguable—Brady played much better in the second half of the 45–7 victory over the Colts when the footballs were fully inflated—but the issue is whether rules were broken.

Kraft accepted his penalties from the league after he initially considered fighting the fine and loss of draft picks. He is a league man, and although he has never acknowledged the Patriots did anything wrong, he felt compelled to back down. He has never doubted that Brady was innocent of any wrongdoing. "Tom Brady has our unconditional support," Kraft said. "Our belief in him has not wavered."

If Brady was breaking the rules, then it adds another talking point to the pro-Manning backers in the Brady vs. Manning argument. Could that explain why Brady outplayed Manning in so many cold-weather games in New England? Manning stayed clear of any Deflategate talk and any talk about Brady. "I'll speak it as clearly and slowly as I can," he said. "He's my friend; he'll always be my friend. I don't know what happened. I don't have much more than that for you."

Brady vs Manning will take you behind the scenes of the NFL's greatest rivalry between two of the all-time best quarterbacks. "I've been playing against Tom for a long time," Manning said. "You do form a friendship as well, besides just a football handshaking a guy after a game. I have enjoyed that. There's that fine line between asking questions that can benefit you as far as how does he train in the off-season, but at the same time, you do try to protect some secrets. I think he and I have a healthy respect, never crossing the line, asking something that is a little too football private for his team and for my team. At the same time, you are always trying to find ways to improve, to keep playing, to get better. There is really nobody better to talk to than somebody else trying to do the same thing."

One thing they don't talk about: Super Bowl rings. Brady has never brought up the medal count.

"I could never do that," he said. "He's had as great a career as anyone who has ever played the position. I feel I've had as great a career as I could have ever imagined or dreamed of. I've been lucky to have been on some great teams. That's what I think about. I want to be part of the reason why we continue to do well. If I'm not doing well, then someone else has to do it. That's how the NFL works."

Brady and Manning are icons of the game who have permanently carved a niche for themselves in its history, both individually and as part of something really special. Brady vs. Manning has been the best long-running show in NFL history, and nobody wants a series finale.

1

FOR THE RECORD

Peyton Manning and his brother Eli talk often during the season, particularly during the week when one of them is facing a team the other has already played.

They are five years apart, and Peyton picked on Eli unmercifully as a kid—he used to pin him down and bang his knuckles against his chest until he was able to name all the schools in the Southeastern Conference (SEC), and when he mastered that, Peyton tested him on the names of all the NFL teams. But as adults, they count on each other as a trusted set of eyes and ears when studying an upcoming opponent.

In the final game of the 2007 season, Eli and the New York Giants were playing Tom Brady and the Patriots. The Patriots already had the number-one seed in the AFC wrapped up, and the Giants had secured a wild-card spot in the NFC. In other years, this game would have had all the ingredients for a meaningless three hours with the goal to rest the starters and make sure nobody picked up any new injuries going into the playoffs.

In the days before the game, Eli's cell phone rang. It was Peyton calling from Indianapolis. He wasn't offering advice on how to

take advantage of the Patriots defense, although he finally seemed
to have figured out how to beat Bill Belichick's complex schemes.
The Colts had lost to New England by four points in the middle
of the season when both teams were undefeated but Manning had
won the previous three games.

Peyton needed a favor from Eli. More specifically, he needed
Eli to ask the Giants defense for a favor.

Brady was having a magical season. He had thrown forty-
eight touchdown passes in the first fifteen games, and the Patriots
had won them all. Two more touchdowns and Brady would break
the all-time single-season record, which happened to be held by
Peyton Manning. He'd had forty-nine in 2004. One more victory
and the Patriots would become the first team to put together a
perfect 16–0 regular season.

Manning probably would have put the record out of Brady's
reach had he played more than one series and thrown more than
two passes in the final game of the '04 season against Denver. The
Colts had already clinched their playoff seeding, and Tony Dungy
only played Manning to keep his starting streak alive. The next
week, when the game mattered in the wild-card round, the Colts
played the Broncos again and Manning threw four touchdowns
against the Denver defense.

Brady and Manning, even when they were not playing against
each other, were linked once again.

Becoming the first team to go undefeated since the league
went to a sixteen-game season in 1978 was motivation, but Brady
and the Patriots had played with a chip on their shoulder all year
after Belichick was turned in to the NFL by the Jets in the first
game of the year for taping their defensive signals. Spygate, as the
scandal became known, exposed a practice that had been going on
for many years and that called into question the three Super Bowls
that Brady and Belichick had already won together.

Belichick was out to prove that the taping was incidental to the Patriots' success, and he was on a mission for the rest of the 2007 season not only to win games, but to embarrass teams. After the opener, the Patriots won their next seven games by a combined 293–113, including a beatdown of the Redskins 52–7. Belichick humiliated Hall of Fame coach Joe Gibbs by running up the score, leaving Brady in the game until he had thrown his third touchdown pass to make it 45–0 on the first series of the fourth quarter. Belichick was taking out his anger on the Patriots' opponents even though he was the one caught cheating. And now, to complete the Patriots' undefeated season against the Giants in the Meadowlands, where Belichick had made a name for himself by winning his first two Super Bowl rings as defensive coordinator for Bill Parcells, would be perfect. He loved his twelve years with the Giants organization and had too much respect for coach Tom Coughlin—they worked together for three years with the Giants—to consider running up the score. He just wanted to win the game.

Coughlin decided he was going to go all-out to beat the Patriots to try to create momentum going into the playoffs after an up-and-down season. It was a questionable maneuver. New York was already locked in to the number-five playoff seed and couldn't afford any more injuries. The risk, Coughlin decided, was worth the reward. That was good news for the Manning precinct in Indianapolis. The outcome of this game meant little to the Colts, but Brady's stats meant everything to Peyton Manning.

He called his younger brother and asked him to relay a message to the defensive leaders: If the Patriots were going to get into the end zone, he sure would appreciate if it happened on the ground. No touchdown passes, please.

"He said it jokingly, but maybe a little serious in the mix," Eli Manning said. "I thought I would pass it on to Antonio Pierce."

It was no joke.

Anytime players say statistics are just numbers and they don't pay attention, they're not telling the truth. Manning might have been funny as guest host on *Saturday Night Live* and a tremendous pitchman in all those television commercials, but he has an ego, a big ego. Manning wanted that touchdown record to be enduring, just as Dan Marino did when he threw forty-eight back in 1984, shattering the old record of thirty-six set by Y. A. Tittle, which had stood since 1963. At least Marino's record lasted twenty years. Manning's was on the verge of being wiped out after just three.

Pierce, the Giants middle linebacker, had created headlines that week by saying that Brady walks around "like he's Prince Charles, like he's the golden boy," and complaining that Brady seemed indignant anytime a defensive player managed to lay hands on him. The Giants did not like Brady. They wanted to knock him around. They were happy to give it their best shot to do Eli's big brother a favor.

Eli walked over to Pierce in the locker room to relay the message from Peyton: "Hey, you know, if you guys can do whatever you can to not let him break the record, that would be great," Eli said. "It would be nice if the defense can go out there and not give up any touchdown passes."

Brady had thrown forty-eight touchdowns, but that was against the rest of the league. Pierce did not want him breaking the record against the Giants. Eli Manning is hard to read sometimes, even for his teammates. "You think the guy is joking, but then you look at his face," Pierce said. "He was serious about that."

Then Pierce laughed. "There might have been a little bit of an incentive for us to try and stop Tom Brady from getting that record," he said.

The Giants defensive players went out to dinner every Monday and Friday night. Pierce told Eli to inform Peyton that if the

Giants prevented Brady from breaking the record, they expected a "parting gift." He had it all planned out. He would round up the crew for a night in Manhattan with dinner at Del Frisco's, one of the best steak houses in New York. Pierce got the word to Peyton that if the Giants came through, he would be expected to pick up the check.

The night before the game, at the Hilton Hasbrouck Heights, the Patriots team hotel in New Jersey five miles north of Giants Stadium, backup quarterback Matt Cassel was being prepared by the New England offensive coaches to come into the game in relief of Brady, but he knew he wouldn't get in until the Patriots were comfortably ahead to secure the undefeated season and Brady had set the touchdown record. Based on how the season had gone, that figured to be sometime in the third quarter. "They were talking to me like, 'What are your favorite passes on the call sheet?'" Cassel said. "I'm like, 'Okay, I'm going to get in there and rock-and-roll.' Then it became a tight game and there wasn't even a question on the sideline. Those guys weren't coming out of the game. Brady definitely wasn't getting taken out of the game. The next thing I know, the fourth quarter rolls around and Brady is taking a knee, and we just went 16–0. I was like, 'Okay, well, maybe next year.'" He wasn't trying to jinx his friend, but Cassel did get his chance in 2008 when Brady tore his ACL in the first game.

The Giants held Brady without a touchdown pass in the first quarter. But on the first play of the second period, he completed a four-yard score to Randy Moss, tying Brady with Manning at forty-nine TD passes. It was also Moss's twenty-second TD catch of the season, tying him with Jerry Rice for the single-season record. Brady didn't throw a touchdown in the second or third quarter, giving Manning hope that he would at least end the season with a share of the record. It was a lot to ask. Brady came into the game averaging more than three touchdown passes per game. By the fourth quarter, it became clear that the Giants defense could no longer contain him; he was operating the highest-scoring offense in NFL history (a record Manning took ownership of in Denver in 2013). The Giants were playing inspired ball and giving the Patriots a huge scare, as they held a 28–16 lead early in the third quarter, still 28–23 going into the fourth.

Brady went deep to Moss down the right sideline on second down early in the fourth quarter, but he was unable to hold on. The Patriots came back with the exact same play on third down, knowing that the Giants secondary couldn't keep up with Moss. This time, Brady and Moss connected on a 65-yard touchdown with 11:06 remaining, which broke the records of Manning and Rice, putting Brady and Moss on top. It gave New England the lead for good. The Patriots eventually won 38–35 but lost to the Giants five weeks later in the Super Bowl when Brady was held to just one TD pass. Brady got the regular-season record. The Giants got the Super Bowl ring. On a smaller scale, they also would have liked to stop Brady from making history against them.

"We tried," Pierce said. "We didn't just try for Peyton. We obviously tried for ourselves. But that just tells you how competitive those guys are."

Brady was later told that Manning had implored the Giants defense through Eli to prevent him from breaking the record. He grinned, noting that the Giants didn't make it easy. "We worked for them that night," he said.

Brady understood that Manning was trying to protect his turf. Six years later, Manning had forty-seven touchdowns going into the Broncos' final two games of season. He needed three to tie Brady and four to take back the record. He tossed four in the next-to-last game against the Texans to get to 51. He was back on top. In the final game, needing a victory to secure the AFC's number-one seed over the Patriots, Manning threw another four in the first half against the Raiders. That gave him fifty-five. With the Broncos comfortably ahead 31–0 at the half, Manning took a seat on the bench.

"He wanted the record back," Pierce said. "Then he wanted to crush that record a little bit. He went up plus five. As much as Brady and Manning are gentlemen on the field and shake hands and head-nod, don't ever get it twisted one way or the other that these guys don't want to outdo the other."

Even when he broke the record, Manning had Brady on his mind. He predicted that Brady would break the record in 2014. "I have zero chance," Brady said with a laugh. "But it's a very nice thing for him to say."

Brady was right. He didn't break the record, and he didn't come close. He threw thirty-three touchdowns in 2014. He says he doesn't care about records. He cares about rings, and it became clear as the years ticked by in their careers that Manning would never catch him. One year apart, they each played the Seahawks in the Super Bowl. Manning and the Broncos lost 43–8. He threw just one touchdown pass, had the first snap fly over his head for a safety, and also threw two interceptions, one setting up a touchdown and the other returned for a touchdown. Brady and the Patriots won 28–24. Brady threw four touchdown passes and passed Joe Montana for the most TD passes in Super Bowl history. He overcame two bad interceptions, the first one costing the Patriots at least a field goal and the second setting up a Seahawks touchdown, but he threw a pair of fourth-quarter touchdown passes, including the game-winner with just 2:02 remaining. He completed 13 of 15 passes in the fourth quarter, including a perfect 8-for-8 on the final drive. He also broke Manning's Super Bowl record for completions, set just twelve months earlier. That postseason gap makes owning all the regular-season passing records even more important for Manning's legacy.

· · ·

It goes beyond the pregame chat and postgame handshake for Peyton Manning and Tom Brady. That's all the public sees. They are supercompetitive athletes, especially when they play each other, but they have a relationship that goes beyond mutual respect. They relate to each other. They are the only two players in the last fifteen years who are bigger than the game. "They are much better friends than anybody knows," Archie Manning said.

Brady and Manning play golf together in California. They've had dinner together in Boston. They speak on the phone and often text each other good luck before games. "I wouldn't say I really root for them to win because of the impact it has on our team and our season," Brady said. "But I always want him to do well."

During the off-season in 2013, Brady was at his home in Brentwood, California, outside Los Angeles. He and Bundchen purchased the four-acre property for $11.75 million in 2008, spent four years having the 18,298-square-foot French-style house built, then wound up selling to Dr. Dre of Beats headphone fame for $40 million in the summer of 2014. The Brady bunch—they have a son, Benjamin, and a daughter, Vivian, and Tom has a son, Jack, who lives with his former girlfriend Bridget Moynahan—moved into a custom-built mansion in Brookline, Massachusetts, in the fall of 2014, about two hundred yards from the front door of Patriots owner Robert Kraft. They downsized to 18,000 square feet.

Manning and Brady played golf a "bunch of times," Brady said, during the off-season in 2013. They had a lot to talk about. Manning had just completed his first season with the Broncos and had lost in devastating fashion to the Ravens in double overtime at home in the divisional round of the playoffs. The following week, the Ravens went into Foxboro for the AFC championship game and defeated the Patriots. Joe Flacco had won the daily double, beating Manning and Brady back-to-back on the road in the playoffs, something Mark Sanchez was first to do, with the Jets in 2010.

Before training camp opened in the summer of 2013, Manning was on the West Coast with his wife, Ashley. "I'm in LA," Manning texted Brady. "If you're around, let me know."

The previous summer, Manning tried to get together with Brady in California, but the Bradys were out of town. This time, they were home. Brady invited Peyton and Ashley to their house for dinner. The Mannings were traveling without their son, Marshall, and daughter, Mosley, twins born in 2011, but the Bradys' two children were at home. The couples sat for three or four hours, two of the greatest players in football history in the privacy of the Brady home. No cameras, no tape recorders, no media, no TMZ. They didn't go into the backyard and throw footballs through a tire, and they didn't play *Madden NFL 13* with Manning picking Brady and Brady picking Manning.

The four of them sat and talked. Tom and Peyton, of course, did chat some football, most of it before joining the ladies at the dinner table. "We've always had a pretty good bond and spoken the same language," Brady said.

Chefs cooked the meal. Ashley and Gisele talked about their kids and their homes, and their conversation centered on "what wives talk about," Brady said. "Sometimes they will listen a little bit to what we are talking about. I think it's fascinating for both of them. It nice for them to be able to relate to each other in a sense, also, because they know what their husbands are like and how we think and what keeps us up at night. My wife will get in the car driving home with me after a game, and she just wants to talk about the game—what happened, why did you do this? I need to relax. I'm sure Peyton is very similar, because his wife is similar to my wife. They're just passionate about rooting for their husbands to do well."

It was the first time Ashley had spent time with Gisele. Peyton

had met Gisele and spoken to her and Brady in the hallway outside
the locker room when the Colts played New England in 2011, the
year Manning was injured. He still made the trip and helped out
the quarterbacks on the sideline.

Bundchen made headlines in February one year earlier following the Patriots' loss to the Giants in Super Bowl XLVI when she
was critical of the Patriots receivers for dropped passes. Though
she didn't name any names, Wes Welker, who was Brady's close
friend, dropped a key pass in the fourth quarter on a Brady pass
that twisted him around.

On her way to an elevator after the game, Bundchen was
heckled by Giants fans, who shouted, "Eli rules" and "Eli owns
your husband." She didn't immediately respond, but was caught
on video speaking to those around her. "You have to catch the ball
when you're supposed to catch the ball," she said. "My husband
cannot throw the ball and catch the ball at the same time. I can't
believe they dropped the ball so many times."

How could Welker not take what she said personally? The wife
of his buddy was calling him out. Welker beat himself up after the
game for not catching Brady's pass. He blamed himself. "Trust
me, I wasn't happy about it, either," he said. "I don't think anybody
was. I understand the frustration. Somebody caught it on camera.
It's not that big a deal. They are good friends of mine and my wife.
She is as sweet as she can be."

Bundchen is one of the most visible women in the world. Ashley Manning keeps a low profile and is rarely shown at games or in
public with Manning. She is never quoted about her husband. But
the women hit it off at the Brady house. "We had fun," Manning
said. "Ashley has known Tom for quite some time. That was the
first time getting to know his wife. It was great. Just the four of
us. It was the off-season, not a ton of football talk, just two couples spending time together. We tried not to talk about football.
Naturally, when Tom and I are alone playing golf or before dinner

that night, obviously it's pretty natural that football is going to come up."

Manning and Brady are selective about what they allow their fans to know about their lives away from the field, but they hardly lead private lives. Brady has tried to control the message on his Facebook page. Two months after winning his fourth Super Bowl, he posted video showing him diving off a forty-foot cliff in Costa Rica into a pool of water, set to the music from *Superman*, which must have caused Robert Kraft's heart to skip a beat. Brady's comment on his page was "Never doing that again! #AirBrady." The next day, a video surfaced on the Internet of Brady teaming up with Michael Jordan in a three-on-three basketball game in the Bahamas. He then Photoshopped a picture of himself in a full body cast lying in a hospital bed with the caption "Jordan's crossover is no joke!" The cast on his left leg is signed by Jordan, and of course Brady is wearing his trademark eyeblack.

Manning is in half of all television commercials, or so it seems, and Bundchen is one of the highest-paid supermodels in the world; *Forbes* in 2014 placed her earnings for the previous twelve months at $47 million. Brady does just a fraction of the commercials that Manning does, and Ashley Manning is rarely seen.

Ashley Manning is one of the twenty-three limited partners of the Memphis Grizzlies of the NBA. She is from Memphis and became part of the group, which also includes singer and actor Justin Timberlake, to make sure the team didn't relocate. She reportedly made a $5 million investment to purchase 2.84 percent of the team. She and Peyton met through mutual friends before he enrolled at Tennessee in 1994. She went to Virginia. They were married in 2001.

"Ashley doesn't really like to be in the public," Brady said. "She has told that to me. She loves to be really low-key. It's really a great quality about her. I married a woman who happens to do what she does and is very good at it. There is a lot of popularity associated with that. I think, all in all, we're all kind of very homey, family-oriented people. We have public jobs. There's nothing I love to do other than play football. I know my wife loves to work and the career she has. That brings on a lot of other things. I know Ashley says she just likes to go sit in the box and, 'No one knows it, no one hears me, no one knows I'm there. I don't need to go out and show my face. I'll see Peyton after the game.' She kind of feels Peyton does his work, comes home, and she is there to take care of the family."

Brady and Peyton have a strong connection, but it can go only so far when it comes to sharing information. It's easier for Peyton with Eli than it is with Brady. After all, they are brothers and play in different conferences. There is never a time when they want the other to lose, except when they are playing each other, and even then, they root for each other to have big games. Peyton leads Eli 3–0 in Manning Bowl games.

The Patriots have always been battling Manning for playoff seeding, whether he has been with the Colts or the Broncos, so Tom and Peyton never root for each other to win, even though they want each other to do well and stay healthy. They share information about how to beat different teams but never discuss their own teams. "Kind of like pitchers sharing how to get hitters out," says Tony Dungy, who coached Peyton in Indianapolis for seven years.

Cassel is Brady's best friend in all the years he's played for the Patriots. He was Brady's backup from 2005 to 2008. When Brady suffered a torn ACL in the 2008 season, Cassel nearly led New England to the playoffs. Brady helped guide him through the season. Brady texted him the night before each game and the morning after. His play in Brady's absence made him a lot of money when he was traded to Kansas City following the season and signed a big contract that included $28 million in guaranteed money. During the years Cassel played in New England, Brady made sure to include him when Manning would come to Boston in the off-season and they would get together.

"When Tommy gets his knee blown out against the Chiefs, one of the first people to call him was Peyton," said Scott Pioli, the former Patriots vice president of personnel. "And he called him more than once, checking in on him. It revealed something to Tommy. It slowed Tommy down in terms of his thoughts toward Peyton. Not that he had any negative thoughts about him, but when you are that competitive with someone, you've got to find ways to hate them, because if you cross that line competing against someone that you genuinely and authentically care about, you might lose your edge."

Three years later, Manning missed the season following neck surgery. His career was in jeopardy. "Tommy told me it just wasn't the same playing the Colts without Peyton there," Pioli said. "He said he felt he lost somebody. That's why he gets so fired up to play Denver. He has never taken time to look at things in a historical context. He said, 'I'm finally realizing it. Facing Peyton has been one of the great elements of my career.'"

Manning won the Super Bowl following the 2006 season, beating Brady in the playoffs for the first time, erasing a 21–3 second-quarter deficit and then holding on to win 38–34 in the AFC championship game. Manning had business in Boston a few months later and was in touch with Brady to have dinner. Brady invited Cassel, Larry Izzo, Dan Koppen, and Will McDonough, a friend of Brady's who has managed both his career and Bundchen's. Heads turned when Brady and Manning and the group walked into a sushi restaurant and headed into a back room.

"They've got a great relationship and they have admiration for each other, too," Cassel said. "Anybody who plays this position knows how difficult it is to play at a high level, let alone be as consistent as the two of them have been over the years. I can only imagine the respect they have for one another, but the competitive fire burns in both of them."

As their lives have changed, their relationship has grown. "We have a lot in common," Brady said. "We both love doing what we do. We have families now, so it's different than the first time we kind of hung out."

Brady puts together a trip each year to travel to Louisville with several of his Patriots friends to attend the Kentucky Derby. Bruschi, Cassel, Welker, Rob Gronkowski, and Lonie Paxton have been on the excursion. One year, Archie Manning arranged a trip to the derby with sons Cooper, Peyton, and Eli and their wives and his wife, Olivia. Archie doesn't know much about horse racing, but he has a buddy in New Orleans who is pretty knowledgeable about the ponies. His friend advised him which horse to pick in each race. The night before the derby, the eight members of the Manning party met with Brady's group at a Kentucky Derby gala. As part of the deal, they had excellent seats together in the same area for the next day's races. Archie shared his friend's picks with Brady and his friends. Archie won three of the first four races, and the Patriots who bet on his tips cashed in too.

Peyton Manning has always been competitive whether playing Amazing Catches in the yard as a kid with his father and brothers or trying to beat Brady to get to the Super Bowl. After winning the three races and realizing his father was on a hot streak, he objected to his spreading the wealth. "Quit sharing those picks," Peyton said. "It's going to affect the odds."

There were more multimillionaires among the Mannings and the Patriots group than just about anywhere else in Churchill Downs, but Peyton was concerned that if too much money was placed on his father's picks, the payoff would be less. Archie wound up picking eight winners, including the derby winner. He went back the next year and didn't pick a single winner. They all thought it was funny, including Brady's group.

In the early part of the off-season of 2015, before things got busy with the workouts and minicamps, Brady and his father were invited to play at Augusta National Golf Course, site of the Masters Tournament. The father-son competition was set up by a friend who was also friends with Rory McIlroy, the number-one player in the world. McIlroy and his father, Brady and his father, and four others were on the course together. They had dinner at the golf club the night before playing three rounds in two days, and just coincidentally, Peyton Manning was there with his brothers Eli and Cooper, Broncos tight end Jacob Tamme, and Peyton's good friend John Lynch, who played for the Bucs and then for the Broncos prior to Peyton's arrival in Denver in 2012. Brady and Manning spoke briefly but didn't have a chance to play the famed course together. Brady went off the first tee with McIlroy. A couple of weeks later, he was playing basketball with Michael Jordan and McIlroy was playing in the Masters.

The two football superstars have relied on each other's friendship for many years, even though one of them was always in the way of the other on the road to the Super Bowl. "He's a great person and a good friend," Brady said. "When you are competing, it's a whole different story. But it's not like we're boxers and we're throwing punches at one another. We've never been on the same field at the same time. I have a lot of respect for him and what he is able to do. I think it's more of an appreciation, especially for a year like he had in 2013, the best year in the history of all NFL quarterbacks."

2

THE FAMILY BUSINESS

Archie Manning was the second overall pick in the 1971 draft by the Saints. He has three sons who played football. Cooper was an accomplished receiver at Isidore Newman High School in New Orleans, even catching passes his senior year from younger brother Peyton, the starting quarterback. Suddenly, all the fighting that had gone on between them—brotherly love—came to a stop. "That's when I had to start kissing his butt or he wasn't going to throw it to me," Cooper said. "We had a big year. He threw it to me a ton. We got beat in the semifinals of the state tournament. That was a great year not only for us to grow closer and have to put up with each other and get along, but my parents also had a blast that year watching us play together. I caught seventy-five balls."

He earned a scholarship to play at Ole Miss, where his father had gone to school. But before he could even play in his first game, he was having numbness in his hands during preseason practices. He went to the Mayo Clinic in Minnesota and was diagnosed with spinal stenosis, a narrowing of the spinal column. He underwent surgery, ending his football career.

Peyton took the news hard that Cooper couldn't play anymore. According to published reports, Cooper wrote him an emotional letter: "I would like to live my dream of playing football through you. Although I cannot play anymore, I know I can still get the same feeling out of watching my little brother do what he does best. I know now that we are good for each other, because I need you to be serious and look at things from a different perspective. I am good for you, as well, to take things light. I love you, Peyt, and only great things lie ahead for you. Thanks for everything on and off the field."

When Peyton elected to enroll at Tennessee, the state of Mississippi all but broke down the front door of the Mannings' home in the historic Garden District of New Orleans. Archie was an Ole Miss icon, the greatest quarterback in the school's history. Peyton was born to play at Mississippi—it all but said that on his birth certificate—but he decided to create his own identity at Tennessee.

"When Peyton was being recruited, he had a hundred schools after him," Archie Manning said. "It really got turned up his junior year. You know him—Peyton kind of attacked recruiting. He did his due diligence. He wasn't going to let recruiting overwhelm him. He was going to overwhelm recruiting. It didn't bother him. In October of his senior year, he was still talking to forty schools. He was playing his season, doing his schoolwork. He handled it. He did recognize at some point, maybe at my suggestion, 'Peyton, you got to start eliminating some schools.'"

Archie explained to him that it wasn't fair to the schools to keep them hanging and prevent them from finalizing scholarships with other quarterbacks. Just about every school in the country wanted Peyton, including Michigan, which made it deep into the process. Of course, if Manning had showed up in Ann Arbor in 1994, either it would have ended any interest Michigan had in Brady or scared Brady away from enrolling one year later, or it would have been Brady vs. Manning dueling it out to see who played in "The Big House," Michigan Stadium, the world's second-largest stadium, seating over 110,000.

Taking his father's suggestion, Manning began to cut his list. He'd return home from football practice, do his schoolwork, and then take recruiting calls every night between eight thirty and ten o'clock. "He would come sit at the foot of our bed and say, 'Well, I cut Arizona State today. Good coach.' One night he came in and said, 'I just cut two schools and nobody thinks they're any good, but they have new coaches who are going to win. Coach Snyder at Kansas State and Coach Barnett at Northwestern.' A few years ago, I reminded him of that. I said, 'You were a prophet.' He had forgotten about that. I'm not saying he was right about everybody, but those two he was right about. He had a feel for it."

Manning took a visit to Michigan and liked the idea that if he wasn't going to pick Ole Miss, then he wouldn't have to play against them either if he got out of the South. "Michigan was a bailout," Archie said.

Michigan, Ole Miss, Tennessee, and Florida were Manning's final four. "I wanted to go to Ole Miss, I wanted to go to Florida, I wanted to go to Michigan," he said. "You have to pick one."

He loved Ole Miss and wasn't afraid of following in his father's footsteps. Even so, there were rumors that Mississippi was headed for probation, and the Mannings couldn't get a clear answer about what punishment awaited the program. That eliminated the Rebels. "They did go on probation," Archie Manning said. "If Peyton had gone there, he would have been able to play in only one bowl game and been on television only one year."

Peyton loved Michigan and offensive coordinator Cam Cameron, but ultimately decided he wanted to play in the SEC. Cameron wound up taking a job with the Redskins and later told the

Mannings that if it had looked as though Peyton was going to come to Michigan, he would have told him he was leaving before he committed to playing in Ann Arbor. Manning has never played well in cold weather in the NFL. Brady has thrived when it's freezing. Perhaps if Manning had chosen Michigan, he would have been better prepared to play in Foxboro in January.

That left Florida and Tennessee, in the other division of the SEC from Ole Miss. Manning looked at the quarterback depth chart and felt he would have a clearer path reaching his goal of starting by his sophomore year if he went to Knoxville. Archie was such a legend at Ole Miss that the speed limit on the Oxford campus was later set at 18 mph, a tribute to his uniform number. Peyton left it up to little brother Eli to rewrite the Mississippi record books. Eli was up to the challenge, and the speed limit around the football stadium on campus was subsequently set at 10 mph, the number Eli wore for the Rebels. Peyton may have pissed off the entire state of Mississippi, but Tennessee was more than happy to provide a comfortable landing spot.

Archie endured a good deal of the criticism for the Tennessee decision. He received nasty letters. He heard of friends talking behind his back. On his way to Jackson once, he stopped at a gas station and said a "good ole boy" gave him a hard time for letting Peyton go to Tennessee. "I let him make his own choice," Archie told the man.

Just like his brother, Eli was the number-one overall pick in the draft, in 2004 by the Chargers. He had declared he would go back to school before playing for San Diego, which was considered a dysfunctional organization. He wanted to play for the Giants, who were picking fourth. The Chargers and Giants couldn't agree on a predraft deal, but after San Diego took Manning and the Giants were on the clock with the fourth pick, they worked out a trade. New York agreed to select North Carolina State quarterback Philip Rivers for the Chargers and also to trade picks in the third and fifth rounds in 2004 and the first round in 2005 in exchange for Manning.

The Manning brothers are close friends. Cooper has lived vicariously through the accomplishments of his brothers and is a successful businessman in an energy investment banking firm in New Orleans. Archie used to stand on the front porch step of their New Orleans home and toss the football as Cooper, Peyton, and Eli would run out for passes. "They preferred when it was raining or wet because it was more fun to slide," Archie said.

The boys made some Amazing Catches. "They would start at one end of the yard and take off," Archie said. "We had a sidewalk that was about a third of the way, so I had to make sure they cleared it. They would cross the sidewalk, I would lay it out in front of them, and they would try to make diving catches. It was up to me to make it an amazing catch instead of a routine catch."

It was an entertaining game, and Peyton has turned out to be quite entertaining on and off the field. Eli is laid-back; nothing bothers him. Cooper has always been the one with the twinkle in his eye and, as a kid, mischief on his mind. When Archie was playing for the Saints, the team was very bad. They were called the 'Aints. Fans wore bags over their heads at the Superdome. Archie's wife, Olivia, would take Cooper and Peyton to the games to watch their father play. Eli was not born yet.

"We were six and four years old," Cooper said. "Some guys were there and left the bags in their seats. My Mom turned around and there we were; we had them on our heads, too. We didn't know what we were doing, of course. We thought Mom would get a laugh out of it. It helped her laugh because we were probably getting beat that afternoon."

Did he force Peyton to wear the bag?

"Monkey see, monkey do," he said. "That was probably the last time I had control over Peyton when he would do what I said. My grip has been slipping slowly."

Archie said when he heard about the boys wearing the bags, he laughed. Now if newspapers had caught the sons of the Saints starting quarterback wearing bags over their heads as the home team was stinking up the field once again, there might have been hell to pay in the Manning household. "Olivia was pregnant with Eli. We were 0–11, 0–12. We were in the dome and they were booing my ass," Archie said. "Cooper asks Olivia if they could boo, too. You almost got to laugh at something like that. Olivia was pretty pregnant and kind of looking for a reason to quit going to the games. And that was it. She was, 'Let's go. You can't boo and you can't come to any more games. So let's go.'"

Cooper still makes people laugh. Peyton was the son who kept his siblings in line.

"Peyton was pretty easy. He tried to please," Archie said. "I guess you could say Peyton was coachable. If you said, 'Don't cross the street,' he wasn't going to cross the street, and he was going to tell Cooper and Eli, 'Don't go across the street.'"

Eli is seven years younger than Cooper, so their relationship was different from that between Cooper and Peyton. Cooper was more of a big brother to Eli. "Peyton and I are two years apart," Cooper said. "We played a lot of sports together. We fought a lot. A lot of hoops games in the backyard that never finished because the game gets close and here come the elbows and here come the fists. I have very distinct memories of my dad begging and pleading with us, saying if we could ever get along, how lucky we were to have each other. Just compete and finish a game as opposed to fighting and fighting."

Archie was a tremendous athlete, the best in the family. He was fast and had a big arm; he just played on some of the worst teams in the NFL year after year and is the best quarterback in league history never to make the playoffs.

"Peyton is a good athlete, but that's not what made him the player he is today," Archie said. "He never ran fast and that always kind of bothered him. He's the only one of my three children that cared and was interested in what I did and dug up film and read stories. I was classified as a runner. I was pretty fast. It bothered Peyton."

"Dad, why am I not fast?" he asked.

"I don't know, Peyton. I don't know," Archie said.

They were years away from knowing each other, but Manning and Brady already had one thing in common: they were slow. In fact, Brady's forty-yard-dash time at the scouting combine in 2000 is legendary for being so painfully slow. He could've been clocked with an hourglass. Brady ran the forty in 5.28 seconds. Manning didn't run at the combine but was timed in his rookie year at 4.8.

"Peyton and Tom, golly, you wouldn't want to see that race," Archie said. "The fact Peyton wasn't fast made him say, 'Well, I want to be a quarterback.'"

Brady grew up with three older sisters. Maureen and Nancy were accomplished softball players. Julie played soccer. Julie married former Red Sox third baseman Kevin Youkilis in 2012. All the girls played in college. They all picked on their little Tommy. "Oh, yeah, it goes with the territory," Tom Brady Sr. said.

Tom Sr. has an estate-planning business with offices in the Bay Area, New York, and, quite conveniently, Boston. He and his wife, Galynn, attended 90 percent of Tom's games at Michigan, traveling to home and away games even when he was second or third on the depth chart. They went to all his Patriots games for the first four years he was starting, but now limit it to home games and a few road games each year. Archie tries to attend as many of Peyton's and Eli's home games as he can, but it became too much of a physical strain to get to road games.

Tom Sr. also let his son make his own decision about where to attend college, but he was distraught when he selected Michigan over Cal–Berkeley, which is just thirty-five miles across the San Francisco Bay from the Brady home in San Mateo. Tommy was his best friend, and he was moving across the country. Brady Sr. turned to a psychologist for help dealing with the separation from his son. He went through eight weeks of counseling. "Tommy and I, he's my best buddy. We spent so much time together," he said. "We'd play golf, go to ball games; I coached his games. When he decided to go to Michigan, it literally broke my heart." The sessions with the psychologist helped. "Oh yeah," he said. "I don't have any qualms about saying it."

Archie Manning and Tom Brady Sr. developed a friendship because of the rivalry of their sons. Just as Brady never brings up to Peyton that he has quite a big lead in Super Bowl championships, the Manning family doesn't brag that Eli beat Brady in Super Bowls XLII and XLVI.

"I'm trying to win a championship for the Giants and myself," Eli said. "It's not Manning vs. Brady. It's the Giants vs. New England. It's bigger than the two people or a last name."

Archie Manning says Peyton never really discusses the games against Brady with him. "He's been on the short end, but I don't think he's scarred by that," he said. "He's proud of the fact that they are recognized as certainly two of the top quarterbacks of an era. I'm glad he likes Tom. I'm glad Tom likes him. I'm glad they have a friendship. It wouldn't be good if they didn't like each other. Then, all of a sudden, there would be this built-in jealousy or hate. There's been a lot written about Peyton and Tom, and everybody wants to proclaim the greatest ever. I don't think you can do that with quarterbacks. Even Tom and Peyton and Drew Brees and Aaron Rodgers vs. Joe Montana or Roger Staubach or Terry Bradshaw, or how in the world can you go back and talk about people vs. Otto Graham, Sammy Baugh, and Johnny Unitas? To have a son who is kind of mentioned in that argument, I'm proud of that and I'm sure Tom Brady Sr. is, too."

Peyton Manning is a serious student of the history of the game. He was a Dan Marino fan growing up. The first start of his pro career, in the opening game of his rookie year in 1998, was against Marino and the Dolphins. Brady lived in Northern California; his first idol was Joe Montana and then Steve Young. Montana retired six years before Brady was drafted by the Patriots. Young retired the year before Brady came into the NFL. In the summer of 2003, Montana had Brady over to his house for lunch in the Bay Area. Brady said it was a dream come true.

Tom Brady Sr. admires Archie Manning for the class with which he's dealt with two sons achieving fame and greatness in the family business as the First Family of the NFL. "My internist would have had to do ulcer surgery four or five times by now," Brady Sr. said. "Archie is obviously a quality, quality guy."

Tom Sr. felt for Archie after the Broncos were crushed in the Super Bowl by Seattle. He texted his regrets. "It wouldn't have made a difference who was playing quarterback," Brady Sr. said. "Obviously, the fans of one guy tar and feather the other guys when the team loses. We are parents, I don't care what you say, you feel that. I just was commenting to him, as a dad to a dad, 'Hey, I feel your pain. I'm proud of your son. I'm proud of you guys.' This is a game. This isn't going to Iraq. Unfortunately, we lose focus. Our life is supposed to be determined by the outcome of a game? We have our priorities certainly misplaced when you are putting that much value on the final score."

Archie Manning still finds it hard to believe he has two sons who have been in five Super Bowls and won three. "Olivia and I try not to take it for granted," he said. "Along the way, we've tried to be sensible and good, supporting parents. Sometimes we look at each other and say, 'Can you believe this?' We're so proud. We just kind of pinch ourselves. Both of them are fortunate to be healthy.

As parents, we've been blessed. They had successful college careers and are getting to play for successful NFL franchises and winning Super Bowls."

Archie never pushed his sons to be quarterbacks. It's more than just having the quarterback genes. How many NFL quarterbacks have sons who turn out better than them? Certainly not Montana, whose two sons bounced around college football. Or Phil Simms, who had two sons make it to the NFL; his older son, Chris, started a playoff game for the Bucs, the first of four stops in a seven-year journeyman career interrupted by a frightening ruptured spleen suffered early in his career against Carolina. His younger son, Matt, was a Jets backup for several years before he was claimed on waivers in 2015 by Buffalo. All those young men had the burden of carrying the family name and trying to live up to the accomplishments of their fathers.

Brady came from a family of athletes, but not even Tom Sr. thought his only boy had a future in professional football. In fact, he was a good enough lefty-hitting catcher with a strong arm at Serra High School in San Mateo, the same school that produced Barry Bonds, to be drafted in the eighteenth round by the Montreal Expos in 1995. His father thinks that if he hadn't already accepted a scholarship to play football at Michigan, he might have been selected in the second or third round. The Manning brothers were destined to be quarterbacks. Not so with Brady. He didn't start playing football until he was a freshman in high school and didn't get on the field as a quarterback his first year even though his team finished 0–8 and didn't score a touchdown. He became the starter by default in his sophomore year when the previous year's number one quarterback decided not to play. Tom's mother played competitive soccer into her forties, and he inherited his athletic ability from her.

"To have all this stuff happen, I'm not sure if the word is *surreal* or whether it's *bizarre*," said Brady Sr. "When Tommy was grow-

ing up, he was a normal kid. He's still a normal son to us. He's
so blessed with a wonderful wife. She's just awesome. They get
along like ham and eggs. I've got three other kids, three daughters;
they're just awesome. Tommy happens to have captured some ce-
lebrity, for whatever that's worth, and untoward wealth. The reality is, he's exactly the same guy; he's more sophisticated, but he's
still the gentle, kind, loving son that we hoped he would be. All
this other stuff is peripheral. He really digs his family, his sisters,
his parents, and his own family. He's a great dad."

Manning could have made a fortune if he'd been able to cash
in the value of the postage from all the recruiting letters he received. Brady was a recruiting afterthought. He didn't need to set
aside ninety minutes every night after doing his homework to field
calls from college head coaches. He put together a recruiting tape
that he sent to schools, trying to sell himself.

Archie Manning sat back and let Peyton manage the recruiting process. Tom Brady Sr. did the same with Tom. He didn't accompany him on recruiting trips. He felt he needed to experience
that on his own. He was privately rooting for him to stay home
and play at Cal, but "I never expressed that to him," he said. Tom
Sr. was not going to influence his son as to where to go to college.

They compiled a list of fifteen questions to ask reps from each
school that was interested. "Tommy had to own the decision, because when things got really tough, I didn't want to be responsible
for him turning around to me and saying, 'Jeez, you really wanted
me to come here, but in my heart I didn't want to,'" Brady Sr. said.

Brady narrowed it down to three schools: Michigan, Cal, and
Illinois.

He fell in love with Michigan and Ann Arbor. "I loved the
social aspect. I loved the team. It was a great school," he said. "It
was more of a feeling. Once I experienced that, I really didn't want
to go anywhere else."

He visited Ann Arbor in the winter. Billy Harris, the defensive backs coach on Michigan head coach Gary Moeller's staff, was in charge of West Coast recruiting. He was concerned about a California kid being turned off by the arctic Midwestern winters. "We gave that old pitch: when you go pro, it might be somewhere where it snows," Harris said. "Thank goodness he went to Michigan, because it snows in New England. Now he can credit Michigan for helping him deal with bad-weather games."

NFL teams have been second-guessed forever because Brady lasted until the sixth round, the 199th pick of the 2000 draft. Still, it wasn't as if the Bradys packed up young Tommy and sent him to Ann Arbor expecting him to return as a first-round draft pick or become the greatest quarterback in NFL history. "Before he had gone off to Michigan, we had homed in on the fact that 'football probably isn't going to be your life,'" Brady Sr. said. "Those athletes go to school and there is not—even though people had hoped and expected it—a future in athletics."

So the father told the son as he was considering his final decision: "There is a very good probability that you will not have the success that you hoped to have. Whatever school you choose, you better decide, in conjunction with the athletics, that you want a degree from that school that means something that is going to get you on to the next level of your life. What school would be the school . . . that you would be proud to have that degree on the wall and it would launch you into your career, if football doesn't work out?"

As a result, "Before he decided on Michigan, that was one of the major, major criteria. It wasn't just football criteria," Brady Sr. said.

Brady wanted to be a Michigan man. He wanted to lead the Wolverines onto the field at The Big House in front of 110,000 screaming fans dressed in maize and blue. He wanted to walk down State Street after the game as the Michigan quarterback, the big man on campus. Football wasn't a significant enough presence back home at Berkeley, although the path to the field might have been quicker, especially after he had been the star of a summer camp at Cal and was promised he would start as a sophomore. Michigan people told him, "You would have to prove yourself to be the best if you are going to lead the best," and Brady wasn't going to run away from the challenge of working himself up the depth chart.

Before allowing him to sign the letter of intent, however, Brady Sr. called Harris. "Billy, the only thing that I know has to happen is we have to have somebody at Michigan who really wants Tommy. He wants to go where he's wanted. Does Gary Moeller want him?"

"Absolutely, he wants him," Harris said.

"I want that in blood. I want you to tell me truthfully that's the case," Brady Sr. said.

"I'll get back to you," Harris said.

Two days later, Moeller and Harris were in San Mateo having breakfast with the Brady men.

"Tommy, we got to change from what we've done," Moeller said. "We can't keep running with the same kind of system. You are our prototypical quarterback."

That sold Brady. He was going to Ann Arbor. He signed his letter of intent.

Brady didn't even have time to buy a couple of Michigan sweatshirts before Harris called. "I got good news and bad news," Harris said. "The good news is, we're going to play golf before next summer, and I'm going to see your family more often. The bad news is, I'm no longer at Michigan."

3

GO BLUE OR BE BLUE

Lloyd Carr walks virtually unnoticed into Zingerman's Deli on the corner of Detroit and Kingsley on the North Side of Ann Arbor, one mile from the center of the beautiful University of Michigan campus. Zingerman's is a bucket-list stop in one of the great college towns in America, the place former Wolverines quarterback and now head coach Jim Harbaugh recommends when he's asked where to eat in town, and the lines often extend out the door and around the corner at lunchtime.

This was a quiet spring morning just past breakfast. The sun was making its first appearance since October. In two hours, the place would be packed, but at the time there were a few people on line downstairs, a group sitting at nearly tables, and in an upstairs dining room, a woman on her iPad on one side and a few students having breakfast on the other. That was about it.

Carr, a dignified man, a proud grandfather enjoying his retirement years, arrives to address one of the great unsolved mysteries of this generation in college football: the Michigan years of Tom Brady. How and why did Carr make him beg for every snap he received in his five years on campus?

Carr still lives in Ann Arbor. He retired following the 2007 season after putting together a 122–40 record in thirteen years. His legacy is set in stone: he won the national championship in 1997, giving him one more than the legendary Bo Schembechler. Michigan football has since fallen on hard times, Rich Rodriguez and Brady Hoke having been unable to get the Wolverines back into national championship contention. Tom Brady was very close to Hoke, who was a defensive assistant under Carr during Brady's years at Michigan. Brady was disappointed that Hoke was fired after the 2014 season, but he was excited that Harbaugh, after a falling-out with the 49ers, was coming back home to resurrect the proud program. Carr, still a visible face around campus, endorsed the Harbaugh hiring and was at his introductory press conference.

A handful of customers at Zingerman's approach and say, "Coach, good to see you. How you been?" as Carr carries a cup of coffee to the upstairs dining room. Nobody ever walks up to him on campus and asks, "What were you thinking when you had Tom Brady?" They could be thinking it, however. Just about everybody outside Ann Arbor is. How did the greatest quarterback in NFL history, a four-time Super Bowl champion and three-time Super Bowl MVP, get so overlooked that his father still holds a grudge against Carr for mistreating his son?

Brady's agony started the day Harris made the phone call to say he was leaving. Harris was Brady's main contact during the recruiting process, but he had taken a job as the defensive coordinator at Stanford, right in Brady's backyard. It was a nice promotion up the coaching ladder. Harris remained friends with the Brady family and even showed up at Brady's send-off party before he left for Michigan. He brought him a University of Michigan flag as a going-away present. Harris departed Ann Arbor for career advancement, but Michigan was in his heart. His two black Labs were named Maize and Blue. Harris was fired by Stanford after four seasons and took a job at Eastern Michigan. He and his wife sold their house in California, but his wife's job at Stanford didn't end for another four months. She lived with the Bradys at their home in San Mateo during the transition.

Harris's decision to leave Michigan before Brady even arrived left him without the one ally on the coaching staff he knew would always be in his corner. Moeller had pledged to Brady in the breakfast meeting that he wanted him to play for him. But in May 1995, a few months before Brady was to arrive on campus, Moeller was arrested following a drunken incident at a restaurant in Southfield, Michigan. He eventually pleaded no contest to disorderly conduct and assault charges and was fined $200. According to reports, he was intoxicated and punched a police officer in the chest.

One week later, Moeller was pushed out. He'd had a record of 44–13–1 in five seasons, with two Big Ten titles and a share of a third. This was more bad news for Brady. First the man who recruited him had taken a new job. Then the head coach who swore he wanted him was fired and replaced by Carr, the defensive coordinator, whom Brady didn't know. Carr was first promoted to head coach on an interim basis, but before the end of the 1995 season, the interim tag was removed. Carr had been a Michigan assistant for fifteen seasons, including the final ten of Schembechler. Brady had been abandoned. "Lo and behold, Tommy has nobody in the coaches' room rooting for him," Brady Sr. said.

The next year, quarterbacks coach Kit Cartwright left for Indiana.

"All the people that helped recruit Tommy to Michigan had left," Harris said. "That's what makes you feel bad. Now if there are any struggles, the people that are usually closest to you are the folks that recruited you."

There was no uncertainty for Manning at Tennessee. Phillip Fulmer was the head coach who recruited him to Knoxville, and he was there long after Manning graduated. David Cutcliffe was his offensive coordinator and quarterbacks coach when he arrived. Cutcliffe left to be the head coach at Ole Miss in 1998, following Manning's senior year. He then recruited Eli Manning to play for him at Mississippi. Cutcliffe later became the head coach at Duke and supervised Peyton Manning's throwing rehabilitation in Durham, North Carolina, following the neck surgery in 2011 that nearly ended his career.

Manning always trusted that the coaches had his back in Knoxville. He was prepared to sit during his freshman year and would have been fine with it, knowing he would rise to the top of the depth chart in his sophomore year. He didn't even have to wait that long.

But for Brady, it wasn't until he walked off the field following the Orange Bowl on January 1, 2000, after throwing for 369 yards and four touchdowns to beat Alabama in overtime, that he was finally appreciated as a Michigan man.

Brady has played with a chip on his shoulder during his entire career with the Patriots. He knew how hard it was for him to get on the field in Ann Arbor, knew he'd almost gone undrafted, and knew it took a freak injury to Drew Bledsoe to get him his first start in the NFL. He still goes out to every practice with the mind-set that he must excel to keep his job. It's what drives him. The Michigan experience made Brady who he is today—but not before it nearly broke him.

Brady was so discouraged at not being given a chance to play that he nearly transferred to Cal the season after redshirting as a freshman. He attempted only twenty passes in his first two years on the varsity team and didn't become the starter until his fourth year in the program. It wasn't until midway through his fifth and final season that Carr gave Brady his full endorsement. Only then did he have the job security not to have to look over his shoulder

at phenom and local favorite Drew Henson, who was from nineteen miles up the road on US 23 in Brighton. But then, almost as
a warning that nothing worth having ever comes easy, Carr still
benched him for one series in the final game of his career in the
Orange Bowl.

It's not uncommon for teams in the NFL draft to overlook
players who later become stars. Trying to figure out why Brady
was never shown the love at Michigan until he was ready to leave
is much harder. "It was a great learning experience for me," he
said. "Everyone has their own journey, and my journey was a very
competitive one. I was forced to compete on a daily basis. It wasn't,
'Okay, if you commit to Michigan, you're going to be the quarterback your second year.' And that's probably how a lot of kids want
it, you know? They didn't promise me anything."

That was part of the message Brady delivered when Wolverines coach Brady Hoke asked him to speak to his team on the eve
of Michigan's 2013 season, a few hours before Brady was to play
against the Detroit Lions at Ford Field in a preseason game. He
was standing in front of ninety players at Schembechler Hall. All
eyes were on him. This was Tom Brady, Super Bowl champion,
but he spoke to them as Tom Brady, who was in one of their seats
nearly twenty years earlier, unsure of where his football career and
his life would take him. Hoke was sitting to Brady's left as he gave
an impassioned speech without any notes.

Every man in this room is counting on you. And every player
that's ever worn this helmet is counting on you. Because you
guys are the ones that are lucky enough to play for Michigan.
And not a lot of other kids around the country can do that.
There's probably a lot of other kids that are sitting in meeting
rooms across the country playing for some other teams. Not
every kid is playing for Michigan. And this place is special to

me. It's special to the guys that I played with. It's special to the guys that played before me. Because we love Michigan.

Now, I didn't have an easy experience. I didn't come in as a top-rated recruit. I didn't come in with the opportunity to play right away. I had to earn it. And you know what the greatest honor I've ever received as a player is? In my fourth year and in my fifth year, I was named team captain. That, to this day, is the single greatest achievement I've ever had as a football player, because the men in this room chose me to lead their team. And these were my best friends. These were the guys that knew that I liked to work, that knew that I loved football, that knew that I loved to play, that knew that I wanted to be the quarterback for Michigan. And all the lessons that I've learned here on State Street and in The Big House, that's still what I bring to practice today. And after fourteen years, I love the game more than I've ever loved it.

Where did I learn the love for the game? Where did I learn to practice? Where did I learn to compete? It was sitting in the same chairs that you guys are sitting in today.

On a wall behind where Brady was speaking was a sign: THE TEAM, THE TEAM, THE TEAM. In his career with the Patriots, Brady has never talked about individual achievement. It's always about the team.

Brady's success in the NFL raises the question of why Carr played Scott Dreisbach and Brian Griese over him for two years and then Griese over him in Brady's third year. Carr avoided any second-guessing at the time, because Griese, who went on to be an NFL journeyman playing for five teams, was the quarterback in the national championship season. Since Brady had not been given a chance to prove he belonged on the field, Wolverines fans had no idea of the talent that was sitting on the bench. Nobody was in The

Big House chanting "We Want Brady," except maybe Tom Sr., his wife, and his three daughters.

Patriots fans chanted, "Brady's better! Brady's better!" when he outplayed Peyton Manning in a 43–21 victory over the Broncos in Foxboro in 2014. It's easy to say now that hearing that made up for the disrespect he received from the Michigan fans and coaching staff, but those were five difficult years in the young man's life; he can never get them back.

Most of the criticism directed at Carr is based in hindsight on what Brady has become in the NFL. "I didn't expect anybody to defend me, and I've never defended myself," Carr said. "My deal was, 'Hey, I'm trying to win. I might be right, I might be wrong, but I'm going to do what I think gives us the best chance.' It is a big issue. It's a big part of who Tom Brady is. Nobody that I know could have handled it better."

Manning began his college career at Tennessee in 1994 third on the depth chart. Brady was buried at number seven when he arrived at Michigan in 1995, behind even senior Jason Carr, the head coach's son, who had thrown just fourteen passes in his first three years and would throw another ten in Brady's freshman year, when he was redshirted.

From the day Manning stepped onto the campus in Tennessee, there was no need for coach Phillip Fulmer to manage the expectations of Volunteers fans. They all knew it would not take long for him to take over. Senior Jerry Colquitt opened the 1994 season as Tennessee's starter, but after tearing his ACL on the seventh play of the first game at UCLA, he was replaced by Todd Helton, who went on to have an excellent baseball career as the Colorado Rockies first baseman. Helton suffered a knee injury in the fifth game, and when he came off the field, Manning, who had played some in the UCLA game and one other before Helton was injured, ran onto the field and never left. The next football game Manning didn't start was the season opener in 2011, the fourteenth year of his NFL career, when he was recovering from neck surgery.

Manning was not an instant hit in the huddle with his teammates, a fact he elaborated on as the keynote speaker at the 2014 valedictory exercises at the University of Virginia. Manning's wife, Ashley, was a 1997 Virginia graduate, and Manning visited her often when he was at Tennessee. The Virginia students selected Manning to give the address, and he was flattered. He took the honor very seriously, not that you would expect anything less from him. Manning doesn't do anything in his life without preparing. Manning told the students:

> It was the first time I ran into the huddle as a quarterback at Tennessee. We were playing at UCLA in the Rose Bowl, ninety-five thousand people in the stands, ABC broadcasting the game on national television, Keith Jackson and Bob Griese. Tennessee was ranked ninth in the country. UCLA was unranked. It was expected to be a blowout. I was third team on the depth chart, not expecting to play the entire game, much less the entire season. On the seventh play of the game, our starting quarterback tears his knee, and he is out for the year. Our backup quarterback was a guy named Todd Helton, who went on to have an eighteen-year Major League Baseball career. Let's just say, Todd was kind of thinking about that baseball signing bonus he was about to get. He wasn't real crazy about going into the game. So we're getting beat 21–0, and my coach turns to me, and he says, "Peyton, you're going in." And, boy, I didn't think I was nervous. I looked down and all the hair on my arms is just sticking up.
>
> So I'm jogging into the huddle, and I remembered something my dad had told me. He said, "Son, if you ever get into the huddle with the starters at any point in the season—it may be in the fourth quarter of a blowout, it may be just in prac-

tice, it doesn't matter—you be the leader, and you take control of that huddle. That's your job as the quarterback. You're
just eighteen years old. Most of these seniors are twenty-one,
twenty-two. It doesn't matter. Be the leader and take control
of that huddle."

So I remember old Dad's advice, and I got into the huddle,
and I said, "All right, guys, I know I'm just a freshman, but
I can take us down the field right now, get us a touchdown,
and get us back in this game. Let's go." Big left tackle, a guy
named Jason Layman, about six five, 330 pounds, grabs me by
the shoulder and says, "Hey, freshman, shut the blank up and
call the blanking play." And I said, "Yes, sir." That was really
great advice from my dad. I really appreciated that.

Archie watched the speech on the Internet. He laughed as
Peyton told the story. "He went in there and gave his little leader
talk, and the tackle told him to shut the eff up and call the effing
play," Archie said. "It was kind of humbling."

It was a beautiful day in Charlottesville, Virginia, with the
senior class sitting in front of Manning on the Lawn. He was insightful and witty. At one point he picked three students out of
the crowd to catch passes from him. He eased their minds by sar-
castically assuring them that if they dropped the ball, there was
no way it would wind up on YouTube. All three caught easy ones.
Manning joked that after he fired Nerf balls at child actors in a
skit on *Saturday Night Live,* he received letters from mothers and
grandmothers who watched the show with their nine-year-olds
and were disappointed in him for throwing the ball so hard at the
kids. He said he wrote back asking why their nine-year-olds were
up late watching *SNL.*

By October of his senior year in high school, Manning was
still talking to forty schools. Brady was down to three. If he chose
Cal, his father could watch him play on Saturdays, and they could

play golf on Sundays. Michigan and Illinois were far from home, and the winters would be brutal—tough for a kid from Northern California—but getting exposed to swirling snow, wind whipping his face, and temperatures around zero late in the season would be good prep work for the big leagues.

Tom Sr. made it clear that the decision would be his, and he would have to own it. If things didn't work out, he didn't want to be responsible for giving his son bad advice. He was there to support him and advise him but not influence him. As the process began to develop, as the skinny kid from San Mateo sent out videos and schools showed interest, Michigan became his choice.

Brady arrived at Michigan for the summer preseason practice and quickly knew there wasn't much chance he'd be seeing action as a freshman. Carr redshirted him. Dreisbach, a redshirt freshman, won the starting job in 1995 but was injured in the fifth game of the year, and Griese started the last nine games as Michigan went 9–4, including a loss to Texas A&M in the Alamo Bowl. Dreisbach returned in 1996 and beat out Griese, a fourth-year junior. Brady at least made it into two games.

The day he addressed the Michigan players in 2013, he didn't tell them about the turning point in his career when he nearly left in 1996. It was only his second year, but he wasn't able to jump over Dreisbach or Griese. Brady loved the school, but he was a football player and he wanted to play. He saw no opening to get on the field in the years ahead. He felt lost.

He set up a meeting with Carr early in the season. The worst fears of Brady Sr. were being realized. His son didn't have an advocate in the coaches' room. Carr was not impressed enough by what he was seeing on the practice field to consider starting him. Brady walked into Schembechler Hall and went up one flight of steps to Carr's second-floor office. There was a lot of history in that building and in the Michigan program, but Brady was ready to walk away.

The coach is from Hawkins County, Tennessee, and the pace of his speech is deliberate. He is not an intimidating man. Brady had just turned nineteen and was 2,372 miles from home, feeling as though a degree from one of the best schools in the country just might not be enough to make him stay.

Carr sat behind his desk. Brady sat in front of him.

Brady said, "Coach, I think I'm going to transfer."

"Why is that?"

"I don't think I'm ever going to play here, and I don't think I'm getting a fair chance."

"If you want to transfer, I'll give you your release, but I think it will be the biggest mistake you ever make. Look, you're in a very competitive situation here. All you guys have talent. The best advice I can give anybody in a competitive situation is that they come in here every single day prepared mentally and physically to compete at their very best. Don't be watching the other guy, hoping he has a bad day or doesn't do well. Just worry about getting better every day."

There was a pause.

Carr continued. "Look, you want to be the best, you've got to stick it out and try to beat out the best. Tom, have you talked to your dad?"

"Yeah."

"What does he say?"

"He will support whatever decision I make."

"Well, why don't you give it some thought tonight and come back tomorrow, and we'll talk again."

There was no doubt in Carr's mind about what Brady was going to do. Carr called his coaches together and told them, "Well, I think Tom's going to leave."

During recruitment, Brady Sr. also told his son, "So many kids

I see transfer from school to school to school to school, and that does a disservice to the kid's adolescence and to the kid's future, because he's running away from problems, and he's not confronting them head-on."

Brady went back to his apartment. If he left Michigan, he would sit out the rest of the 1996 season and the NCAA would have to rule whether he had to sit out 1997 as well. Carr was prepared to give him his release. He didn't want an unhappy player. Brady slept on his decision. He agonized over it.

"I really wasn't sure where my career was going to go," Brady said. "I just wasn't sure if I would ever get an opportunity to play."

Brady had just one school on his list if was going to leave Michigan. He would transfer back home to Cal–Berkeley. The coach, Keith Gilbertson, who had recruited Brady out of high school, had been replaced in 1996 by Green Bay Packers assistant Steve Mariucci, who had a reputation as an excellent quarterbacks coach. As it turned out, Mariucci was hired as the 49ers head coach after one season, which would have added him to the list of coaches who left campus before Brady even arrived, but Brady's decision was more about getting to play than about the coach. Brady debated in his mind about Cal.

"I was just really thinking if that was going to be a great opportunity for me," he said.

As he promised, Brady went back to see Carr at Schembechler Hall the next day. Carr was sitting behind his desk again. Brady was in front of him again. This time, Brady leaned over Carr's desk to get his point across. "Coach," he said with more confidence than he had the day before, "I've decided I'm going to stay at Michigan, and I'm going to prove to you I'm a great quarterback."

That's what Carr wanted to hear. He wasn't looking to run Brady off and get back his scholarship. He liked him. But he also made no promises about playing time. "He was always competitive from the first day, but I think what happened from that point on is, I would say he began to enjoy the struggle," Carr said. "He went out with the intention of showing his teammates what kind of quarterback he is."

Schembechler came up with the Michigan motto: Those Who Stay Will Be Champions.

The Michigan players touch that sign on the way out of the locker room on Saturdays. In his speech to Team 134, the Michigan team of 2013, Brady closed by speaking of the Schembechler saying that shaped his future: "You stick around, you fight, you work, you do everything you can every day for each other, and you'll be champions."

Griese took over as the starting quarterback as a third-year sophomore in 1995 after Dreisbach tore ligaments in the thumb on his throwing hand in practice. Michigan was 4–0 at the time. Dreisbach had surgery at the University of Michigan Hospital and didn't play again that season. Jason Carr, a fifth-year senior, was Griese's backup.

Dreisbach returned as the starter in 1996. Griese was the backup and didn't get a chance to win the job back until Dreisbach injured his elbow and suffered a concussion in the first half of the annual Thanksgiving weekend game against Ohio State, which was undefeated and ranked number two in the country. Michigan trailed 9–0 at the half, but Griese rallied the Wolverines to a 14–9 upset victory in Columbus, throwing for 120 yards, including a 69-yard touchdown to Tai Streets on the second play of the third quarter. The job was his for the rest of the year.

"It was a stellar performance," Carr said back then. "He came into a pressure situation and made no mistakes. It was really something to see."

Griese then started in the loss to Alabama in the Outback Bowl following the 1996 season. Brady may have decided to stay at Michigan, but his talk with Carr didn't produce an immediate change in his status. His résumé for the season: two games, five passes, three completions.

Brady was still a long way from playing, but his attitude had changed. He was out to win practice every day. He had committed to staying at Michigan. He wanted to prove to Carr that he was the best option at quarterback. He watched film until midnight. His teammates in his apartment building could hear him leaving at six a.m. to work out. Brady began scheduling visits with Greg Harden, Michigan's director of athletic counseling, who became his mentor. Harden couldn't do anything to get him on the playing field, but he became a big influence in Brady's life, helping him deal with his frustration, just as Brady Sr. had undergone counseling to help him deal with Tom's going to college so far away from home.

"Tommy was smart to grab help being offered," Brady Sr. said. "Greg was a major help in his life. Tommy was not getting a chance to play, and Greg helped him process the experience."

Griese had been traveling an even bumpier road than Brady. He was a lightly regarded high school player and came to Michigan as a walk-on. He didn't earn a scholarship until right before his freshman season when another player left the program. Then Griese was redshirted. His father, Bob, had been an excellent quarterback, winning the Rose Bowl for Purdue and then two Super Bowls for the Dolphins, including the victory that capped the Dolphins' magical undefeated 1972 season. He missed most of that season, however, after suffering a broken leg and dislocated ankle, but when his replacement, Earl Morrall, struggled in the AFC championship game, Don Shula went back to Griese. He helped beat the Steelers and then the Redskins in Super Bowl VII. Bob Griese was elected to the College Football Hall of Fame and the Pro Football Hall of Fame.

Brian Griese was to receive his degree in the spring of 1997, and even though he had one year of eligibility remaining as a fifth-year senior, he seriously considered giving up football and going to graduate school. He had not shown enough to be a midround draft pick or even to be drafted at all, and there was no guarantee he would beat out Dreisbach. He had a talk with his older brother, who convinced him to take one more shot at winning the job and getting to the Rose Bowl, just like their dad.

This was not good news for Brady. He was antsy to play, and the more experienced Griese presented another obstacle. Dreisbach also was back again. Carr had to make the right decision. The pressure was on him to win. When Moeller was forced out, Carr initially was named to replace him on an interim basis for the 1995 season by athletic director Joe Roberson. He was not considered a candidate for the job. Tony Dungy, then the defensive coordinator of the Minnesota Vikings, who was a Michigan native and later Manning's coach with the Colts, was on Roberson's list. Near the end of the season, Carr had done well enough to have the interim tag removed. He was 9–4 in his first season and 8–4 in his second—not acceptable by Michigan's lofty standards—and the 1996 group of seniors was the first in school history not to play in the Rose Bowl.

"It was a big year because we had lost four games in each of those previous four seasons and there was pressure," Carr said. "By that time, going into Tom's third year, we all knew that if he got a chance, if we needed him, he was ready."

Carr waited until just a few days before Michigan opened the season against Colorado in 1997 to announce that Griese would be the starting quarterback over Dreisbach, who was getting a cast removed from a sprained right wrist days before the game. "I think his decision making has improved, and I think he has shown great leadership skills," Carr said of Griese.

There was immediate discontent in the Brady household. Carr's decision was between Griese and Dreisbach. Brady was barely mentioned in any of the accounts of the quarterback competition that summer and didn't appear to be in Carr's thought process. "Tommy went in and said, 'I beat him out. You know I beat him out,'" Brady Sr. said. "Carr said no."

Brady's position on the depth chart was not the hot topic of conversation at the Michigan football training table. "Look, we're college kids. What do you know? It's an intense competitive environment where everybody essentially is trying to be the next man up or step into a role in the national spotlight," said Dhani Jones, a Michigan linebacker from 1996 to 1999. "I think Michigan was stacked with so many great quarterbacks. Everybody wants to come in and be The Man. I don't think Brady got the short end of any stick. I think that he actually came in at the appropriate time. Everybody is like, 'He should have started the entire time he was there.' Maybe if he started the entire time, he wouldn't be where he is now on the Patriots."

Jay Feely, the Wolverines kicker, was extremely close to Brady. Feely met his wife, Rebecca, when they were students at Michigan. Brady was in their wedding party. Feely knew how much not playing was getting to Brady. "I think he was probably very frustrated," he said, "the same as any guy who wasn't getting the opportunity to succeed or fail. I think that's what every guy wants, whether it's in college or the NFL. You want to be on the field. When you don't get on the field, you don't know whether you're good enough."

Feely said there wasn't any talk on the team that Brady deserved to be playing. "Nobody knew how good he could be. I don't know if *he* knew how good he could be. Everybody knew all along he was a great leader. That was one of his greatest qualities, his ability to bring guys together. He was always the central figure, even when he was the third-string quarterback. People are naturally drawn to him and his personality. But I don't think anybody in any way could honestly tell you that they saw the potential that was there to become one of the greatest ever."

Griese made Carr look smart in 1997. The Wolverines went 12–0, and their 21–16 victory over Washington State in the Rose Bowl allowed Carr to announce to the team in the locker room after the game that they were national champions. They were number one in the Associated Press writers' poll. Nebraska finished number one in the coaches' poll after beating Tennessee and Peyton Manning 42–17 in the Orange Bowl. Michigan beat Ryan Leaf, who in the coming months would be competing with Manning to be the first pick in the 1998 NFL draft. Griese was the MVP of the Rose Bowl, passing for 251 yards and three touchdowns. Bob Griese, his father, broadcast the game for ABC.

"I think it worked out pretty well," Carr said at Zingerman's. "Here's the thing. Griese had to compete just like Tom did to become the starter. There were people who questioned why Griese was the starter in 1997. Well, I think he did okay. We won the national championship."

As spring practice opened in 1998, Brady had a clear path to the starting job. Griese, a fourth-round pick of the Broncos, was gone from Ann Arbor. Dreisbach was back but had enjoyed limited success when he'd previously had the chance to play, and he was not durable. But there was trouble ahead for Brady.

"Drew Henson is growing up in the town next door. He's the local hero," Brady Sr. said. "He's the guy who has the six-page *Sports Illustrated* spread about him as the next Jim Thorpe or something. I have no doubt that Lloyd Carr had tremendous pressure on him to make the hometown boy the quarterback of the Michigan Wolverines. I also don't have any doubt, although I have no proof, that Lloyd Carr made a deal with the devil that Drew Henson would be his quarterback. So when Tommy comes through the ranks and goes from the bottom of the depth chart to competing for the starting job, Drew Henson, before he even steps on campus, is taking snaps with the first team."

When it was suggested to Carr that Brady was handicapped in his years at Michigan because he didn't recruit him and he wasn't his guy, Carr snapped, "What kind of question is that? The coach's job, the coach here, your job is to win."

Henson was a football, baseball, and basketball star at Brighton High School—he hit seventy home runs and threw fifty-two touchdown passes—and once Carr received a commitment from him to play for Michigan, making sure he received playing time was the only way to keep him from playing baseball full-time. Two months before Henson showed up for his first summer practice, the Yankees drafted him in the third round and gave him a $2 million signing bonus, planning that he would eventually become their third baseman. It didn't help Michigan that Yankees owner George Steinbrenner was a big Ohio State supporter and that by enticing Henson with a baseball career, he could also hurt the Buckeyes' arch rival.

Carr waited until August 27, just ten days before the 1998 season opener at Notre Dame, to name Brady as the Wolverines' starting quarterback. "Now at the same time, I had a freshman named Drew Henson," Carr said. "My stance has always been, 'Let's compete.' You're always trying to get better and you're always competing."

He made the announcement at Schembechler Hall that Brady would start, but just by the tone of his comments, it was clear he would be looking for the first opening to get Henson on the field. He had been practicing with the team for just two weeks after spending most of the summer in the Yankees minor-league system.

"I've been accused that I promised him playing time. All that stuff," Carr said. "I promised him the same thing I promised all the great athletes I recruited: an opportunity to compete. I have no problem with people questioning me for that. I was looking to the future. Henson, make no mistake, was talented. Tom, when he came here, was a great quarterback."

On the day he picked Brady to start, Carr said, "Tom Brady has paid his dues. He has worked extremely hard. He's a bright guy, he has a good arm, and he has the respect of his teammates. I'm anxious to see Tom play. He's got all the right stuff."

Brady won the job over Henson and Dreisbach, who was now a fifth-year senior, and Jason Kapsner, a third-year sophomore. When he was asked about Henson, Carr said he was "rapidly improving" and predicted he would see action in his freshman year.

"Drew has made excellent progress," said Carr, adding that Henson "has gotten better almost daily. He's picked up the offense well. He is without question the most talented quarterback I've been around. It's just a matter of continuing to compete and continuing to prepare. He's going to play some this year because he's not just 'another guy.' He's got everything you want. He is a guy who really adds a lot of mobility to that position."

Why Brady over Henson? "I think it goes back to the fact that Drew Henson has been here two weeks and Tom Brady's been here three years," Carr said. "Tom Brady knows the offense; he's a talented guy. Tom Brady is a fighter, he's a competitor, so I don't sell him short at all."

Brady sat for three years, but he finally had his chance. It didn't get any bigger than opening at Notre Dame. Touchdown Jesus and all. Michigan was the defending national champion, but two lost fumbles by the Wolverines in the third quarter led to two Notre Dame touchdowns that broke the game open after Brady had built a halftime lead. The Irish won 36–20. Carr was determined to get Henson experience by playing him one series per game.

"I'm getting a little bit old, but I have a pretty decent recollection of things that occurred," Brady Sr. said. "Our first game was at Notre Dame, and Drew Henson came in when we were down on the 2-yard line ready to score, to do a quarterback sneak. I think his first snap as a Michigan Wolverine was on Notre Dame's 2, and he fumbled the ball."

Michigan recovered and kicked a field goal. The irony is Brady has become one of the best quarterbacks in NFL history on short-yardage sneaks for first downs or touchdowns. Carr benched Brady late in the game with the outcome decided and Henson came in and threw a touchdown pass.

The next week, Michigan had its home opener against Syracuse and senior quarterback Donovan McNabb. Michigan Stadium was packed with 111,012 fans. Syracuse took a 17–0 lead in the second quarter, and Brady was temporarily knocked out of the game and replaced by Henson. When Michigan trailed 38–7 in the fourth quarter, Brady was benched and Henson came back in. The fans went wild at the mere sight of Henson. Two starts and Brady had been benched twice. He was outplayed by McNabb but would get a degree of retribution when he was better than McNabb in the Patriots' victory over the Philadelphia Eagles in Super Bowl XXXIX following the 2004 season.

The reaction that day at The Big House—the fans booing Brady and cheering Henson—helped create a quarterback controversy. "I put Henson in, some of the crowd—he's a local kid and had an unbelievable high school career—they are happy to see him play. We go down and score a touchdown and that ignites all of this," Carr said. "In the local paper, we had two writers following the team. One of them sides with Brady and the other takes Henson. I remember telling Tom, 'Look, this is what it's like being the Michigan quarterback.'"

Brady faced adversity when not playing. Now he was facing adversity while playing. What did the Michigan fans know about him? He was a California kid who nearly transferred, had to wait until his fourth year before he had a chance to start, and now was 0–2 taking over a team that had just won the national championship and was ranked fifth in the country in the Associated Press preseason poll. Henson was a local hero so good he was able to dictate to any college program interested that they couldn't bring in a quarterback in the class before him.

Carr didn't waver. He stayed with Brady, who then rewarded his coach's faith by ripping off eight straight victories. The winning streak ended at Ohio State in a 31–16 loss when Brady completed 31 of 56 passes for 375 yards and got the crap kicked out of him with seven sacks and many other big hits. "No man ever took the beating he took that day," Carr said. "He was bloodied but unbowed."

Michigan finished 10–3 with a share of the Big Ten championship, ending the season on New Year's Day with a 45–31 victory over Arkansas in the Citrus Bowl, the same bowl Manning had won after his sophomore and junior years. The Wolverines finished twelfth in the rankings. That should have been good enough to make Brady the unquestioned starter going into the 1999 season as a fifth-year senior. Henson skipped spring practice to play baseball and wasn't back with the team until summer camp. However, Carr was still going to make Brady fight for every snap right until his final game. He didn't let anybody outside of the team know that Brady would start until his team took the field for the season opener at home against Notre Dame. The Wolverines were ranked seventh in the preseason polls.

When he was asked a few days before the game who was starting, Carr said, "What time's the game?" When he was told it was three thirty, he said, "Three thirty? You'll see then."

It was Brady, but this time with a big, fat asterisk. Instead of working Henson into each game for one series, Carr came up with a bizarre plan: Brady would start and play the first quarter. Henson would play the second quarter. At halftime, he would decide who played the second half.

"I had two extremely talented guys, and I told them from the beginning that I was going to give them an opportunity to compete," Carr said. "Tom handled it. I can assure you he didn't like it. Neither did Henson. But Tom handled it like a champion. And I think it's because of the way he handled it, there's no one who didn't have great respect for him as a leader, as a teammate, and that includes me."

Brady had been voted captain by his teammates for the second year in a row. He had to set an example with his attitude and hard work. He knew he couldn't complain about Carr's rotation because it could divide the team. He just had to suck it up and hope that Carr would eventually just let him be his quarterback.

"I honestly could say I think I was completely oblivious to it. I can say that I probably didn't even think about it," Dhani Jones said. "I will say this: if I was Tom, I'd be frustrated. As a quarterback, you either want to know that you are in control or you're not in control. Who wants to come on and off the field? If I'm looking at it from Brady's perspective and seeing Henson out there and me out there and Henson out there and me out there, I'm pissed."

It might have been the strangest quarterback controversy in college football, but it didn't top what Tom Landry did in a Cowboys game at Chicago in 1971. He was unable to choose between Craig Morton and Roger Staubach. These were the days when most quarterbacks called their own plays. It was way before coaches would use hand signals to send in plays, and the coach-to-quarterback radio helmet was a concept as foreign as cell phones. Landry was one of the few coaches calling every play on the sideline. He would get the play to the quarterbacks by shuttling guards as his messengers. For the game in Chicago, instead of alternating the guards, he alternated Staubach and Morton every down, giving them the play on the sidelines. Obviously, that was a bad idea. After losing to the Bears, Landry settled on Staubach and the Cowboys went on to win their first Super Bowl.

Carr's plan worked early in the season, as Michigan opened with victories over Notre Dame, Rice, Syracuse, and Wisconsin. Brady earned the right to play the second half three times. Carr picked Henson in the game at Syracuse. "It was a turf field and Henson could run," Carr said. "He had good mobility."

Henson helped win the game as Brady stood on the sidelines at the Carrier Dome. In the locker room after the game, the team circled around the captains as they said a few words.

"It's a great win," Brady told his teammates to open his speech. He was hurting inside, but he was a team player. The team had won. That was the important thing.

"That was one of the most remarkable memories I have of him," Carr said. "I would say in athletics I've never seen a better example of leadership."

Brady started the next week against Purdue and won the right to play in the second half. In the sixth game, against Michigan State, Carr again picked Henson to open the second half. This time he played poorly, and Carr switched back to Brady, who nearly brought the Wolverines from behind. Carr then decided to end the platoon system and just put it all on Brady. The next week against Illinois at home, the Wolverines held a 27–7 lead but wound up losing 35–29 to a 24-point underdog. It was not Brady's fault. The defense fell apart. He threw for 307 yards.

That was the last time Brady lost in college. He did throw three interceptions against Penn State at Beaver Stadium, but he brought Michigan back from a 27–17 deficit in the fourth quarter to win 31–27. He won his last five college games, saving the best for last in a 35–34 overtime victory over Alabama in the Orange Bowl. Michigan finished fifth in the polls.

Somehow it seems fitting that when Michigan trailed 14–0 in the second quarter, Carr benched Brady for one series and put in Henson one last time. The Wolverines went three-and-out, and

Brady played the rest of the game. He rallied his team from 14–0 and 28–14 deficits. Michigan blocked a 36-yard field goal on the final play of the fourth quarter to send the game into overtime. On the first play of overtime, Brady rolled right and threw a 25-yard touchdown pass to Shawn Thompson. Alabama came right back and scored but the game ended when the Crimson Tide's Ryan Pflugner's extra point was wide right. Brady had played the game of his life, but consistent with the lack of appreciation he felt at Michigan, the Most Outstanding Player award went to sophomore wide receiver David Terrell, who caught ten passes for 150 yards and three touchdowns. Terrell would go on to become the first pick of the Chicago Bears, the eighth player selected in the 2001 draft, the same year Brady won his first Super Bowl. He was cut by the Bears after four seasons, and at Brady's urging, the Patriots signed his former Michigan receiver in the spring of 2005. Terrell didn't make it to the regular season as he was among the final cuts.

Brady Sr. was outside the gate at Pro Player Stadium following the Orange Bowl waiting for his son after the last game of his college career. It would usually take twenty-five or thirty minutes. After forty minutes, there was no sign of the Michigan quarterback. Brady Sr. decided to walk up the tunnel to look for his son. After a few steps, he saw Tom and Michigan quarterbacks coach Stan Parrish making their way toward him. Parrish was carrying Brady's duffel bag.

"Parrish said to me, 'Mr. Brady, I've been coaching twenty-five years, and I have never seen an athlete go through what your son has gone through and perform the way he performed and carry himself in such an outstanding manner.' He said, 'In twenty-five years of coaching, this kid has overcome more than any kid that I have ever seen.'"

Brady Sr. took a deep breath when relaying the story. "I talk about it, I get emotional about it," he said. "I will tell you this: Tommy never once complained to us about it. Not once."

Carr gets defensive when talking about how he handled Brady in his five years at Michigan and lists his accomplishments: he was 20–5 as a starter, beat Ohio State, beat Michigan State twice, won the Big Ten, and won two bowl games, including the Orange Bowl against the SEC champion, Alabama, in the final game of his college career.

"If you watched the last four or five games, you would see a guy that was unbelievable under pressure," Carr said. "The game at Penn State, go back and look at the last five minutes of that game. He brought us from behind against Ohio State to win and there's never been a better performance ever at Michigan than Brady's performance at the Orange Bowl.

"So here's the thing: people say he was not the starter. Well, you're watching a guy two years. Maybe the fact that I played Henson some in there may have influenced people. But it's all there on tape. Those last five games, he was sensational. What came to the surface there, going back to the Ohio State game, was his toughness, his leadership, his passion to win. All those things are part of who he is. I love Tom Brady, and no one respects him more than I do."

Henson had the starting job to himself in his junior year and led Michigan to a 9–3 record and a share of the Big Ten title. He then left to concentrate full-time on his baseball career with the Yankees. If he had returned for his senior year to play football and if he played as well as he had in his junior year, the expansion Houston Texans were expected to take him with the first overall pick in the 2002 draft. They selected David Carr instead. Henson couldn't make it in baseball and tried to make a comeback in football. He signed with the Cowboys in 2004, and Bill Parcells started him in a Thanksgiving game against the Bears. Henson had an interception returned for a touchdown in the first half, so Parcells benched him at halftime and put in veteran Vinny Testaverde. Henson played with the Vikings and then his hometown Lions, but he had spent too much time away from football. His dream was to be a major-league baseball player. He had more talent as a quarterback but didn't give himself a chance. It was 2008; he was only twenty-eight, but his football and baseball careers were over.

Brady does not have bitter feelings for Carr, but Brady Sr. does. "I absolutely do. I don't harbor it against Michigan. I have Irish Alzheimer's. I forget everything but my grudges," he said. "I harbor it against Lloyd Carr. The way I feel about it really has no bearing. What's important is how Tommy feels about it. As a parent, I feel Tommy got screwed and many of my friends who were at Michigan, who were strong Michigan advocates and graduates— they felt he got screwed too. That's just the way it is. This wasn't a Michigan decision. This was a Lloyd Carr decision."

Brady learned from his years at Michigan never to take anything for granted. Even as a four-time Super Bowl champion, he goes out to practice every day with the goal to impress Bill Belichick enough to allow him to start the next game. He hates giving up first-team reps. Michigan taught him to fight for everything he wanted.

When Carr retired after the 2007 season, he received a very nice note from Tom Brady. "It was wonderful," Carr said. "We exchange mostly text messages. The one when I retired was special because look at what he has become. He's a Hall of Famer."

Carr has traveled in person several times to see Brady play in the NFL. He went to Miami. He went to Cleveland. "I had a lot of respect for him," Brady said. "I really enjoyed playing for him. He taught me a lot. It certainly wasn't easy, but I think that was the best thing for me. I really needed to be toughened up. I don't think it would have worked out in the long run had I not learned the will to compete and win. The whole competition at Michigan really helped establish that part of my character."

The national championship is Carr's legacy at Michigan, but so are the frustrating years of Tom Brady's college career.

"Did I think he was going to have a good career in the NFL? Absolutely. Did I think he was going to be a Hall of Famer after six or seven years in the league? I don't claim that," Carr said. "I'll say this: since I've retired, I've had a lot of time to think about a lot of things. In my opinion, if you took the greatest quarterbacks in the history of Michigan football, nobody played better than Tom Brady at Michigan."

4

THE FRANCHISE QUARTERBACK

Bill Polian had been hired by Jimmy Irsay to run the Colts, and it was the perfect match—an owner passionate about his franchise and willing to open up his checkbook working with a team president who knew how to build championship contenders and spend money wisely.

Polian constructed the Buffalo Bills teams that went to four straight Super Bowls in the first four years of the 1990s. The Bills lost to the Giants, Redskins, and then the Cowboys twice and became the butt of jokes. As time passed, however, the Bills have been celebrated for getting to four straight Super Bowls rather than being ridiculed for losing all of them.

By the time they had lost the first three, Polian's time in Buffalo was up. He worked in the NFL office in New York for a brief period before Jerry Richardson hired him to put together the expansion Carolina Panthers, who were starting play in 1995. Polian knew his first priority was getting a quarterback. By the time he arrived in Buffalo in 1984, the Bills had already selected Jim Kelly as part of the great quarterback draft of 1983, which included future Hall of Famers John Elway and Dan Marino, but Kelly decided to sign with the Houston Gamblers of the USFL. He was from western Pennsylvania and had dreamed of playing at Penn State until Joe Paterno told him he wanted to make him a linebacker. Kelly had a linebacker's mentality, but he had a quarterback's arm. He went to the University of Miami instead, enjoyed the warm weather, and chose the hot Houston summers over the frigid Buffalo winters. He played in the USFL for three years until the league folded in the summer of 1986, and then Polian brought him to Buffalo. Kelly fell in love with the city and remained after his Hall of Fame career was over.

Polian knew he had to find a franchise quarterback to be the foundation of the expansion team. North Carolina was a college football haven but had been starved for an NFL team. The Panthers were awarded the first pick in their inaugural 1995 draft, and Polian traded down to the fifth spot and picked Penn State quarterback Kerry Collins. By their second season, the Panthers and the Jacksonville Jaguars, their expansion brothers, were in the conference championship game. They both lost, however.

Next stop: Indianapolis.

At the end of the 1997 season, Polian left the Panthers and was hired as the Colts president. He had one year remaining on his contract, and the Colts agreed to give up a third-round draft choice as compensation for Carolina to release him.

Polian walked into a gold mine. The Colts had just finished off a 3–13 disaster to earn the first pick in the draft. The day after the season ended, Irsay fired Bill Tobin, the director of football operations, and coach Lindy Infante, who made the playoffs with a 9–7 record in his first season, but got blown out by the Steelers in the playoffs, and then opened the '97 season with a ten-game losing streak.

By now, Polian had developed a reputation as a master builder, although one with a nasty temper. He sealed his 2015 election to the Pro Football Hall of Fame in the newly created contributors category by rescuing the Colts from obscurity. Jim Harbaugh had been the Colts quarterback the previous four years and had come close—a jump ball nearly caught in the end zone by Aaron Bailey in the 1995 AFC title game in Pittsburgh—to taking Indianapolis to the Super Bowl. Harbaugh was a beloved figure in Indianapolis—he once changed a driver's tire on the way home from a game—and has since developed into one of the best head coaches among all former NFL quarterbacks. Polian knew he was taking a quarterback with the first pick and Captain Comeback was not in the plans. Polian traded Harbaugh to the Ravens for a third-round pick six weeks after the season ended.

"Look, you've been great, but the new guy is going to play," Polian told Harbaugh.

Harbaugh was so competitive and so popular in the locker room that it would have been tough for any rookie if he had remained. Polian didn't want controversy as he began the rebuild. This was a new regime, and Polian was sitting with the first pick and two quarterbacks from which to choose: Peyton Manning and Ryan Leaf. He wanted a smooth transition.

Manning was the sure thing, the best quarterback prospect since John Elway. Leaf was the wild card—amazingly high upside but potential to be a big-time bust. Of course, it now seems like a no-brainer. Manning has gone on to a record-setting career and a Super Bowl win; he's one of only three quarterbacks to take two different teams to the Super Bowl. Leaf was the biggest draft dud of all time and had played himself out of the NFL by the time he should have just been getting warmed up. He lasted three years in San Diego—he missed his entire second season after a training-camp shoulder injury, which required surgery—and one in Dallas. He went about the next decade making headlines for all the wrong reasons and spending more than two years in jail for breaking into a house in Great Falls, Montana, and stealing prescription pills.

Polian walked into a conference room at the Colts headquarters on West Fifty-Sixth Street in Indianapolis for his first meeting with the scouts he inherited. He had his own ideas about Manning and Leaf but wanted to hear from the men in the field who had spent countless nights away from home scouting talent to bring to the Colts.

"I basically said two things: 'I'll learn to speak your language; you don't have to worry about speaking mine. Just go right ahead and do the things you had been doing under Bill Tobin,'" Polian said. "'And give me a preliminary opinion on Manning-Leaf. You don't have to go into the reasons; we'll get into that later on.'"

Polian had seen Manning play three times in person when he was working for the Panthers. He had seen Leaf play once. Eight scouts were in the room. Four voted for Manning. Four voted for Leaf. In the next meeting, he asked for one sentence about why they had made their choices. "What was interesting was that the Peyton people were not anti-Leaf," Polian said. "The Leaf people were pretty vehemently anti-Peyton."

He had four months to make a decision. He started to "zero-base it," as he put it, to go back through the whole process with his scouts and involve Jim Mora, whom he had hired as the Colts head coach, along with key offensive assistants Bruce Arians and Tom Moore. He went to the Colts video department and asked for a montage tape of every pass Manning and Leaf had thrown in their careers. "They kind of looked at me like, *What?*" Polian said.

Manning had thrown 1,381 passes at Tennessee. Leaf had thrown 880 passes at Washington State. That was a lot of tape to put together. This was before plays were easily accessible by computer. The scouting staff did as Polian asked, and right before the combine, he circulated the tape to his staff.

Six weeks before the draft, Chargers general manager Bobby Beathard, always known for taking chances and making big trades, held the third pick overall. He wanted Manning, and to a much lesser extent Leaf, but knew he had to come out of the draft with either one to fix San Diego's quarterback issues. The Chargers had finished 4–12 with Stan Humphries and Craig Whelihan at quarterback. Beathard had to move up one spot to guarantee that he'd get Manning or Leaf. He paid a fortune by trading his first- and second-round picks in the 1998 draft, his first-round pick in 1999, kick returner Eric Metcalf, and linebacker Patrick Sapp to the Cardinals to jump up just one spot.

"I think the consensus opinion is that two like that don't come along very often," Beathard said. "If we're going to be successful in getting that type of quarterback, we're going to have to give up something, and we really did."

Beathard insisted he would be happy with whichever quarterback the Colts didn't take. If that was his way of talking up Leaf and trying to trick Polian into taking him, Polian was too savvy to fall for that. Beathard liked Manning better.

Manning separated himself from Leaf at the combine in Indianapolis. On one of the first nights, Leaf had a 7:00 p.m. appointment with the Colts in their hotel suite at the Holiday Inn not far from the RCA Dome. Polian, Mora, Arians, and Moore were there for their allotted fifteen minutes. Interviews took place during a three-hour window until 10:00 p.m. Leaf didn't show up. "The scout who was in charge of trying to run him down was just flying around trying to reach somebody on the phone," Polian said. "Where is he? What is he doing?"

Sixteen years later, agent Leigh Steinberg said Leaf intentionally skipped the meeting to dissuade the Colts from taking him because Leaf wanted to play for the Chargers. The Leaf camp said at the time that there was confusion over the time of the meeting, but that apparently wasn't true. He just blew it off. The Colts were livid that Leaf skipped the meeting, but Polian denied that he had been manipulated into taking Manning. If Polian had liked Leaf better than Manning, he would have taken him. But that would have been hard. Leaf was a jerk and a knucklehead. Manning was a coach's dream.

The following night, Manning had his appointment with the Colts. Mora, the former New Orleans coach, had gotten to know him over the years through Archie Manning, who was doing the Saints games on the radio. Polian had never met Peyton. He told him he had seen him play a few times in college. "So we sat down and took out our binders, and he took out his binder, and he began to ask us questions," Polian said.

The horn blew after fifteen minutes. Manning had to move on to the next team. The Colts had interviews scheduled with other players. They never got to ask Manning a single question. He asked them all of his. "He got up and left and said, 'Nice to see you. See you down the road,'" Polian said. "I think it was Tom Moore who turned around and said, 'Well, he just interviewed us,' which, of course, as we got to know him, was his modus operandi."

Manning asked about the Colts offensive philosophy, their practice philosophy. "Nitty-gritty football," Polian said. "He had them all written out. Of course, he hasn't changed one iota."

Polian and his contingent planned to be at Leaf's campus workout, so they didn't attempt to reschedule an appointment with him at the combine. Manning had definitely taken the lead, but it was not yet a done deal. Polian approached Mora in mid-March with the idea of sending the tape that the video department had produced to Bill Walsh, the three-time Super Bowl champion coach of the 49ers who was one year away from returning to the 49ers as vice president and general manager. He was unattached in the spring of '98 and agreed to consult with the Colts on the two quarterbacks. Polian shipped the tape to Walsh, who was living in the Bay Area.

By late March, Polian was still waiting to hear from Walsh. He had already watched the tape three times himself and had charted each of the 2,261 throws. "You get paralysis by analysis," he said. "You begin to see ghosts."

On a quiet Sunday afternoon in April, he called Arians and Moore into his office. "It looks to me like Peyton's got a ceiling on his arm at about sixty yards. Beyond sixty yards, he's not all that accurate," Polian said.

"That might be true," Moore said. "But we won't throw any passes over sixty yards."

"You think I'm seeing ghosts?" Polian asked.

"Yeah, you are," Moore said. "Go look at somebody else."

Polian and his entourage took off for Knoxville to run Manning through a private workout. The perception was that Manning had just an average arm, definitely weaker than Leaf's. The Colts played in a dome, so except for outdoor games late in the season and in the playoffs, he didn't need to have a rocket arm like Elway's to cut through the nasty weather. Polian discovered at the workout that Manning's arm was a lot stronger than he had seen on tape.

Moore ran Manning through one of his favorite drills to test arm strength. The receiver stands five yards away. The quarterback has to throw the ball without a drop. The receiver moves back five yards at a time. They keep moving apart five yards at a time. "It's the perfect measure of arm strength and revolutions on the ball," Polian said. "Peyton's arm was plenty strong. Interestingly, he threw a heavy ball, the opposite of what people thought or said. That issue disappeared. He looked terrific in the workout. His footwork was perfect. It was a very, very impressive workout. Of course, it was a very impressive interview. We spent a lot more time with him." This time around, Manning even let the Colts ask some questions.

Tennessee coach Phillip Fulmer then gave the Colts a detailed analysis of Manning as a player. There were no doubts about his character. When the Colts group boarded their plane out of Knoxville, Polian turned to Moore and said, "So much for the stuff about arm strength."

They were off to Pullman to check out Leaf. They didn't run the workout; it was scripted. Multiple teams were present, and Leaf did it in shifts. As Beathard was walking out, Polian, Arians, and Moore were walking in. Polian watched Leaf throw and turned to Moore. "Wow, his arm isn't as strong as Peyton's."

Polian noticed that Leaf's "body definition" wasn't very good. "It was pretty obvious that he hadn't spent a lot of time in the weight room," he said.

He interviewed Leaf at great length. Washington State coach Mike Price was in the room at Leaf's request, even though Fulmer had not been present when the Colts had interviewed Manning in Knoxville. The interview with Leaf went horribly. Polian felt he wasn't professional, wasn't mature, not a football junkie like Manning. At the combine, Manning had asked the Colts whether, if they drafted him, he could come to Indianapolis the next day to start working out and learn the playbook. It was explained to him that college rules prohibited them from doing that right away. Classes had to be over even though he had already graduated.

"What are you going to do to get me up to speed?" Manning asked. "Can I go to a high school in Indianapolis? Can I cross the line into Kentucky? I'm going to be there. We are going to find a way around this rule, right?"

"We will find a way to get you the data," Polian said.

Leaf never asked those questions. He wouldn't even commit to coming to Indianapolis the day after the draft for a get-acquainted session if the Colts picked him. "I hadn't planned on it," he said.

He also hadn't planned to show up on the day rookies were allowed to report in early May. He had a trip planned to Las Vegas with friends. Polian's mind was made up. Then Walsh checked back in.

"He was strongly Peyton for a lot of principally technical reasons," Polian said. "We had a long discussion about technical things. He was sold on Peyton's balance, his ability to stay alive in the pocket, and his accuracy."

Walsh was doing this as a favor to Polian and didn't send him a bill. But Polian felt that wasn't right and sent him a "gratuity," he said, in the form of a check. The draft was still weeks away, but Polian reconvened his brain trust and conducted another Manning vs. Leaf vote. "Clearly, it was trending Peyton," he said. "The early returns were showing Peyton."

They brought him to Indianapolis when they wanted to double-check a minor physical issue. There was no problem. That's when Manning promised to win a championship for Polian if he took him but said that if he passed on him, he would regret it, because he'd come back and kick his ass.

What kept coming back to Polian was Leaf's immaturity, while Manning seemed equipped to handle the demands placed on an NFL quarterback. Polian received a call from Beathard. It was clear he wanted Manning, but he never made an offer to Polian to trade up one more spot. The Colts would have considered a deal only if they had Manning and Leaf dead even and could gain valuable extra draft picks. That might have been the case in January, but now the draft was ten days away.

"Give me a call and let me know who you're going to pick," Beathard said.

Polian called Mora into his office.

"What do you think?" Polian said.

"I think Peyton," Mora said.

"I think you're right. This is what we believe in. If we don't take this kid, we're turning our backs on everything we think we stand for," Polian said.

Arians and Moore were 100 percent for Manning. The scouts were still split. That didn't surprise Polian. "They had done all the work. They were married to the guy they were married to," he said.

Irsay, then just thirty-eight years old and in his second year as the Colts owner after his father, Robert Irsay, had died, was going to be investing an awful lot of money in Polian's decision. He sent a private plane to Knoxville to pick up Manning and bring him to Miami, where they dined at the Surf Club in early April, a few weeks before the draft.

"I'll win for you," Manning told him. Irsay said Manning's words sent chills down his spine. Manning looked straight at Irsay with piercing eyes and shook his hand as firmly as it could be shaken.

"Peyton was impressive," Irsay said. "He would've been great as an astronaut, too. NASA if not the NFL."

Now Irsay wanted to know whom Polian was going to select with the first pick. Manning, he said.

Irsay wanted to know why. "Shows you what a great scout I am," Polian said. "I said if we bust out Ryan, it's a total bust. We don't recoup anything. It's hit-or-miss. If we bust Peyton, if we're wrong on Peyton, which you can always be, the worst we get is Bernie Kosar. Not bad, but not an apt comparison, given what we know today. Jim and I both laughed, and that was essentially it."

The first day of the draft was on a Saturday. Archie Manning called Polian on Tuesday to ask when he would have a decision. Polian knew he was taking Manning, but if nobody was forcing him to make a decision with the draft four days away, he wasn't about to do it. The Colts had the right to sign Manning before the draft, and Polian could have had negotiating leverage with Tom Condon, Manning's agent, because the first pick was going to sign a bigger contract than the second pick. He chose not to use it. He didn't tell Archie. He finally told Peyton on Thursday, but made him promise not to say anything publicly. Irsay was going to be at the Theatre at Madison Square Garden to present a Colts jersey to Manning onstage, and Polian didn't want to take the spotlight away from his owner.

At the NFL's Friday draft event, on a boat that circled Manhattan for two hours, Manning had a secret. He knew the Colts were taking him, but he played dumb. Leaf said he didn't know, but based on Steinberg's account, he was hoping Indianapolis took Manning. Finally, on Friday night, about twelve hours before Commissioner Paul Tagliabue would announce the pick, word leaked that the Colts were indeed taking Manning. "I was taught to be a person of process," Polian said. "We went through the process. The process led us to the right answer."

The Colts and Chargers met in the third preseason game that summer in Indianapolis. The Chargers won 33–3, and Leaf outplayed Manning. He was 15 of 24 for 172 yards with an interception and a fumble and was sacked three times. Manning was 11 of 21 for 123 yards with two interceptions and no sacks.

"The whole Ryan-Peyton thing—we don't get into that," Manning said after the game. "That just slows me down from what I'm trying to do. All it does is take time away from that. I hope he does well. There's no controversy between him and me. All I want to do is play well for my team."

Leaf threw some bouquets Manning's way. "Peyton's the real deal. Everybody knows that," he said. The question after the game, Polian said, was whether Manning was a bust and whether he would ever make it.

The Colts and Chargers met again in the fifth game of the season in Indianapolis. This time, the Colts won 17–12. Manning and Leaf were each an abysmal 12 of 23. Manning threw for 137 yards with one touchdown and one interception. Leaf threw for 137 yards with no touchdowns and one interception. Manning was not sacked. Leaf was sacked four times. It was the first victory of Manning's pro career.

That was the last time they ever stepped on the same field. When Manning was starting to consistently put up big numbers, Leaf's career was just about over.

Manning could have owned New York in a much bigger way than his brother Eli did after winning two Super Bowls with the Giants. Peyton has a much more engaging personality, which is appealing to advertisers.

For the first month after the 1996 season, it looked as though Peyton could be the Jets best quarterback since Joe Namath. Bill Parcells had just worked his way out of his deal in New England and taken over as the Jets coach and general manager. New York had been a dreadful 1–15 under Rich Kotite and had the first pick in the '97 draft. The Jets quarterback was Neil O'Donnell, whom Parcells inherited and quickly learned to dislike. Kotite had signed O'Donnell to a five-year, $25 million contract in 1996, shortly after his two interceptions helped cost the Steelers a chance to beat Dallas in Super Bowl XXX.

Parcells-Manning was a match made in football heaven: Manning was obsessed with football, and Parcells was obsessed with players who were obsessed with football.

Just two events needed to happen and Manning could be the new Namath, minus the pantyhose, fur coats, and Super Bowl guarantees. Parcells had to assure Manning he would take him with the first pick in the draft. Manning had to declare for the draft and give up his senior season at Tennessee. He was going to be graduating in three years, so he could leave after his junior year and still have his degree, which was important to him and his family.

Manning was facing an April 4 deadline to declare for the April 19 draft. Parcells officially became the Jets coach after Tagliabue brokered a compensation settlement between the Jets and Patriots on February 10. He had already been hired and was working as the Jets GM after he left the Patriots shortly after coaching them in their loss to the Packers in the Super Bowl. Tagliabue's ruling made him the coach as well.

Parcells sat in his office at Weeb Ewbank Hall on the campus of Hofstra University in Hempstead, New York, studying tape of Manning. He was outstanding in his final game of the season, throwing for four TDs and 408 yards in Tennessee's 48–28 victory over Northwestern in the Citrus Bowl. The Jets were a team lacking in talent and poorly coached by Kotite, just off the worst season in team history. The Jets had some offensive playmakers in wide receivers Keyshawn Johnson and Wayne Chrebet, but Parcells knew he needed a lot of impact players on defense to get the program turned around.

He studied every throw Manning made as a junior. He liked what he saw. "I think the player is a very good player, and I'll just leave it at that," he said.

The NFL wants players to stay in school and discourages teams from speaking publicly about underclassmen. Parcells used that as a cover for one of the most dreadful mistakes he made in his Hall of Fame career. When Archie Manning called him twice before Peyton announced on March 5 that he would be returning to Tennessee for his senior year, he was all but begging Parcells to tell him whether or not he would take his son with the first pick in the draft. Peyton wanted to make an informed decision and needed answers from Parcells. He didn't want to enter the draft with the intention of playing for Parcells in New York and then have no control if Parcells traded the pick. He wanted clarity about what Parcells was thinking.

"Peyton wanted me to call him," Archie said.

He told Parcells he thought there was a good chance Peyton was going to return to school. That represented a change in thinking, because Peyton later said that during the 1996 season, he was "pretty intent on leaving." If Parcells guaranteed that Manning would be his pick, the feeling around the league at the time was that Manning would turn pro.

"I'm telling you, he's pretty torn," Manning told Parcells. "He'd like to be the first pick in the draft; he's got no problem with New York or the Jets. At the same time, he wants to play his senior year."

Parcells knew that if Manning came out and he selected him, he would be the Jets quarterback for the next fifteen years. He also knew that if he traded the pick, he could fill many of the Jets' holes. One close friend of Parcells suggested that he didn't believe in Manning as much as others did, and at that time in the NFL, before it became a league dominated by the passing game, Parcells wasn't convinced he needed a superstar quarterback to win, especially one coming to New York with as much hype as Manning. "I wasn't in any place to talk," Parcells said. "The league was very adamant about not making any commentary about what players should do. They were on your ass about it. They were watching the Jets. They were watching us like hawks."

Parcells said all he told Archie was to let him know if Peyton was coming out. "All this conjecture about if we just told him he would have come out—that's bullshit. He was committed to staying in school. That's what he wanted to do. He enjoyed college," Parcells said. "Nothing I can do about it."

Parcells never gave the Jets a chance. Backroom conversations happen all the time in the NFL. It would be foolish to suggest otherwise. If Parcells was unsure about Manning and didn't want to commit to taking him in early March, he had that right, although it was the wrong decision. But to say he was concerned about NFL rules makes little sense. If he wanted Peyton, all he had to do was tell Archie.

Was it all a moot point? Archie thinks Peyton would have stayed at Tennessee anyway, but he admits, "If Bill had come out and said, 'Peyton, you're my guy, I'm going to pick you,' it may have made it a little bit harder. But I swear he wanted to be a senior."

Manning finalized his decision to stay at Tennessee on a Sunday. Three days later, he walked into a packed press conference at Thompson-Boling Arena on the Tennessee campus to make his announcement. The anticipation was similar to that of three years earlier, when he revealed he was going to Tennessee instead of Ole Miss, Florida, or Michigan. The arena was filled with teammates, alumni, and students. Coach Phillip Fulmer and offensive coordinator David Cutcliffe were present. Not one person there wanted Manning to leave, and a huge roar went up when he said he was staying.

After the press conference, Archie and Peyton drove to a friend's house in Knoxville. Peyton was amazed that there had been so much suspense in the arena. "Do these people really think if I was going to leave, I would have had a press conference? Would I have gotten up there with Phil Fulmer, David Cutcliffe, my teammates, students, and alumni and say I'm going to go?" he said to his father in the car. "They didn't figure that out. I would have called that one in."

Manning had already begun working out with his teammates and hanging out with friends, and because he had taken between eighteen and twenty-two hours of classes in several semesters, he was a year ahead of schedule to get his degree in speech communications. He graduated with a 3.61 GPA. "I was in such a rush my first three years, I didn't have much chance to breathe," he said.

He evaluated all he had at Tennessee and decided to be a kid for one more year. He would lighten his course load in the fall and relax. He would take graduate classes. "I thought, *I'm not sure I'm really ready to leave this,*" he said. "It was one of the best decisions I ever made. I got to be a senior in college. It's not a year you can ever get back. There was no guarantee the Jets were even going to draft me."

Would Parcells have taken Manning if he'd declared for the 1997 draft? "Yeah, we probably would have," he said. "That's a retrospective view, too. You know what I mean?" Parcells wound up trading the pick to the Rams, who selected offensive tackle Orlando Pace. Parcells now had the sixth overall pick. He traded down a second time and took linebacker James Farrior at number eight. Farrior became a much better player after he signed as a free agent with the Steelers in 2002 than he ever was with the Jets. Parcells passed on Pace when he traded out of the top spot and then traded away the chance to pick offensive tackle Walter Jones at the number-six spot. Pace and Jones are in the Pro Football Hall of Fame.

Manning wanted to return for his senior year to beat Florida, but he lost to the Gators for the third straight time as a starter. He'd also played as a backup in a shutout loss to Florida as a freshman. He wanted to win the national championship. Tennessee was 11–2 and finished seventh in the polls after losing 42–17 to Nebraska in the Orange Bowl. Michigan, with Tom Brady as a backup quarterback, won the writers' poll, and Nebraska won the coaches' poll to share the national championship. Manning wanted to win the Heisman but finished second to cornerback Charles Woodson, Brady's teammate at Michigan.

"Peyton Manning came back to win the Citrus Bowl again," quipped Florida coach Steve Spurrier. "You can't spell Citrus without the UT." Manning had won the Citrus Bowl after his sophomore and junior seasons.

When Spurrier was hired to coach the Redskins in 2002, his comments from five years earlier were mentioned to Manning. "The Tennessee-Florida rivalry is extremely intense. It was always 'Spurrier beat Peyton,'" he said. "I thought their defense was pretty good, too. Since I've been in pro ball, I've played in a few golf tournaments and been to a few banquets with Steve. We told stories and had a few beers together."

Spurrier couldn't wait to return to college ball after compiling a 12–20 record in two seasons in Washington. One of those victories came against Manning and the Colts.

Had Manning come out in 1997 and skipped his senior year, he and Parcells would have been quite a combination. They are pretty much the same person when it comes to football. Attention to detail. No shortcuts to winning. Holding everybody accountable. The two strong-willed personalities might have clashed every now and then, but if Parcells had had Manning, he surely would have coached the Jets for more than just three years. They could have won multiple championships together.

And Parcells would have enjoyed coaching Manning. "I would have liked it very much," he said. "I can tell pretty much what kind of guy he is. I would have liked it."

Parcells and Manning didn't know each other back then but went on to become good friends. Years ago, Manning was the guest of a lawyer friend of Parcells's for a round of golf at McArthur Golf Club in Hobe Sound, Florida, to which Parcells belongs. It's the course designed by pro golfer Nick Price. After the round, everybody was socializing, but there were Parcells and Manning off to the side engaged in a deep talk about football. When Parcells was running the Dolphins and the Colts were practicing at the Dolphins facility before Super Bowl XLIV, Parcells went down to the weight room to hang out with Manning, Jeff Saturday, and Dallas Clark.

Manning had a very tight inner circle, and when his career was in jeopardy following his fourth neck surgery and he was working out and trying to decide in 2012 whether to give it another shot, Parcells and former Giants quarterback Phil Simms were on his short list of consultants. "I was able to converse with him in a language that he understood," Parcells said. "How much do you got on your comeback route? How much on your long ball? Where are you on this or that? He was very candid."

Manning wanted Parcells to watch him throw, but they never did hook up, just as they didn't connect in 1997. Cutcliffe, who'd known Manning as an eighteen-year-old, guided him through the football part of his rehabilitation at Duke. Parcells was available for moral support. "I like the son of a bitch a lot. I really do. He's trying to win. And you can tease him," Parcells said.

Manning did a commercial for Buick. The car is giving him instructions as he drives. "So I leave him a little message," Parcells said. "If that Buick can tell you who is open on Sunday, why don't you just bring that Buick down to the sideline with you?"

Parcells rejected criticism of Manning's history of not being able to win big games in college or the NFL. "They like to kill heroes now," he said. "They do like to kill them."

5

BRADY'S DRAFT DAZE

Just a few days before Tom Brady won his second Super Bowl, defeating the Panthers in Houston following the 2003 season, he was intercepted in practice by safety Rodney Harrison, who proceeded to show Brady up by high-stepping around the field at the Texans' indoor facility. Bill Belichick was running the two-minute session to finish things up, and the competition between the offense and the defense was typically intense. The Patriots were transitioning into their Super Bowl game mind-set. Brady is always in a game mind-set. The trash-talking and yelling between Brady and Harrison carried over into the locker room. "Some bad words being said," Harrison said.

Before they left the field, Brady tried to get even before Belichick ended the practice. "He was so pissed, he chased me around the field for about thirty seconds trying to throw footballs at me, screaming expletives at me," Harrison said. "He's very competitive. He wants to win. Practice is a game situation. It's not like he practices one way and shows up for a game another way. His personality is the same in practice as it is in the game. He's fiery. He's intense."

He slaps high fives and butts heads in games. He does it in practice, also. He took the approach at Michigan that if he wasn't the best quarterback on Tuesday, Wednesday, and Thursday, he wouldn't be playing on Saturday. Even with Super Bowl titles on his résumé, this mentality hasn't changed. He hates to give up practice reps to his backup, even when his buddy Matt Cassel was behind him and desperate to get on the field. Brady never wants to give Belichick any reason to think he's not the best quarterback for his team. In a 2014 game at Kansas City, one of the worst of his career, Brady was benched early in the fourth quarter of a 41–14 loss. When rookie Jimmy Garoppolo came in and threw the first touchdown pass of his career, he was greeted by high fives on the sidelines, but not one of them came from Brady. Critics say he came off as a spoiled brat. The reality for Brady: nothing personal, but why congratulate somebody who wants your job?

The Michigan experience hardened him. Then he came within fifty-five spots of not even getting drafted.

Brady's career at Michigan ended with his nearly flawless performance against Alabama in the Orange Bowl. He was feeling pretty good about his chances to go relatively high in the 2000 draft. He had recovered from being beaten down and built back up at Michigan, and now the NFL was taking its turn slapping him around. He was taken in the sixth round, the 199th player overall, the 7th quarterback selected in a bad quarterback draft and the 7th player the Patriots selected. He was picked with a supplemental draft choice, the 33rd player taken in the round. Brady was so stressed from the ordeal and so relieved to be picked, his first reaction was just being thankful that he didn't have to be an insurance salesman.

The struggles at Michigan helped mold Brady as a very young man. The motivation provided by the NFL humiliating him on draft day has driven him since the moment he arrived in Patriots training camp at Bryant College in Smithfield, Rhode Island.

"Well, I still carry it," Brady said. "It's always a part of you. There is still a reason why I was drafted that late. I'm still not the biggest guy. I'm not the strongest guy. I don't run the best. I don't throw the ball the hardest."

Peyton Manning arrived in New York two days before the 1998 draft. It was not his first trip to New York. In fact, he had been at the Downtown Athletic Club in December of 1997 for the Heisman Trophy announcement. On the day before the draft, the NFL kept Manning and the other players it brought in for the draft busy making appearances. Brady was not invited to the 2000 draft by the NFL. Those invitations were reserved for players expected to be picked early in the first round. Brady was back home in San Mateo watching the draft on television with his family and waiting for the phone to ring.

It would be a long wait, a long and emotionally draining wait. All these Super Bowls later, Brady is at peace with the indignity of being an afterthought, even by the Patriots. If Belichick had thought Brady was going to be a star, he never would've waited until the sixth round to take him. But then if Brady had been picked by somebody other than Belichick, maybe he never would have become Tom Brady.

"I had the luxury of being under the radar. That's how I look at it," he said. "I also realize that there's people behind you trying to take your job just like I did. You got to prove it every day. That's what I tried to do every day when I was in the position where I wasn't playing. There is no entitlement. I never feel entitled to my position. I feel like I got to earn it every day, I got to earn the respect of my teammates every day. I learned that a lot in college. That was a great lesson for me about competition.

"I actually think it was harder for those guys who are the first-round picks and the top overall pick because the pressure is on right away. You have no time to learn. They throw you in there and you go. 'Okay, let's see how well you do.' Usually it doesn't go well. How could it? There's just too much for you to learn in too short a period of time. That's why I think it's pretty remarkable what Peyton's done, what Eli's done, because you have guys like David Carr, JaMarcus Russell, I'm not putting David Carr in that group, but first overall picks that don't turn out the way the team had hoped."

Ryan Leaf, picked one spot after Manning, is the biggest draft bust in history. Brady is at the opposite end. He was passed over 198 times. Brady's hero, Joe Montana, was the last pick in the third round in 1979, pick number 82. Bill Walsh, the quarterback genius, wanted Phil Simms with the first pick in the second round but his plan was blown up when the New York Giants surprisingly picked him seventh in the first round. Then Walsh had to be talked into taking Montana and out of taking Steve Dils, who had been his quarterback at Stanford, but Walsh's innovative West Coast offense and Montana's football smarts, quick release, and nimble footwork turned out to be the perfect football marriage. Johnny Unitas was a ninth-round pick of the Steelers in 1955, was cut before the season, and then worked in construction for one year and played for the semipro Bloomfield Rams. The next year, the Baltimore Colts signed him, and he went on to win two NFL Championships, one Super Bowl, and three MVP awards. Kurt Warner's rise to Super Bowl champion was even more spectacular. He was undrafted out of Northern Iowa and became a scared rookie free agent cut by the Packers when he was trying to make it as a backup to Brett Favre. He packed groceries at Hy-Vee to make a living, lit up the Arena League, and excelled in NFL Europe. He made it onto the field for one game with the Saint Louis Rams in 1998. He was second on the depth chart in the summer of 1999 behind new starting quarterback Trent Green, a big-money free agent signed from the Redskins, until Rodney Harrison of San Diego crashed into Green's knee in a preseason game. Green suffered a torn ACL and was lost for the season. Dick Vermeil cried at the press conference after the game but expressed full faith in Warner, a complete unknown. He went on that year to win the regular-season MVP and Super Bowl MVP. He played in two more Super Bowls, first losing to Brady and the Patriots, and then, after signing with the Cardinals, losing to the Steelers. Warner, Peyton Manning, and Craig Morton are the only quarterbacks to start for two different teams in the Super Bowl.

Each NFL team invests millions and millions of dollars in scouting. General managers, coaches, and scouts spend countless hours interviewing players at the combine in Indianapolis. They work them out on campus. They bring them into their facility. They watch tape until their eyes can take no more. They still make franchise-altering mistakes. Brady didn't have the measurables that would have predicted success, other than being six foot four. He was skinny, actually scrawny. He was slow, actually turtlelike. His arm wasn't nearly as strong as it is today. He couldn't get on the field for three years at Michigan, and then once he became the starter in his last two years, he had a hard time keeping Drew Henson off the field.

"One of the real troubling parts was the Michigan situation," Belichick said on the *Brady 6* documentary produced by NFL Films. "The fact that really they were trying to replace him as their starting quarterback. You say, 'Okay, they don't really want this guy as their starting quarterback. They want another guy. Well, what's the problem here?' It's a little bit of a red flag there. There was nothing we could really do about the whole Henson situation. We just had to evaluate what we saw. And we saw Tom time and again his senior year start the game off well, and then so many times Tom would come back in and rescue the situation and pull out the win for Michigan against great competition, in the biggest game. He just took his opportunities and tried to make the most out of them."

The one crucial element teams can't measure is a player's heart. As the NFL would find out, Brady played with a lot of heart.

The 1983 draft was the Year of the Quarterback. John Elway, Todd Blackledge, Jim Kelly, Tony Eason, Ken O'Brien, and Dan Marino were all taken in the first round—in that order. Marino slipped because of a poor senior year at Pitt and unsubstantiated rumors of drug use. Elway, Kelly, and Marino are in the Pro Football Hall of Fame.

The 2000 draft was not a quarterback draft. Chad Pennington, a game manager with just an average arm, was the only quarterback selected in the first round. The Jets, after trading Keyshawn Johnson to the Bucs for two number-one draft picks, had a record four first-rounders. The other came from the Patriots when the Jets agreed to let Belichick out of his contract so he could coach New England. Pennington won the only two AFC East titles that Brady did not, from the time he took over for Drew Bledsoe in 2001 through the 2014 season. Pennington won the division for the Jets in 2002, the season after the Patriots' first of three Super Bowls in four years, by outplaying Brady in a late-season game. He also won the AFC East with the Miami Dolphins in 2008, but that was the year Brady was lost for the season after tearing his ACL in the first quarter of the first game. Pennington and Brady had a nice rivalry going for a while, but Pennington required four surgeries on his throwing shoulder—he kept blowing out his rotator cuff and labrum—and his career ended with an ACL tear playing basketball in the off-season in 2011.

Pennington was a legitimate NFL starter, and he, not Brady, was the one getting compared to Montana early in his career. But his body betrayed him. Pennington was hurt so often and so severely that he twice earned the Comeback Player of the Year

Award. He completed 66 percent of his passes in his eleven-year career, second best on the all-time list through the 2014 season behind Drew Brees, who was at 66.2 percent.

Giovanni Carmazzi was the next quarterback to be drafted after Pennington, but not until the third round. He played at Hofstra, which no longer has a football program. Two days after Montana was inducted into the Hall of Fame in the summer of 2000, the 49ers played the Patriots in the Hall of Fame preseason game at Fawcett Stadium in Canton. Carmazzi was in totally over his head. The game was too fast for him. "Let it be duly noted that his career begins rather ingloriously with back-to-back sacks," Al Michaels said on the ABC telecast.

Carmazzi was the first quarterback off the bench for the 49ers; he played the entire second quarter and was 3 of 7 for 19 yards. He was outplayed by fellow 49ers rookie quarterback Tim Rattay from Louisiana Tech, the small school that produced Terry Bradshaw, whom Walsh had taken in the seventh round. Brady came in after Drew Bledsoe and Michael Bishop and played the only series the Patriots had the ball in the fourth quarter. He was 3 of 4 for 28 yards and looked as though he belonged. "I think we walked out of that game feeling that we had probably taken the right guy," Belichick said on *Brady 6*.

Walsh and 49ers coach Steve Mariucci must have known after that game that they'd taken the wrong guy. They scouted Brady at a predraft workout in San Francisco held for Bay Area small-college players and for players who went to high school in the Bay Area. Brady did nothing to convince the 49ers to invest a draft pick in him. Walsh had actually said after drafting Carmazzi that he was concerned another team would take him before the 49ers had their chance in the third round. Maybe it was the football gods getting even with Walsh for hitting the lottery with Montana. He passed on Brady, the next Montana, who would have walked the twenty-seven miles from his home to the 49ers office in Santa Clara—that's how badly he wanted to play for the Niners. Carmazzi never got on the field in the regular season in two years in San Francisco; he eventually played in NFL Europe and briefly in the Canadian Football League.

The Ravens took Chris Redman in the third round. Later in his career, he was cut by Belichick when he tried to make the Patriots as a backup to Brady. He had twelve career starts. The Steelers selected Tee Martin from Tennessee in the fifth round. He took over for Manning and won the national championship in his only season as a starter but never started a game in the NFL. The Saints took Marc Bulger in the sixth round but cut him before the season. He then spent time on the Saints practice squad and the Rams practice squad and eventually had a nice career with Saint Louis, taking over for Kurt Warner. Sixteen picks before Brady finally went off the board, the Browns, in their second year as an expansion team, picked Spergon Wynn, who didn't complete even 50 percent of his passes at Southwest Texas State after transferring from Minnesota. Brady had just ripped apart the Alabama defense in the Orange Bowl but had to endure watching Wynn go ahead of him.

Recent Michigan quarterbacks had not become elite players in the NFL. Harbaugh had his moments, but Elvis Grbac, Todd Collins, and Brian Griese, the three most recent Wolverines quarterbacks drafted before Brady, all had backup-type talent.

"At that time, there were three rounds the first day and four rounds the other day," Brady Sr. said. "The first day, Tommy and I played golf in the afternoon. The second day, Sunday, we just kind of hung by the television. At the beginning of the fifth round, Tommy said he had to go upstairs. We were lying on the bed with my wife in the room, and halfway through the sixth round, he said, 'I got to get out of here.' He got up and went downstairs and grabbed a baseball bat and went for a walk."

He was gone for twenty minutes.

The conference table in the Patriots war room at Foxboro Stadium was cluttered with multiple telephones, computers, thick binders, and six water bottles. Scott Pioli, who was Belichick's right-hand man on personnel issues, sat between Patriots owner Robert Kraft and Belichick. Scouts and other members of the personnel department gathered around the table. Belichick had dispatched quarterback coach Dick Rehbein to Ann Arbor in the weeks leading up to the draft to scout Brady, and he came back with a very positive report. He also sent him to Ruston, Louisiana, to work out Rattay. Brady was his guy. That's whom Rehbein wanted.

Bobby Grier, the Patriots vice president of player personnel, also endorsed Brady. He had done his homework, contacting Michigan coach Lloyd Carr. Grier had been at New England for twenty years, first as an assistant coach and then in personnel. But Belichick had been given final say by Kraft when he was hired, three months before the 2000 draft. Belichick then fired Grier after the draft. As early as the third round, Belichick considered Brady. He had inherited an 8–8 team that regressed in each of Pete Carroll's three seasons. Belichick had been a defensive assistant in New England in 1996 when the Patriots lost to the Packers in the Super Bowl, and he developed a strong friendship with Kraft during that year. When Bill Parcells engineered his departure to the Jets, Belichick was Kraft's first choice to replace him. Belichick was a public relations nightmare in his five years as the Cleveland Browns head coach, and Art Modell fired him after the 1995 season. His press conferences were painful. Modell was moving the team to Baltimore and wanted to start off on a positive note in Charm City, but Belichick exuded negativity. Belichick was looking for a job, and Parcells immediately went to Kraft and made a pitch to add his former defensive coordinator, even without any openings on the staff.

As much as Kraft had grown to like Belichick for being in-
clusive, Kraft had such a bitter relationship with Parcells that he
couldn't rationalize keeping such a close ally of the Tuna's. He
believed he needed a clean break and hired Pete Carroll. Belichick
accompanied Parcells to the Jets. Enough time passed by 2000,
and after he fired Carroll, Kraft was ready to reunite with Belichick. But Parcells stepped down as the Jets coach within minutes
after the final game of the 1999 season against Seattle, which by
contract immediately promoted Belichick to head coach. The Jets
knew the Patriots wanted Belichick, but they wanted him also.
Parcells made a preemptive strike by resigning before the Patriots
could request permission to speak with Belichick.

Belichick had been paid a $1 million bonus by Jets owner
Leon Hess in January 1999 as an enticement not to speak with
other teams and to stick around until Parcells quit, whenever that
might be. Hess died four months after making the payment to
Belichick. When Parcells resigned as the Jets coach, the team was
weeks away from being sold for $635 million by the Hess estate to
Woody Johnson.

On the morning after the regular season ended, the Patriots
sent a fax to the Jets requesting permission to speak with Belichick, who had already been named Jets coach. Kraft wanted to
hire him as coach and director of football operations, and Belichick wanted the job. Jets president Steve Gutman denied permission. The next day, Belichick held a rambling press conference. He
read from a handwritten note on loose-leaf paper and resigned as
the "HC of the NYJ." The Patriots and Jets then began a lengthy
fight over Belichick, much as they had over Parcells three years
earlier. Kraft had interviewed former Panthers head coach Dom
Capers and was just about to give up on Belichick and hire Capers
when Parcells called him in his office a few nights before the Rams
were to play the Titans in the Super Bowl. He introduced himself

as "Darth Vader," and they worked out a deal that included sending New England's first-round pick in 2000 to the Jets.

Parcells could have been vindictive and made Belichick sit it out. At the time, however, there was no reason for Parcells or anybody associated with the Jets to believe that allowing Belichick to remain in the AFC East would prevent them from having their own success. Belichick was just 37–45 in five years in Cleveland, then spent four years working as an assistant again for Parcells. If Parcells had thought Belichick would get to six Super Bowls and win four of them in his first fifteen seasons in New England, Kraft would not have been able to offer enough to get Parcells to let Belichick out of his contract.

Once Parcells and Kraft made the deal, Belichick got in his car and drove the four hours from his home on Long Island to Foxboro to sign the contract. "When I hired him, there was an outcry against the move," Kraft said. "I had one media person send me a tape of him doing press conferences in Cleveland. We had to build a new stadium. They said this guy wasn't going to help you, he's not media friendly."

Belichick was taking over a team that was $10.5 million over the $62.172 million salary cap. Belichick and Pioli cut players and restructured the contracts of others to meet the cap requirements. They were left with a roster of forty players. "People don't realize how much of a mess we took over," Pioli said. "What we did have was three quarterbacks. Drew Bledsoe, John Friesz, and Michael Bishop."

Bledsoe was in the prime of his career. Friesz was a capable veteran backup. Bishop, a seventh-round pick in the 1999 draft, was the developmental quarterback. There was no need for another quarterback when the depth chart on the wall was blank at other positions.

"We were completely inactive in free agency," Pioli said. "We didn't sign anyone because we were over the cap."

They didn't have their first-round pick. That went to the Jets for Belichick. After Belichick and Pioli picked Hawaii tackle Adrian Klemm in the second round, the Patriots debated taking Brady in the third round. "He was in the mix of players based on where we evaluated him," Pioli said. "It was a pretty quick conversation."

They had more pressing needs. The Patriots took Arizona State running back J. R. Redmond. They talked about Brady again in the fourth round but took Michigan State tackle Greg Robinson-Randall. They talked about him in the fifth round, when they had two picks. They took Boise State tight end Dave Stachelski and Missouri defensive tackle Jeff Marriott. Belichick needed bodies at positions where he didn't have many bodies. He didn't need bodies at quarterback. Bledsoe had been in the NFL only seven years, had been the first overall pick by Parcells in the 1993 draft, took the Patriots to one Super Bowl, and was durable. He'd started all sixteen games in four of the previous five years.

As Brady went for a walk around the block with the baseball bat in his hands, the Patriots brain trust was trying to replenish a thin roster. They were keeping an eye on him on their draft board, but the waiting around was eating up the Bradys. Team after team was crushing his dream.

"We thought there were several teams that were going to be taking him," Brady Sr. said. They were sure the Chargers would be the team. Leaf was already a bust, and it was a year before they would take Drew Brees in the second round. San Diego coach Mike Riley first came in contact with Brady when he was an assistant coach at Southern Cal; he wanted to recruit him, but coach John Robinson told Riley he was all set at quarterback. Riley saw Brady at the scouting combine in Indianapolis and Brady Sr. said Riley told his son, "I missed you the first time. I won't miss on you again."

Every time the Chargers were on the clock, the Bradys were hoping general manager Bobby Beathard would listen to Riley. If it couldn't be the hometown 49ers, then the Chargers would be a great spot. An easy trip down the California coast for the family to watch him play. The Chargers didn't call Brady's name.

Brady's third start in 2001 after Bledsoe was injured came against San Diego. He led a huge comeback with 10 points in the last 3:31 to send the game into overtime and then brought the Patriots into position for Adam Vinatieri to win it with a 44-yard field goal on the Patriots' first possession of overtime. The Chargers quarterback for that game was Doug Flutie, a folk hero in New England from his days at Boston College. He also played for the Patriots from 1987 to 1989 and would finish his career as Brady's backup in 2005.

By the time the draft entered the sixth round, the grade the Patriots assigned Brady had him all alone on the left side of their board, with lower-rated players in the column to the right. "The conversation came up that we either completely misevaluated this guy or there is something wrong with this guy that we don't know about," Pioli said.

Pioli remembered interviewing Brady at the combine. He had an edge to him, "a rare combination of calm confidence that never even got close to arrogance," he said. "I still see him that way. He has a way about him that is really hard to articulate. He is truly and authentically genuinely humble and not disingenuous."

The pictures from the scouting combine of Brady shirtless, in gym shorts, with his bones sticking out, were not going to get him drafted. They might have gotten him thrown off Cape Cod beach resorts. "Bad body," Pioli said. "Some boys wind up being great high school players who hit full body maturity at age eighteen. Look at what happened to Phil Simms's body from the time he came out of Morehead State to the time he was physically a grown man. Tommy's body hasn't fully matured yet."

Mel Kiper, the well-respected ESPN draft analyst, ranked Brady as only the tenth-best quarterback in the 2000 draft. He wrote some complimentary things about him in his analysis. "Smart, experienced, big-game signal caller getting very high grades in the efficiency department this past season . . . He's a straight dropback passer who stands tall in the pocket, doesn't show nervous feet, and does a nice job working through his progressions. He's not going to try to force the action, rarely trying to perform beyond his capability." Kiper was clearly not sold on Brady, however, or he wouldn't have listed him two spots behind Tim Lester, who played at Western Michigan and was not among the eleven quarterbacks drafted in 2000. He summed up Brady by saying, "He doesn't have the total package of skills," but was impressed with his play against big-time opponents in his final season. "At the pro level, his lack of mobility could surface as a problem, and it will be interesting to see how he fares when forced to take more chances down the field," Kiper wrote.

The Patriots had two picks in the sixth round at numbers 187 and 199. They were not worried that another team was about to grab Brady just as they were set to take him. If they lost out on him, so be it. If they were going to take him, it would be only when they had exhausted their list of players who could fill in the depth chart. This was not the 1991 draft, when the Jets, who didn't have a first-round pick, were frantically trying to trade up to get Southern Mississippi quarterback Brett Favre, the top-rated player on their entire board. The Jets had forfeited their first-round pick by selecting Syracuse wide receiver Rob Moore in the first round of the 1990 supplemental draft. Their first turn in 1991 didn't come until the seventh spot in the second round. Unable to make a trade, the Jets cringed when the Falcons took Favre one spot ahead of them. The Jets settled for Browning Nagle. That didn't work out well.

The Jets lost out on Favre in 1991 and potentially lost out on Manning in 1997, but if Parcells had listened to his Midwest scout, Jesse Kaye, he would have drafted Brady for the Jets in the sixth round before Belichick had a chance to take him. Parcells had picked Pennington in the first round, and with veteran Vinny Testaverde expected back as he rehabilitated from a torn Achilles suffered in the first game of the 1999 season, and with Parcells favorite Ray Lucas third on the depth chart, Parcells was not thinking about another quarterback. Kaye all but stood on a table campaigning for Brady, but Parcells didn't listen.

Sometimes, you just have to take the advice of the people around you. Belichick listened to Rehbein.

"He had a strong influence," Pioli said.

Parcells did not listen to Jesse Kaye.

"I don't remember that," Parcells said.

Even so, according to a Jets executive who was in the draft room in 2000, Kaye indeed lobbied Parcells hard to take Brady in the sixth round.

For the eight years that Belichick worked for Parcells with the Giants, the one year they worked together with the Patriots, and their three years with the Jets, Parcells was the mentor, Belichick the protégé. They had a falling-out after Belichick walked out on Parcells and the Jets, reconciled six years later at a Hall of Fame luncheon for Harry Carson, and for many years lived two floors apart in the same building in their winter homes in Jupiter, Florida. Parcells was inducted into the Hall of Fame in 2013—Belichick left Patriots training camp to attend the ceremony—and Belichick is a certainty to join him in Canton one day. His career accomplishments have now exceeded Parcells's and the primary reason is that Belichick took Brady.

Pennington was the first quarterback the Jets had taken in the first round in seventeen years. Instead of Brady in the sixth round, Parcells took North Carolina safety Tony Scott. Brady might never have received an opportunity with the Jets. It's hard to predict how these things turn out, but picking Scott didn't do the Jets much good. He played in twenty-three games in two years, was cut, and never played in a regular-season game again. He was claimed by Belichick in the summer of 2002 and released six weeks later. He was signed by Seattle in 2003 and released in the summer.

Eight picks after the Jets selected Scott, the Patriots passed on Brady for the sixth time. This time, it was for Virginia defensive back Antwan Harris with pick number 187. The picks go quickly at this point in the draft. Teams want to finish up and begin competing for undrafted free agents. It was beginning to look as though that's where Brady was headed as he came in from his walk, 2,692 miles from the Patriots war room. He was on the verge of falling right through the draft. Pioli looked at the Patriots board and the overlooked quarterback from Michigan was by far the highest-rated player remaining. Players are stacked in columns according to their grade, and Brady was not only by himself in the highest-rated column remaining, but the column to his right, which had lower-rated players, was empty. Only one or two remained in the next column.

"Okay, we've got to pull his name," Pioli said.

Brady was coming back into his house, baseball bat in hand. The phone was ringing.

"Coach Belichick would like to talk to you," the voice on the other end said.

Brady was ecstatic. The agony was over. He was on his way to Foxboro.

"It's amazing the number of stories that I hear now of how many people loved Tommy coming out but for whatever reason they weren't in a position to take him," Pioli said. "Revisionist history is amazing, but there are a lot of people that have inserted themselves into Tommy's football life story in order to give themselves credibility."

Bills coach Rex Ryan was a defensive assistant in Baltimore. He said Matt Cavanaugh, the Ravens quarterbacks coach, loved

Brady, but was unable to convince general manager Ozzie New-some to take him. Ryan was not grading quarterbacks then but says Brady was "Captain Comeback at Michigan." He says he can't imagine, if he'd been making the decision, that Brady would've lasted until the sixth round. "I don't get it," Ryan said. "I swear to God, I always think, if I was coaching, would that guy have lasted? Would I have missed on him? I don't see how the hell I could. He never ran a forty worth a damn? Big deal. The guy is a winner."

Brady developed a sense of humor about the agony of the draft. He posted his college résumé on his Facebook page during the 2014 season. His achievements and job experience were under the heading "Thomas E. Brady, Jr." He graduated with a bachelor's degree in general studies in December 1999 with a GPA of 3.3 out of 4.0 from the College of Literature, Science and the Arts at the University of Michigan.

At the bottom of the résumé on his Facebook page, Brady added a caption: "Found my old résumé! Really thought I was going to need this after the fifth round." Even though he has found a way to joke about it, Brady has never forgotten about the indig-nity of nearly getting passed over. It still motivates him. When he was told in the locker room after a playoff victory over the Ravens following the 2014 season that he had passed Joe Montana as the all-time leader in playoff touchdown passes, he smiled and said, "That's cool. Not bad for a sixth-round pick."

Sadly, the man who loved Brady the most didn't live long enough to watch him develop into a superstar. Dick Rehbein, who had been diagnosed with cardiomyopathy in 1988, died in Au-gust 2001. He passed out running on a treadmill at training camp and was taken to the hospital. He lost consciousness after under-going a stress test and could not be revived. Rehbein's family takes pride in the role he had in bringing Brady to New England.

"I really wish Dick was still here to see this, but my husband's legacy is with Tom, and I feel proud that my girls have something to associate their dad with," Rehbein's wife, Pam, told ESPN.com. "It's an awesome thing for them to have."

Just as at Michigan, Brady didn't have a clear path to the starting job in New England, but it was not an impossible journey. Belichick was never a huge fan of Bledsoe, but he was a favorite of Kraft's and the team had a lot invested in him. Kraft was uncomfortable with all the power that had been given to Parcells, who was already with the team when Kraft purchased the club in 1994. After Parcells departed, Kraft overreacted and didn't give Pete Carroll enough input into personnel decisions. He reverted to the power structure that existed with Parcells when he hired Belichick. He went back to the one-voice approach. He trusted Belichick's decisions, even if that eventually would lead to Bledsoe leaving New England.

"We knew we had a good quarterback, not a great quarterback," Pioli said. "Quarterback wasn't our biggest problem."

The first time Kraft met Brady was in the parking lot at Foxboro Stadium a few weeks after he was drafted. The team had its offices in the stadium, and the players, coaches, front-office staff, and owner would exit through the same door. Kraft was parked right in front. As he was getting into his car around eight p.m., Brady walked up to Kraft with a couple of pizza boxes in his arms.

"Hi, I'm Tom Brady," he said.

"I know who you are. You're our sixth-round draft choice from Michigan," Kraft said.

Brady looked Kraft right in the eye. He shook his hand firmly. "I'm the best decision this organization has ever made," Brady said.

Brady had a strong training camp as a rookie and made the roster as the fourth-string quarterback. No team ever keeps four quarterbacks on the active roster, but with salary cap problems preventing the Patriots from keeping a full fifty-three-man roster, there was room for Brady, who came at a nominal price. Belichick could have tried to sneak him through waivers and signed him to the practice squad, but felt it was not worth the risk of another team claiming him. The Patriots could afford to use a roster spot on a player they didn't intend to play all season. Besides, there was something about this kid that Belichick really liked.

Brady didn't look any closer to getting any playing time going into his second training camp. In March, the Patriots signed Bledsoe to a ten-year, $103 million contract, the largest in NFL history. It saved $1.5 million in cap space and reconfirmed New England's commitment to Bledsoe with $24 million in guaranteed money over the first three years of the deal.

"Bledsoe really was the face of the franchise after we bought it," Kraft said. "We had a great coach in Bill [Parcells], but it was always, 'Was he staying or wasn't he staying?'" Kraft sold his brand by selling Bledsoe as the star. He had a special place in his heart for Bledsoe, but Belichick did not endorse Kraft's giving him the new contract, especially with Bledsoe coming off a poor season. "Bill was in transition," Kraft said. "Would he have preferred we wait? Probably."

The Patriots' new privately financed $325 million stadium was under construction and scheduled to open in 2002. There was not a penny of public money going into the building, and Kraft didn't want to sell public seat licenses. Economic times were bad, and after the September 11 terrorist attacks, financing "dried up," Kraft said. He had to personally buy $56 million of blue steel for the stadium because he couldn't get a loan. Waiting would've set back the opening of the stadium until 2003.

When he signed Bledsoe to the deal, he was sending a message to his fan base. The Patriots had finished 5–11 in Belichick's first season, and the fans clearly had not bought in, but at least Kraft was telling them that Bledsoe was not going anywhere. Brady was not going anywhere on the depth chart, either. Belichick signed veteran Damon Huard in March to be Bledsoe's backup, and Bishop was still on the team. Brady is a gym rat and worked on getting stronger and preparing himself to make a run at Bledsoe's job. He might have been the only person in New England who thought he had a chance to beat him out that summer. By early August, Belichick cut Bishop. That moved Brady to third team. By the end of training camp, he had moved ahead of Huard and was closing in on Bledsoe. Belichick admitted that Brady performed at a higher level than Bledsoe in the summer. If Belichick had made his decision based on who played better in training camp and in the preseason games, Brady would have started the opener in Cincinnati.

"We were talking about it. It was an ongoing conversation," Pioli said. "There were a lot of things at play. We had a quarterback under contract that was established in a lot of ways. He was the face of the franchise. His skills hadn't completely deteriorated."

Belichick met with Kraft and told him Brady had a "tremendous" training camp. "But we had a quarterback who had taken us to a Super Bowl who was great," Kraft said.

Belichick never mentioned to Kraft that he even thought about starting Brady to open the season. "All he ever said is he had the most impressive training camp of anyone," Kraft said.

Bledsoe's new contract and Brady's inexperience prevented Brady from winning the job, but now it seemed only a matter of time. Belichick's decision not to bench the franchise quarterback goes back to his tumultuous tenure in Cleveland. Art Modell hired Belichick after the 1990 season, when he was the hottest candidate in the NFL. The Giants had just won their second Super Bowl, and Belichick's defense was responsible. He used a four-three scheme to beat the Chicago Bears in the divisional round, a three-four alignment to eliminate the two-time defending champion 49ers in San Francisco in the NFC title game, and then only two down linemen with nine others flooding the passing lanes to stop Jim Kelly and his high-octane "K-Gun" offense in the Super Bowl.

Belichick arrived in Cleveland, and his quarterback was in place. Bernie Kosar, who was from nearby Boardman, Ohio, had already taken the Browns to three AFC title games in his first five seasons but lost them all to the Denver Broncos. He was the biggest Browns hero since Jim Brown. Belichick was just 6–10 with Kosar in his first season and was 2–5 in 1992 when Kosar broke his ankle. After ten weeks on injured reserve, Kosar returned in the final game of the season and broke his ankle again. The Browns finished 7–9. The following year, Belichick signed Vinny Testaverde, who was Kosar's backup at the University of Miami and the former number-one overall pick by Tampa in the 1987 draft. Belichick was moving away from Kosar, and it wasn't long before he brought Testaverde into a game in relief and then started him. He was forced to go back to Kosar when Testaverde suffered a shoulder injury, but the relationship between Belichick and Kosar was destroyed. Late in a game that was already lost to the Broncos, Kosar changed a play sent in from the sideline, threw a touchdown pass, and boasted that he had drawn the play up in the dirt.

Modell met for three hours after the game with Belichick to discuss Kosar. The next day, Belichick and Modell met with Kosar, and Belichick released him. "Basically, it came down to his production and a diminishing of his physical skills," Belichick said at a press conference.

Kosar went to Modell pleading to keep his job, but Modell sided with his coach. Belichick was vilified for giving up on the local hero. Testaverde was still out with a shoulder injury, and Belichick was forced to start Todd Philcox for the next three weeks. The Browns lost all three games, and their season, which had started 5–2, was washed away. They finished 7–9. The next year, with Testaverde at quarterback, the Browns made the playoffs with an 11–5 record. Belichick and Testaverde then beat Parcells and Bledsoe in the wild-card game in Cleveland before losing in Pittsburgh. Modell announced in the middle of the 1995 season that he was moving the franchise to Baltimore in 1996, sabotaging his team. The Browns were 4–4 at the time but won only one of their last eight games, and Belichick was fired.

Modell was as close to Kosar as Kraft was to Bledsoe, and the two players' popularity in their communities was similar. That weighed on Belichick's mind when he decided to stick with Bledsoe for the start of the 2001 season, even though his instincts told him Brady was ready and better. He didn't want to go through another Kosar situation with the fans, at least not yet. He had admitted he hadn't handled Kosar correctly and was trying to learn from his mistake. Brady had thrown just three passes as a rookie, and Patriots Nation was not ready for Belichick to make the switch to a second-year player they knew little about. Bledsoe was a leader in the locker room, and there was a clique, comprising offensive linemen Bruce Armstrong, Max Lane, and Todd Rucci and tight end Ben Coates, who were known as FOBs, or Friends of Bledsoe. They were his guys and formed a powerful faction. Belichick went for self-preservation over instincts. The job belonged to Bledsoe when the Patriots got on the team plane for Cincinnati.

The Patriots lost to the Bengals, 23–17. Bledsoe's numbers were very good: 22 of 38 for 241 yards with two touchdowns and no interceptions. He was sacked four times. He was now 5–12 as Belichick's starter. Two days after the Patriots returned from Cincinnati, the United States was attacked. It was September 11, 2001. The nation was in shock and in mourning after terrorists hijacked two planes and took down the World Trade Center buildings in New York, slammed a third plane into the Pentagon, and crashed a fourth in Shanksville, Pennsylvania, after the passengers overwhelmed the hijackers, who were targeting the White House or the Capitol.

The nation had no appetite for football. The players had no desire to play. The Jets threatened to boycott their game against the Raiders in Oakland. The World Trade Center had been visible from Giants Stadium, and it would have been insensitive to hold the Giants home game against the Packers so close to ground zero so soon after the tragedy. The Giants and Jets players were too busy visiting fire stations and helping out families of the victims to even think about playing a game. Pete Rozelle's greatest regret as commissioner was playing games the weekend after the assassination of President John F. Kennedy in Dallas on November 22, 1963. Two days after the September 11 attacks, NFL commissioner Paul Tagliabue postponed the games for the weekend of September 16–17 and rescheduled them to be played at the end of the regular season. The Patriots would not be playing in Carolina as planned.

The Patriots' second game would be the third on the original schedule, the home opener against the Jets. The battle between the Jets and Patriots had grown into the so-called Border War, which started when Parcells went from New England to New York in 1997, then signed Patriots restricted free agent running back Curtis Martin, whom he had drafted in 1995, to a poison-pill offer sheet in 1998 that Kraft elected not to match. The Border War culminated with Belichick's drive north on I-95 in 2000. Nevertheless, the animosity between the teams and animosity Boston fans feel for all New York teams was set aside on September 23 at Foxboro Stadium. The Patriots fans greeted the Jets warmly as they ran onto the field. It wasn't just New York that was attacked by terrorists; it was the entire country. The parking lot was filled with American flags. As fans entered the stadium, they were also given American flags. The pregame program was emotional and patriotic.

In the locker room prior to the game, Testaverde, who was now playing for the Jets, had gone over and looked at two posters on the wall with pictures of missing police officers and firefighters from 9/11. Testaverde got a lump in his throat. Ron Kloepfer was among the twenty-three missing police officers. "High school teammates. I know him. It's just sad," Testaverde said. "He was a great guy. Fun to be around."

The Jets won 10–3. It was a victory for the city of New York. It was no coincidence that the Jets, Giants, Mets, and Yankees all won the first game they played after the attacks. The Jets-Patriots game itself was not memorable—except for one play that changed the course of history in the NFL.

On the official play-by-play, it was recorded thus: 3-10-NE 19 (5:11) D.Bledsoe right end to NE 27 for 8 yards (M.Lewis). FUMBLES (M.Lewis), ball out of bounds at NE 27.

Drew Bledsoe dropped back to pass but couldn't find an open receiver. He scrambled to his right, attempting to pick up a first down. He was being chased by defensive end Shaun Ellis. When he neared the Jets sideline, he was met by Mo Lewis, a six-three, 258-pound Pro Bowl linebacker. Lewis led with his right shoulder and hit Bledsoe with tremendous force in the shoulder and chest. It was a brutal hit. The NFL is a game of brutal hits. Bledsoe was briefly knocked unconscious.

"It was third down and I was heading toward the sidelines," Bledsoe said. "It was two yards short of a first down and I tried to turn back, and when I did, I gave Mo Lewis my full chest and he blew me up."

On the previous play, Bledsoe had completed a 17-yard pass to Bert Emanuel that was overturned by a successful instant-replay challenge by Jets coach Herm Edwards. If the play had stood, the Patriots likely would have run the ball on first down. Instead, Bledsoe was forced to scramble on third down.

The Jets went three-and-out on the next series, and when the Patriots took over at their own 39 with 3:36 left in the game, trailing by seven points, it was Bledsoe back under center. Unaware that he had a sheared blood vessel in his chest, he shook off the hit from Lewis and played the next series, which ended with the Patriots losing the ball on a fumble.

The notation on the play-by-play the next time the Patriots had the ball: New England Patriots at 2:16, 1-10-NE 26 (2:16) 12 Brady now at QB (Shotgun) T.Brady pass to P.Pass to NE 30 for 4 yards (M.Lewis, R.Mickens).

"The reason I ended up coming out of the game is because I had a concussion also," Bledsoe said. "I couldn't think straight. I didn't know my plays. I went back in the next series, and I didn't know which way was right and which way was left. That's why I ultimately came out of the game. It wasn't because of the big injury."

Belichick immediately regretted his decision to let Bledsoe return for the one series. "I shouldn't have put him out there," Belichick said. "Watching him play, he wasn't himself. He got his bell rung. When I went over to him he seemed coherent and said he was okay. But after watching him, I didn't think he was. I told him what decision I had made. He understood."

Brady ran onto the field, and it wasn't as though he put any fear into the Jets defense. He had 70 yards to go to get the tying touchdown, and Belichick had used his last two time-outs to stop the clock on the Jets' previous offensive series. Brady quickly completed five of six passes for 46 yards and suddenly the Patriots were on the Jets 29, but only fourteen seconds were left. Brady spiked the ball to stop the clock on first down. He then threw three straight incompletions and the game was over. Nobody was declaring that the Tom Brady era had arrived.

After the game, Bledsoe was walking off the field when he was approached by Ron O'Neill, the Patriots trainer. "Hey, Bub, you need to come with me," O'Neill said.

"Okay, I'm just going to go in for the team prayer," Bledsoe said.

"Nah, I think you need to come with me. You don't look right," O'Neill said.

As Bledsoe started up the tunnel toward the Patriots locker room, his chest really started to hurt. There was a lot of internal pain. He told O'Neill and Dr. Bert Zarins, "I'll just go home, sleep on it, and will see you tomorrow."

Bledsoe knows where he'd be now if he'd gotten his way. "Had they allowed me to do that, I would have died," he said.

Bledsoe said Zarins was aware of the concussion but said "what ultimately concerned him is when you have a concussion, normally your heart rate starts to slow way down. Instead, my heart rate was increasing, was getting faster and faster."

This was now full-scale crisis mode. Bledsoe's uniform was cut off because he couldn't get his arms above his head. He took a quick shower. They had clothes for him to wear in the trainer's room. He was getting groggy. He was taken out of the locker room on a gurney to a waiting ambulance parked in full view of fans and media. He was bleeding out internally at the rate of a liter per hour. "There are seven liters of blood in my body," he said. "Yeah, it was bad."

He was rushed to Massachusetts General Hospital on Fruit Street in Boston. His younger brother, Adam, rode in the ambulance with him. The hospital was thirty miles away, and it took forever as the ambulance tried to maneuver around traffic leaving the stadium on Route 1 North. Adam Bledsoe thought his brother, the quarterback of the New England Patriots, had died as they were nearing the hospital. It took until 2013 for Adam to tell his brother how scared he was.

"He said we were driving to the hospital and they couldn't give me anything for pain because I'm allergic to morphine and Advil is a blood thinner, and they figured I was bleeding," Bledsoe said. "There was yelling every time there was a bump because it hurt bad. Then we got about ten minutes away and he said I just went out. Just went lights-out. He thought I died in the ambulance. I didn't wake up until the next day."

When he did awake, his wife, Maura, was there. So were Belichick and Brady. Even though he didn't have a great relationship with Belichick, he wasn't surprised to see him by his bedside. "It's different when somebody's life is on the line," he said. "Obviously, you're showing up."

The doctors hooked Bledsoe up to a machine that took the blood that was seeping into his chest, cleaned it, and put it back into his body. They waited for it to clot and for the bleeding to stop. The doctors wanted to give the bleeding a chance to stop on its own. Otherwise they would have to cut Bledsoe's chest open, which could have been career-ending. "There were a couple different times I met double the criteria for opening my chest cavity and they chose not to do it," he said. "They chose to wait, which was very cool."

Bledsoe remained in the hospital four days as Brady prepared to start the first game of his NFL career against Peyton Manning and the Indianapolis Colts. Bledsoe's injury gave Belichick the opening he was looking for to start Brady. "It gave us the chance," Pioli said. "It was more than just Bill that was ready to make that change."

The Patriots beat the Colts, 44–13. Brady threw for just 168 yards with no touchdowns or interceptions. Manning threw three interceptions and the Patriots returned two for touchdowns. Brady threw for only 86 yards the next week in a dreadful 30–10 loss at Miami.

Belichick was now 6–14 in his first twenty games and there

was an uneasiness around the Patriots offices. Pioli said he and Belichick feared Kraft would fire them at the end of the season if they didn't turn things around. "We were in trouble. Me and Bill were in trouble," Pioli said. "We were 1–3 after 5–11. We were in a lot of trouble. We never did talk about it. It was the eight-hundred-pound gorilla in the corner. You know it's there."

Kraft was not happy, and Belichick and Pioli were getting paranoid. Kraft's franchise quarterback had suffered a life-threatening injury, and the anti-Belichick momentum was building in New England. "I remember calling Bill and I said, 'You just keep doing what you are doing. I believe in you,'" Kraft said. "In the NFL you really judge the season, if you are going at a high level, by what happens from Thanksgiving on. It's a great business, but it's a sick business."

Bledsoe was fortunate to be alive. He wouldn't be cleared to play until November 13. The Patriots were 5–2 with Brady and 5–4 overall, but Bledsoe fully expected Belichick to give him back his job, or at least the chance to compete for his job, and that he would start that Sunday against the Saint Louis Rams.

"I'm itching to get back in," Bledsoe said at a news conference he held with his doctors. "I'm going to do everything in my power to be on the field on Sunday. Ultimately, that's not my decision. But I can't wait."

Instead, Belichick made the decision he'd wanted to make in the summer: Brady was his quarterback. It's a teaching point Brady now uses. "I try to express this to the younger players, and it's the attitude I took: You always feel you should be the one in there regardless of whether you should be or shouldn't be," Brady said. "The coach makes the choice. I always wanted to get in there and show them what I could do."

Bledsoe said Belichick never made any promises that when he was healthy, he would have the opportunity to win back his job. It's just something he expected. "There are no promises in profes-

LEFT Four-and-one-half-year-old Tommy Brady (his family and close friends still call him Tommy) warms up in the parking lot at Candlestick Park before the 49ers beat the Cowboys in the NFC Championship Game on January 10, 1982. The Bradys were longtime season-ticket holders of the 49ers, and Tommy's favorite player was Joe Montana. Who knew this little kid would go on to play in more Super Bowls than his hero? Brady never played an NFL game at Candlestick. *The Brady Family* RIGHT Why is this little boy crying? The Brady family was sitting in end-zone seats right behind where Dwight Clark made "The Catch," in the '81 NFC title game to beat Dallas. Tommy was crying because fans in front of him stood up and he couldn't see Clark's catch. Eighteen years later, the 49ers broke Brady's heart by passing on him in the 2000 draft to take Hofstra's Giovanni Carmazzi. *The Brady Family*

LEFT Archie Manning never made the playoffs in his fourteen-year NFL career and never imagined that Eli (far left) and Peyton (right) would grow up to be Super Bowl champions. The front yard of their house was the scene of their "amazing catches" game, with Archie as the QB and the boys diving for his passes. *The Manning Family* RIGHT The Manning boys may have battled one another as kids, but now they are as close as brothers can be. Cooper (second from left) had his career as a wide receiver cut short by a neck injury before his freshman year at Mississippi, but he has lived his football dreams through the spectacular careers of Eli (far left) and Peyton (second from right). *The Manning Family*

The Brady Bunch is a tight-knit family who have been very supportive of Tom through his early struggles at Michigan to his incredible success in New England. From left: Tom; his aunt Kathy; his father, Tom Sr.; older sisters Julie, Nancy, and Maureen; and mother, Galynn. All the Brady kids played college sports, and Tom Sr. admits they inherited the athletic genes from their mother. *The Brady Family*

LEFT Brady at Michigan. Tom Brady put on an incredible performance against arch-rival Ohio State in 1998 at the Horseshoe in Columbus, Ohio. Although Michigan's eight-game winning streak came to an end in a 31–16 loss, Brady was 31 of 56 for 375 yards. He took a beating from the Ohio State defense with seven sacks, but his coach, Lloyd Carr, said Brady was "bloodied but unbowed." *University of Michigan* RIGHT Peyton at Tennessee. Peyton Manning poses for his senior-year football publicity picture after deciding to return to play his final season rather than enter the NFL draft. Manning loved the college life. Although he lost for the third time to Florida, failed to win the SEC, and finished second in the Heisman voting, Manning has never second-guessed his decision to play his senior year. *University of Tennessee*

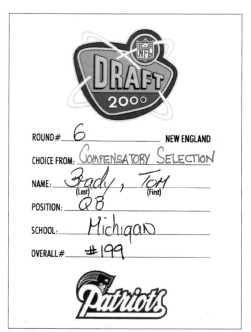

It's the most famous late-round draft card in NFL history. It's so famous that the actual card the New England Patriots used to write down Tom Brady's name as the 199th player selected in the 2000 draft is on display in the Pro Football Hall of Fame in Canton, Ohio. Brady was the seventh quarterback picked and the seventh player drafted by the Patriots. *Pro Football Hall of Fame*

Peyton Manning played the first fourteen years of his record-setting career with the Indian-apolis Colts. He was the reason the Colts won at least twelve regular-season games for seven years in a row, making it to two Super Bowls and winning one. It's hard to believe now, but the Colts scouts were split 50/50 between Manning and Ryan Leaf before the 1998 draft. *AP Images*

Tom Brady was just hoping he would be drafted so he didn't have to become an insurance salesman. In his first fifteen seasons, he went to six Super Bowls and won four, tying him with Terry Bradshaw and Joe Montana for most ever by a quarterback. Brady had a good arm at Michigan, but as he be-came bigger and stronger in the NFL, there wasn't a throw he couldn't make. *AP Images*

Aloha. Peyton Manning and Tom Brady have been good friends for a long time, but the only time they were Pro Bowl teammates came in Honolulu in 2005, the last time Brady played in the all-star game. They could have been together even more, but Brady played only twice out of the ten times he was elected. In the days leading up to the Pro Bowl, Manning would hold court for hours at the outdoor restaurant at the hotel the players stayed in for the week. *AP Images*

Peyton Manning at long last was able to hold the Lombardi Trophy after the Colts beat the Bears in Super Bowl XLI. Two weeks earlier, he beat Tom Brady in the AFC Championship Game, his first playoff victory over his most intense rival, with a late touchdown drive to seal a Colts comeback from an eighteen-point deficit, the largest ever in a conference title game. *AP Images*

Tom Brady and Brazilian supermodel Gisele Bundchen were married in 2009. In the off-season, they spend a lot of time in New York, where they have an apartment near Madison Square Park. She is the world's number one model. He is the greatest quarterback of all time. She makes more money than him. In 2011, Tom and Gisele attended a gala at the Metropolitan Museum of Art in Manhattan. *AP Images*

Tom Brady and Peyton Manning get together after their 2012 game in Foxboro. After playing against each other twelve times when Manning was with the Colts (Brady led 8–4, including 2–1 in the playoffs), this was their first meeting after Manning signed with the Broncos. Brady beat Manning three straight times in the regular season from 2012 through 2014, but Manning beat Brady in the 2013 AFC Championship Game. *Copyright © Gabriel Christus/Denver Broncos*

Peyton Manning added another record to his long resume when he threw the 509th touchdown pass of his career on October 20, 2014, to push Brett Favre into second place. It came on an eight-yard pass to Demaryius Thomas with 3:09 left in the first half of a 42–17 victory over the 49ers. In an entertaining scene, the Broncos receivers played keep-away with the record-setting ball until handing it over to Manning. He helped plan the prank in practice but didn't think his receivers would go through with it. *Pro Football Hall of Fame*

When he was a free agent in 2011, Peyton Manning picked the Broncos over the Titans and 49ers to resume his career after the Colts cut him months after his fourth neck surgery. He made the right choice, and in his second year in Denver, he beat Tom Brady in the AFC Championship Game (he was 1–1 against him in title games when he played for the Colts) and soaked in the adulation from the home crowd while on the podium. *Gary Myers*

Two years after little brother Eli won Super Bowl XLVI by beating Tom Brady on Peyton's home field in Indianapolis, Peyton wasn't so fortunate on Eli's home field against the Seahawks in Super Bowl XLVIII. From the moment the first snap sailed over Manning's head for a safety, the Broncos were overmatched and lost 43–8. On the podium in the interview area after the game, Manning bristled when asked if he was embarrassed. *Gary Myers*

As Deflategate hung over Super Bowl XLIX, Tom Brady had a lot of pressure on him to perform well and eliminate the noise, as the Patriots call distractions. On media day in Phoenix five days before the game, Brady was relaxed and cordial. He threw the winning touchdown pass with just over two minutes remaining to beat Seattle 28–24, tying him with Terry Bradshaw and Joe Montana for most Super Bowl titles, with four. It was Brady's first title in ten years. *Gary Myers*

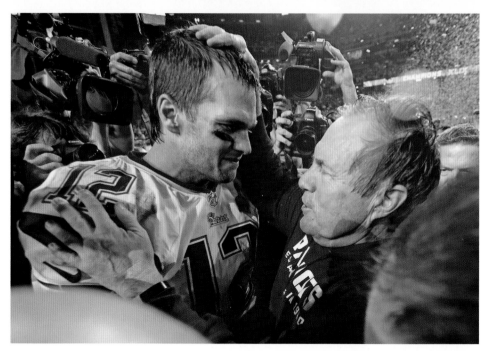

They have never gone out to dinner or sat down to discuss the great success they've had together—they've been to six Super Bowls and won four—but Bill Belichick and Tom Brady are the best coach-quarterback combination in NFL history. They embraced after beating the Seahawks in one of the best Super Bowls of all time. "Way to go, man. That's tremendous. Great job," an emotional Belichick told Brady, who responded with a huge smile, "What a win, huh?" *AP Images*

Tom Brady has stood the test of time. He raised his fourth Lombardi Trophy on February 2, 2015, which came thirteen years after his first one and ten years after his previous one—the two longest stretches for any quarterback in NFL history. He's won his four Super Bowls by a total of thirteen points. He lost his two by a total of seven points. *AP Images*

sional sports, and anybody who thinks there are, they're just plain foolish," Bledsoe said. "That's no slight on anybody. That's just the way it is. When I came back and my job wasn't waiting there for me, I certainly was really pissed about that. I didn't feel that it was right. I felt like I had been wronged."

He split practice reps with Brady his first week back leading into the Saint Louis game. The Patriots lost to the Rams, the best team in the league, but by only seven points. They were just 5–5 but gained confidence by playing the Rams so tight. Belichick decided splitting the reps was hurting the offense and that this was now officially Brady's team. "Tom started last week against Saint Louis, this week against New Orleans, and he's probably going to start next week against the Jets," Belichick said. "That's the way it was. That's the way it's going to be. I think it's pretty clear-cut."

Brady went out and threw four touchdown passes to beat the Saints, and the Patriots went undefeated the rest of the way, right through the Super Bowl.

The Patriots won their last six regular-season games, then beat the Raiders in the "tuck rule" game in the snow in the divisional round of the playoffs in Foxboro. Oakland cornerback Charles Woodson, who'd played with Brady at Michigan, forced a Brady fumble on a blitz as he began his arm motion to throw; Raiders linebacker Glenn Bickert recovered at the Oakland 42 with 1:47 left. The Raiders led 13–10 and the Patriots were out of time-outs. Oakland merely had to kneel down three times and the game was over. But the play was challenged by the replay assistant in the press box, and referee Walt Coleman reversed the call, citing the little-known and now defunct tuck rule. It was ruled an incomplete pass rather than a fumble. Brady then threw 13 yards to David Patten, missed on two straight passes, and ran for 1 yard, and then Vinatieri drilled a 45-yarder through the blizzard to send the game into overtime. The Patriots won the toss and Brady moved them into position for Vinatieri to win it with a 23-yard field goal after running fourteen plays that took New England from its own 34 to the Raiders 5. The Raiders complained after the game that they got screwed, and that feeling has never changed. They lost to the fine print in the rule book.

The Patriots had truly survived and moved on. The next week, they went into Pittsburgh and beat the Steelers in the AFC championship game. Bledsoe came in late in the second quarter after Brady sprained his ankle; Bledsoe played the rest of the game.

Brady was back for the Super Bowl one week later against the Rams. His legend was born that day in New Orleans. The Rams had just erased a 17–3 deficit with two touchdowns in the fourth quarter, tying the game on Kurt Warner's 26-yard touchdown to Ricky Proehl with 1:30 remaining. The Patriots took over on their 17 with 1:21 remaining. John Madden, the most respected football voice on television, famously told the 86.8 million people watching that Belichick, with no time-outs and poor field position, should run out the clock and play for overtime. The Rams had all the momentum, but Belichick was going for it right then. Brady completed 5 of 7 passes for 53 yards, which helped move the Patriots to the Rams 30-yard line. Vinatieri then kicked a 48-yard field goal to win Super Bowl XXXVI.

"Yeah, baby. Way to go, 12," Bledsoe said as he hugged Brady on the field. "You are the man. You are the man."

Brady, just twenty-four and a half years old, was the youngest quarterback to win the Super Bowl. Less than three months later, Bledsoe was traded to the Buffalo Bills for a first-round draft choice.

6

RESPECT FOR PEYTON

Tedy Bruschi and his defensive teammates entered the Patriots meeting room in the week leading up to a game against the Indianapolis Colts to watch tape of Peyton Manning going through his antics at the line of scrimmage, waving his arms like Leonard Bernstein conducting the New York Philharmonic at Lincoln Center.

Bruschi arrived in New England in 1996 when Bill Parcells picked him in the third round. Manning was drafted by the Colts two years later, and it wasn't long before Colts offensive coordinator Tom Moore realized that Manning was so far ahead of the curve intellectually that he could give him a few run-pass options in the coach-to-quarterback radio helmet and let Manning decide which play to call based on what he saw at the line of scrimmage.

Moore slowly gave Manning the responsibility in his rookie year, and by 2000 the Colts had fully transitioned to a no-huddle attack with Manning running the show at the line.

"Everybody has special talents, and one of your jobs as coaches is to make sure that you give a guy an opportunity to be the very best that he can be," Moore said. "Peyton had a special talent from the standpoint of recognizing defenses, knowing the offense, getting you into the right play, getting you out of the bad play. He had the greatest recall of any player I've ever coached. The whole thing evolved as the years went along. Well, what the heck, if we're going to make audibles and he had the recall and application to get us out of bad plays and get into good plays, then let's just go no-huddle and not waste our time in the huddle."

That was just the beginning. By the time Manning was screaming "Omaha! Omaha!" later in his career, as he worked furiously to get the play calls to his teammates, the league knew that half of what he was doing was real and the other half was dummy calls to throw off the defense.

"It's like one of those things—if I could read Chinese and you didn't," former Colts tight end Dallas Clark recalled. "But you're looking at it thinking, *What in the world is that?* People look at him and go, 'What is he doing?' Peyton loves playing those mind games. I watch it now and go, 'That's what I love.' I just smile. That is awesome. Those guys are having the time of their lives. They might not be thinking it right now, because Peyton is yelling and cussing at them, but it's fun. That's fun football."

Bruschi and the Patriots dominated their games against the Colts once Manning arrived. The Colts and Patriots were in the AFC East and played twice a year until there was a minor re-alignment in 2002 sending Indianapolis to the AFC South. In the years from Manning's rookie season through 2004, the Patriots won ten out of twelve games, including the 2003 AFC championship game, in which Manning was intercepted four times—Ty Law got him three times in New England's 24–14 victory—and a 2004 divisional-round game in the snow won by the Patriots 20–3, in which the Colts punted or turned the ball over on nine out of their ten possessions.

The Patriots were not confused by Manning at the line of scrimmage. They were amused.

Once the tape was turned on in the meeting room, the players were entertained. They watched him wave his arms, frantically run up to the center, back up, scream to his left, scream to the right, wave his arms some more and call for the ball to be snapped with just seconds remaining on the play clock. In the Patriots' view, the only person he was confusing was himself.

"We didn't respect the Colts at first because they just had a problem beating us," Bruschi said. "We used to laugh at Peyton in the meeting rooms because we used to be able to confuse him so well. And you could see the look on his face and the little gy-rations—he let it be known that we'd get to him. Then we would watch film. 'Oh man, look at what I did here. I was supposed to be over there, but I lined up all the way over there and I hopped around, and he's up there gyrating like he's got no control.' Then all of a sudden the play clock winds down."

New England wasn't the only team that made fun of Man-ning's gestures. Prior to the first of the Manning Bowl games be-tween Peyton and Eli, on the opening Sunday night of the 2006 season, the Giants video staff, on instruction from the defensive coaches, prepared special tapes of Manning's hand signals at the line of scrimmage. The buildup to the game was intense. The Colts were a Super Bowl contender and indeed would go on to win Super Bowl XLI. The Giants were coming off an NFC East champion-ship in Eli's second season and had big expectations.

The Giants players were forced to watch the tapes of Peyton so many times, they were sick of them. "They put together tons of film," said linebacker Antonio Pierce, the leader of the Giants defense. "We were supposed to try and figure out and guess what it was. You will see the shovel. The shovel was a dig route. The pistol. That was a slant. Then he would change it up."

The regular-season schedule had come out in the spring, and the coaches had months to prepare for the first few games. Just as Peyton, Eli, Archie, and the oldest son, Cooper, grew tired of answering questions from the media about the family tree, the Giants defense had reached its limit for watching Peyton tapes during training camp and in the week before the game. To keep themselves from falling asleep and thus getting fined by Tom Coughlin, the defense set Manning's arm-waving to music using an electronic gadget. "It started off as a teaching tape," Pierce said. "The next thing you know, we're watching a music video with Peyton Manning."

Peyton threw for 276 yards with a touchdown and an interception. Eli threw for 247 yards with two touchdowns and an interception. The Colts won the game 26–21.

By the time the Patriots arrived in Indianapolis for the AFC championship game at the end of the 2006 season, Bruschi and his teammates were no longer laughing at Manning. He had defeated them in the regular season in 2005 and 2006 in New England and put up a total of 67 points. Manning never thought it was him against Brady. He knew he had to outscore Brady, but he also had to outsmart Bill Belichick's defense. Belichick won seven of his first eight games against Manning and had gotten deep inside Manning's head. Manning had finally found a way to get him out.

"You get super focused and you can't prepare enough," Manning said. "You know it's going to be a dogfight. I've always felt like it was a pretty good two-headed monster coming at me, between arguably one of the best coaches of all time, certainly a great defensive coach, and then Tom at the quarterback position. It was always tough. You grinded to get ready for that game because you knew you had to be on top of your stuff."

The Patriots and Colts each finished 12–4 in 2006, but San Diego had the best regular season in its history, 14–2, and Baltimore was right behind at 13–3, so New England and Indianapolis were both relegated to the wild-card round with records that in most years would have been good enough to earn the top seed in the conference. The Colts beat the Chiefs and the Patriots beat the Jets in the opening round. The next weekend, the Colts went into Baltimore and beat the Ravens 15–6 in a game without any touchdowns. It was the third time Manning had failed to get his team into the end zone in the playoffs but was the first time he won. Then Brady put up 11 points in the last 4:36 in a wild 24–21 comeback victory in San Diego. The Colts earned home field in the championship game because they'd defeated the Patriots during the regular season.

Colts coach Tony Dungy couldn't say it at the time, but he knew there was tremendous pressure on Manning to beat New England. He knew what Manning's detractors were saying, although he didn't agree with them: "Belichick was in his head, we'd never beat these guys, he's going to choke in the big games," Dungy said.

It was Brady vs. Manning for the third time in the playoffs. Manning needed this game much more than Brady. It was a legacy game. Brady had surpassed Manning and now Manning was trying to close the gap.

"They are great friends, but I don't think either of them likes to lose to the other," said center Dan Koppen, who played with Brady in New England and Manning in Denver.

"They took two different roads," Bruschi said. "It's a kid that had a chip on his shoulder, was the 199th pick, and nobody expected anything out of him, and there was a guy that was given the keys to the kingdom. A lot of credit to Peyton that he's taken those keys and he's still driving. The keys are well deserved, but Brady *made* the keys. He wasn't given them. That's a different approach, a different mentality."

The atmosphere in the RCA Dome was electric for the AFC championship game. This was not Manning's best team. They were better in 2005 when they were 14–2 but lost a tough game to the Steelers in the divisional round. Manning was better in 2004, when he threw forty-nine touchdown passes. This was his second championship game, his first at home, so this was his best chance to get to the Super Bowl. Brady already had three Super Bowl titles.

This was a game the Colts should win. It was a game Manning had to win, or the can't-win-the-big-game label, which haunted him at Tennessee and stuck with him as he didn't win a playoff game in the NFL until his sixth season, might be impossible to shake. "I don't think he would let that dictate his career," Clark said. "Dan Marino is his favorite quarterback, so to have that happen to his hero, to not win one Super Bowl, I don't think he was going to put that pressure on himself." But the pressure was there for the championship game and it was all on Manning.

The Patriots caught a break on their second series. Brady fumbled on a third and 1 from the Colts 4, but guard Logan Mankins fell on the ball in the end zone for a touchdown. New England then scored touchdowns fifty-three seconds apart early in the second quarter to take a commanding 21–3 lead. First, Corey Dillon scored on a 7-yard run, and on the second play of the Colts' next possession, Asante Samuel intercepted Manning's pass intended for Marvin Harrison and returned it 69 yards for a touchdown. There was still 9:25 left in the second quarter, so there was plenty of time, but no team had ever come from 18 points down in a conference championship game, and now Manning had to do it against a defense that had tormented him in two previous playoff games. The doubts about Manning being able to perform in big spots had returned.

He was able to get the Colts 3 points closer at the half at 21–6.

After halftime, Manning scored on a 1-yard run and then threw a 1-yard touchdown pass to Dan Klecko, the former Patriots defensive lineman turned fullback turned pass-catching machine. Manning's two-point conversion pass to Harrison brought the Colts even at 21–21 with four minutes left in the third quarter. Manning had wiped out a 15-point halftime deficit in eleven minutes. This was Manning at his best and finally he was showing it in the playoffs. The Patriots went ahead by 7 on Brady's 6-yard touchdown pass to Jabar Gaffney three minutes later. The Colts tied it when center Jeff Saturday recovered running back Dominic Rhodes's fumble in the end zone. The Patriots went ahead by three. The Colts tied it. The Patriots went ahead 34–31 with 3:49 left on Stephen Gostkowski's 43-yard field goal. The next 3:49 would define Manning's career. The elite quarterbacks *will* their team to victory in game-deciding moments. Amazing Catches with his father and brothers in their front yard in New Orleans was fun. They were playing for bragging rights. This was intense. It was time for Manning to show he was great. It didn't start well. He threw three straight incompletions, and the Colts punted. Brady had the ball on his own 40 with 3:22 left and the Colts down to two time-outs. The Patriots were in prime position to run out the clock and make it to another Super Bowl.

On first down, the Patriots were penalized for having twelve men on the field, a crucial 5-yard setback. Brady then completed two passes for 11 yards and was incomplete on third down, forcing the Patriots to punt. They had used only sixty-five seconds. Manning came back on the field with the ball at his own 20 and 2:17 remaining. Dungy saved him one time-out. If Manning ever was going to prove he was a championship quarterback oblivious to the pressure and able to do more than win 12 games in the regular season but come up short in the playoffs, now was the time.

In four plays using only twenty-four seconds, the Colts had

a first down at the New England 11. Manning completed three passes: 11 yards to Reggie Wayne, 32 yards to tight end Bryan Fletcher, and 14 yards to Wayne. New England's Tully Banta-Cain was penalized 12 yards for roughing the passer on the last completion to Wayne, and now the Colts needed to manage the clock, get in the end zone, and not leave Brady enough time to pull off any last-minute playoff heroics. Unless the Colts turned it over, at the very least they would send the game into overtime with a chip-shot field goal by former Patriots hero Adam Vinatieri.

Joseph Addai ran for 5 yards. Then he ran for 3. Belichick called his first time-out with 1:02 left. It was third and 2 on the 3. The Colts could get a first down without getting a touchdown. Manning had numerous options. Play action, rollout, fade pass. He gave it to Addai. He scored. The Colts led 38–34, their first lead of the game, but there was exactly one minute left, and New England still had two time-outs.

Manning took a seat on the Colts bench and prayed. He prayed he had not left Brady too much time. He prayed his defense could get him to his first Super Bowl. "I don't know if you are supposed to pray for stuff like that," he said.

Manning couldn't look as Brady took over at his own 21 after the kickoff with fifty-four seconds remaining. He threw incomplete to Reche Caldwell on first down; forty-nine seconds remaining. Brady then hit tight end Benjamin Watson for 21 yards. Belichick didn't use a time-out. Brady went no huddle out of the shotgun but was taking too much time. He snapped the ball with thirty-one seconds left and completed a 15-yard pass to fullback Heath Evans. Belichick then called his second time-out with twenty-four seconds left and the Patriots at the Colts' 45. Brady could have taken a couple of Hail Mary shots at the end zone but instead threw over the middle on a pass intended for Watson, who was double-covered. Marlin Jackson, the Colts first-round pick in

2005 and a Michigan man like Brady, cut in front of Watson and intercepted his fellow Wolverine.

Jackson's interception was so clean, it left no opening for the replay assistant to even consider issuing a challenge to bail out Brady as the tuck rule had five years earlier. Manning quickly put his helmet on to run off the final sixteen seconds with one kneel-down. He was finally going to the Super Bowl. He had finally beaten Brady in the playoffs. This time it was Brady's heart that was broken. "Even when we were up 21–3, you knew at some point they were going to come back," Brady said.

He said it was "frustrating for all of us when it ends like this, because the expectations are so high." Brady had also become accustomed to pulling out these high-stakes games in the final minutes. He knew it never should have come down to the final drive, and when Jackson picked him off with 16 seconds remaining, he didn't overanalyze things. "It was over; that was my only thought," he said.

Was the monkey off Manning's back? Was there vindication?

"That's been the number-one question I've been asked so far," Manning said after the game. "But I don't get into monkeys and vindication. I don't play that card."

It might not have been a full-size gorilla that had been airlifted off Manning's back, but it sure was bigger than a monkey. He'd lost the first three playoff games of his career before breaking through in 2003 in a 41–10 victory over the Broncos. Now in his ninth season, he had made it to his first Super Bowl. Although Marino never won a Super Bowl and made it to only one in his career, it came in just his second season and his first full year as a starter. Joe Montana was 4–0 in the Super Bowl with eleven TDs and no interceptions, and he made it to his first Super Bowl in his third season. Steve Young won his only Super Bowl as a starter in his fourth season after taking over for Montana; he implored teammates on the sideline to take the monkey off his back in the final moments of the 49ers victory over the Chargers. Brady won three Super Bowls in his first five years in the league, even though he didn't start until the third game of his second year.

Manning downplayed the historical significance of the victory over the Patriots in the moments after the game. He still had a Super Bowl to play against the Bears in two weeks, and the season would be a failure if they didn't beat Chicago. Many years later, at the Broncos facility, Manning opened up about what it meant to beat New England. "We felt pretty good after winning that game," he said. "We thought we'd beaten a really good team. Fact is, we shouldn't have won that game. We were down. Sometimes it's worse to be down at home than away. Everybody is on you. You hear occasional boobirds come out [when you're] down 21–3. It was kind of a symbolic game in many ways. We had been down and gotten over the hump. That was obviously a special win."

Bruschi was not laughing at Manning anymore. He was still trying to disguise defenses, but it was no longer working. Touchdown passes were sailing over his head. It was the 2006 AFC championship game that altered Bruschi's respect for Manning. "At the end of the game, it was important for me to go up to Peyton and say, 'You deserved it. You earned it,'" Bruschi said. "I was, really, it's strange to say, but I was proud of the kid. I was proud of him because we had just beat on them for so long, and they got us. I'm not dead inside. I know the pressure the guy has been going through, everyone calling him a bust, an individual statistical quarterback. For me, finally he got it done. I was proud of him for doing that."

Manning threw for 349 yards, but he completed only 27 of 47 passes with a touchdown and an interception. His quarterback rating was just 79.1. Brady threw for 232 yards, completing 21 of 34 passes with a touchdown and an interception. His quarterback rating was 79.5. Neither quarterback played one of his best games, but it was the most dramatic game they ever played against each other. It was the signature game in the Brady vs. Manning series.

"I think it means something special to win the game when they play against each other," said former Giants quarterback Phil Simms, who did the game for CBS.

Manning went on to beat the Bears 29–17 in Super Bowl XLI, a sloppy game in a downpour in Miami, the worst weather ever for a Super Bowl. The game began with Chicago's Devin Hester returning the opening kickoff 92 yards for a touchdown. But the Bears were no match for the Colts. Manning threw for 247 yards and a touchdown and was named Super Bowl MVP. He had never beaten Florida. He had never won the SEC championship. He had never won the national championship. Now he won the Super Bowl, and making it even better, he beat Brady, his nemesis, on the way to getting his ring.

"I think for the nostalgia of the rivalry, the Manning and Brady rivalry, it gained so much more traction by us winning a Super Bowl and by us coming back from that huge deficit to go to the Super Bowl," Clark said. "That's as close to Hollywood writing as you can get."

The AFC championship game victory and Super Bowl victory were significant to Dungy on many levels. He was the first African American coach to win the Super Bowl. He had taken over a joke of a franchise in Tampa in 1996 and by 1999 had them in the NFC championship game in Saint Louis. They were going up against Kurt Warner and the Greatest Show on Turf, which had set a record that season by scoring 526 points. Dungy was a defensive whiz, and the Bucs held the Rams to just eleven points, by far their season low, but Tampa could manage just two field goals in the loss. The next two years, the Bucs lost in the playoffs in Philadelphia without scoring a touchdown.

That made it three straight playoff games the Bucs were unable to get into the end zone. Dungy was fired after the 2001 season. The Bucs were turned down by Bill Parcells as the first choice in their coaching search and eventually sent $8 million, two first-round picks, and two second-round picks to the Oakland Raiders for Jon Gruden, who'd had a falling-out with Al Davis. Gruden inherited a team in Tampa that was stacked on defense but needed a new offensive approach. Gruden supplied it. He took Dungy's players and his quarterback, Brad Johnson, and won the Super Bowl, beating Davis and the Raiders, 48–21. The win was a positive reflection on Dungy's ability to pick the right players, but from a coaching perspective, it accentuated his offensive shortcomings.

Dungy had no trouble finding another job right away. Colts president Bill Polian had fired Jim Mora after a 6–10 season that included two losses to Brady and the Patriots. The Panthers, Polian's former team, had fired George Seifert, who had won two Super Bowls with the 49ers. Dungy was offered jobs in Carolina and Indianapolis. He picked the Colts. He picked Manning. Dungy had met Manning once before on a limousine ride from their hotel in Philadelphia to the Maxwell Club awards dinner after the 1997 season. Dungy had been named coach of the year in the NFL, and Manning was receiving the trophy for college player of the year. Dungy told Manning on the ride over that he wished he could draft him in Tampa, but there was no chance of moving into position to get him. Five years later, they met again, this time in Dungy's office in Indianapolis after he had been hired by the Colts. Dungy was stunned when Manning remembered everything about that night, including the name of Dungy's wife, Lauren, and the name of the hotel they stayed in.

Manning's reputation as a perfectionist, leaning heavily on the overbearing side, was no secret. Dungy's reputation as a coach who couldn't develop an offense was well known as well. Dungy believed he had to win Manning over and convince him he wasn't going to just run the ball and rely on the defense to win games, which had been his formula in Tampa. Dungy had retained Moore as the Colts offensive coordinator. When Dungy played quarterback at the University of Minnesota, Moore was on the offensive staff. "We've got a lot of money spent on offense," Dungy told Manning. "This is an offensive team. We're not going to change what we do."

He was just asking Manning to cut down on the turnovers and let the defense work for him. There was nothing wrong with punting on fourth down and living to see another day. He promised Manning he was going to give him a championship defense, but it would take time. However, in their first year together, Manning and Dungy were humiliated 41–0 by the Jets in the playoffs, making it four playoff games in a row in which Dungy's team had not scored a touchdown. The next two years, they lost to the Patriots, the second time once again not scoring a touchdown. Dungy and Manning didn't lose faith in each other, but the pressure was building on both of them. Manning couldn't win a big game. Dungy literally couldn't get his team across the goal line. Dungy kept preaching to his players what he learned from his mentor Chuck Noll in Pittsburgh. Be consistent. "We don't have to elevate our play to beat the Patriots," Dungy emphasized. "We just have to play our game in the big setting."

As he admitted, "It was a message to Peyton, but that was the way I believe you win."

Dungy and Manning were in this together. Each of them had a reputation he was trying to overcome. Beating the Patriots in the championship game vindicated them. They were winners. The victory over the Bears in the Super Bowl was anticlimactic. Manning had just outdueled Brady. If he couldn't beat Rex Grossman, the worst quarterback ever to start a Super Bowl, that would be trouble.

"It's strange, but I bet Peyton would say the same thing, too—

that game against the Patriots was the satisfying one, that was the big game," Dungy said. "We knew if we were going to get there, it was going to happen that way. We were going to go through New England and finally prove we could beat them in a big game. The way it happened, us scoring all those points in the second half, this defense that supposedly had our number, we finally did the job against them when it counted. That was the biggest game by far. That was our emotional Super Bowl."

Three years earlier, the Patriots defense embarrassed Manning in the AFC championship game by intercepting him four times and sacking him four times. Polian was so incensed at the way the Patriots defensive backs were manhandling his receivers that he helped push through new legislation. It helped that Polian and Dungy were on the competition committee, which presents rule changes for the owners to vote on each spring. Starting with the 2004 season, the officials were told to make illegal contact a point of emphasis. After Manning had brought the Colts to within 21–14 in the 2003 championship game, he missed on 8 of his last 10 throws as New England defenders all but took up residence in the uniforms of the Colts receivers. "We just wanted to pound them and hit them and get those white jerseys dirty in Foxboro," Bruschi said. "That's the mentality we had against those guys."

The Patriots had three penalties assessed by referee Walt Coleman's crew: false start, false start, and delay of game. Not one illegal contact. Not one illegal use of hands. Not one pass interference. Coleman had also been the referee in the tuck-rule game two years earlier.

The new point of emphasis loosened things up in 2004, and Manning broke Dan Marino's touchdown record of forty-eight, which had been set in 1984. Manning threw forty-nine TDs, and his 121.1 quarterback rating was a single-season record, shattering the previous record of 112.8 set by Steve Young in 1994. Manning's previous best was 99.0 in 2003.

The crackdown on the defensive backs, however, didn't help Manning when the Colts returned to Foxboro in the 2004 divisional round. Manning's longest completion was just 18 yards. The Patriots were called for five penalties for 35 yards. There was one defensive holding. The Colts declined an illegal contact and accepted the play instead.

The 2006 AFC championship game was the last time Manning and Brady met in the playoffs before Manning's career in Indianapolis came to an end, but their regular-season rivalry continued. Brady won in the regular season in 2007. Manning won in 2008 against Matt Cassel, with Brady sidelined with a torn ACL. Manning won 35–34 in 2009 when Belichick elected to go for it on a fourth and 2 deep in his own territory with a 34–28 lead rather than punt the ball back to Manning. It backfired and the Patriots lost. The Patriots won in 2010 at home in a 31–28 shootout, the last Brady vs. Manning matchup when it was Patriots vs. Colts. New England held a 31–14 fourth-quarter lead but Manning threw touchdown passes to Blair White with 7:57 and 4:41 remaining to bring the Colts within three points. Then after the Indianapolis defense was able to get Manning the ball on his own 26 with 2:25 left, he drove to the Patriots 24 with 37 seconds on the clock. He went down the right sideline for Pierre Garçon but was intercepted at the 6 by James Sanders.

That would be the last pass Manning would ever throw against the Patriots as a member of the Colts. He missed the next season following neck surgery, and the Patriots beat the Colts 31–24. The rivalry with Brady would resume in 2012 with Manning in a different uniform.

7

GOOD-BYE, INDIANAPOLIS

It didn't end the way it should have for Johnny Unitas in Baltimore, Joe Namath in New York, or Joe Montana in San Francisco. They were the biggest names in the history of their franchises, but they all finished their careers with other teams. It didn't end the way it should have for Peyton Manning in Indianapolis, either.

The problem started in the spring leading into the 2011 season. Manning had neck surgery in May, the NFL players were locked out March 11 by NFL owners in a labor dispute, and Manning was one of the named plaintiffs in an antitrust lawsuit against the league, so the Colts' contact with him was minimal. Team president Bill Polian said he was "barraged" by league counsel and team counsel not to talk to Manning. The league was advising all teams not to speak with any of their players during the shutdown. The lockout lasted 136 days, until July 26.

Polian could not be in touch with his franchise quarterback, even after he had neck surgery. "Dr. [Hank] Feuer, our neurosurgeon, had some contact but not a lot. Our trainer had some contact but not a lot," Polian said. "Only the bare minimum, because the constant refrain was, 'Don't talk to him, don't talk to him, don't talk to him.'"

When the lockout ended, Polian had a lengthy phone conversation with Manning. Manning reported to the training facility the next day and told Polian he was fine and expected to be ready for the start of the season. The Colts then signed Manning, a free agent, to a five-year, $90 million deal.

Polian said Manning told him he didn't need as much money as Brady. "You figure out something that works so we can keep people on the team," Manning said.

"You need to get as much as Brady," Polian said. "There's no reason to do otherwise."

There was a $28 million option inserted for 2012 to protect the Colts in the event Manning's neck was worse than they thought. The minimal contact in the off-season prevented the Colts from getting a precise picture of what was going on, and as a result, Polian left the Colts exposed at backup quarterback. As practices started in early August, Manning was not on the field. There was no indication when he was going to be able to throw.

"Believe me, as training camp went on, we became more and more concerned, because he wasn't coming along the way you wanted him to," Polian said. "He, of course, was becoming more concerned and more irritable about it. I never blame a player who's hurt for feeling that way."

Panic began to set in. Colt owner Jimmy Irsay and Polian had loaded up to make one last run with the core group that had been to the Super Bowl two years earlier, but Curtis Painter was the next man up at quarterback. Painter was best known for coming in for Manning in the third quarter of the fifteenth game of the 2009 season when the Colts had a lead on the Jets. Before the game, Polian had ordered his coach, Jim Caldwell, to take Manning out in the third quarter, because the Colts already had the number-one seed locked up. Polian didn't care that his team was 14–0 and wanted to become the second 16–0 team in NFL history; Brady and the Patriots had done it in 2007. He wanted to protect Manning. Painter came in with a 15–10 lead with 5:36 left in the third period, but on his second series, he was strip-sacked, and the Jets returned the fumble for a touchdown. They desperately needed the game to make the playoffs and went on to win it 29–15. It didn't take a body-language expert to see how upset Manning was after the game.

"No regrets," Polian said.

"Deep down, I wanted to go for the undefeated season, but I didn't stop it, because you can make an argument for either," Irsay said. "I know it gets debated fiercely. I can see why. Personally, I like going for it, and let the chips fall where they may."

The plan was devised to make sure Manning was healthy for the playoffs. He took the Colts to the Super Bowl, but they lost to the Saints.

Considering that there was now so much uncertainty about when Manning would be able to play, Polian was not going to trust the 2011 season to Painter. He convinced Kerry Collins, his number-one pick for the Carolina Panthers in 1995, to come out of retirement on August 24. He signed him to a one-year, $4 million contract. Collins had retired after the 2010 season with the Titans, his fifth NFL team. The Colts were still holding out hope Manning would return in September. At least Collins had a lot of experience, and he had played in a championship game with the Panthers and a Super Bowl with the Giants. He was a leader and gave the Colts a better chance to win than Painter. But he had to take a crash course in the offense to get prepared for the season, which was just fifteen days away.

The Colts played their final preseason game in Cincinnati, and the front office staff gathered the next morning at nine a.m. to cut the roster to fifty-three. "One of the assistant trainers came in and said, 'Dr. Feuer needs you in the back. It's an emergency,'" Polian said. "I excused myself and walked back, and Hank was sitting there. He said, 'I got to show you this MRI.'"

Polian took a look.

"He needs a spinal fusion," Feuer said.

"Wow" was all Polian could think of saying.

Polian stayed for about thirty minutes and walked back into the staff meeting. This was going to be the fourth procedure on Manning's neck. It was the most serious.

"Guys, I've got the worst news possible. Peyton's gone for the year," Polian said.

The May surgery in Chicago was to repair a bulging disc. He subsequently needed follow-up surgery. All during training camp, Chris Polian, Bill's son and right-hand man, stayed in touch with Denver GM John Elway regarding a trade for quarterback Kyle Orton. Now the Colts were desperate. "We were prepared to pay whatever it took, but not a first-round draft choice," Polian said.

Orton stayed put in Denver, started the season, and eventually lost his job to Tim Tebow, who took the Broncos on a magical run to the second round of the playoffs. Manning underwent spinal-fusion surgery in Los Angeles on September 8, and Collins was the starter in the September 11 opener in Houston despite having been on his farm enjoying retirement just two weeks earlier. The Colts lost to the Texans 34–7; Collins was rusty. He was sacked three times and lost two fumbles.

The game ended Manning's streak of consecutive regular-season starts at 208 games. Including the playoffs, he had started 227 consecutive games. Both were the second-longest starting streaks for a quarterback in NFL history, trailing only Brett Favre, who had started 297 consecutive regular-season games, 321 including the playoffs, until missing a game late in his final season in 2010. Manning had started every game of his career, beginning with the first game of his rookie season.

Collins started the second game, a home loss to the Browns.

He suffered a season-ending concussion in the third game against the Steelers in another loss. It was now officially time for the Colts to turn their attention to Stanford quarterback Andrew Luck. The motto of their season became "Suck for Luck." Two years after winning their first fourteen games, the Colts lost their first thirteen. They played the rest of the season with Painter and Dan Orlovsky at quarterback. Painter was 0–8 and Orlovsky was 2–3 after Collins started 0–3.

Polian missed a chance to put himself in a better position to survive Manning's injury by not trusting his instincts in the 2011 draft. He knew it was time to start thinking about a successor to Manning, just as the Packers did with Brett Favre when Aaron Rodgers fell to them in the 2005 draft. Instead, the Colts took Boston College tackle Anthony Costanzo with the twenty-second pick in the first round. "The thing I second-guess is, we took Costanzo and not either Andy Dalton or Colin Kaepernick," Polian said. "We might still be there, had we done that. Because if you go 7–9 or 8–8 with one of those guys, even 6–10, you probably survive. That hurts me badly for the coaches and all the other people that got let go largely because we didn't do that in the draft. But we didn't know that Peyton wasn't going to play, believe me. We were as much in the dark as any group has ever been. It was absolutely the perfect storm."

Polian's friends in the league question why he didn't talk to Peyton or his father, Archie, or have a third party call during the lockout to get updates on Manning's status. Polian banged his hand against a table and said, "I can't tell you how strongly it was emphasized to all of us: do not talk to him; you will jeopardize the lockout. It will be a court case, the union will run to court, the lockout will be over, you will ruin the National Football League."

. . .

Manning was such a dominant personality and such a perfectionist that the organization was often on edge. "Look, he's not a saint. No man is," Irsay said.

His attention to detail could be overwhelming. He made sure all the clocks in the building were set to the same time. "He was so thorough and intense and such a perfectionist, you wanted him to get as comfortable as he could before game time," Irsay said. "He was a thoroughbred. He was wired to do what he does, and his intensity 99 percent of the time was an asset. But even as a rookie, it was kind of like, 'Don't throw your arm out in warm-ups.'"

Polian made a mistake by not placing Manning on season-ending injured reserve after his spinal fusion surgery. It wasn't realistic or in Manning's best interests for him to play in 2011. It also gave him and his teammates false hope that he could get back on the field. Polian knew how much Manning wanted to play. "He played every game as though it were his last game," he said. "I remember telling him during his rookie year, 'Don't play with clenched teeth.'"

By the end of September, it was a lost season in Indianapolis, and Polian could have ended all speculation that Manning would suit up by simply putting him on IR. "We wanted to give him the incentive to come back and it was more psychological than anything else," Polian said. "The doctors said, 'Hey, there is a chance, probably slim, but as long as there is that chance, let's keep him active. It will give him hope that he can come back.' That was the principal reason. The secondary reason is we didn't want to send a message to the team that he's gone for the year and there is no hope."

Manning is so competitive that he was determined to work toward playing again before the end of the season, if only to quiet speculation that his career was over. The atmosphere had changed in the Colts building. They were losing for the first time in forever and Manning was cranky. The losing took its toll on the entire organization.

"It wore down everyone," tight end Dallas Clark said. "We all saw the writing on the wall where, okay, we're oh-and-whatever, we got a lot of big contracts coming up, and if you're running this business, what are you going to do? And you got Andrew Luck coming up, who is the clone of Peyton. We're all aware of the business part of the whole thing. No one was getting along. We all kind of knew we're probably not going to be in this business next year. The reality is, the ride is coming to an end here. We had a heckuva run, and that was pulling at a lot of people."

By late in the year, Manning was pushing to get on the field, but the Colts didn't even know if he could throw the ball to compete at an NFL level. Manning proposed playing only in the red zone in a Thursday night home game against the Texans in the next-to-last game of the season. Once the Colts moved inside the Texans 20, Manning would come in and try to finish off the drive. Back in September, two days before it was determined he needed the spinal fusion surgery, Manning had proposed the same setup.

That arrangement would have been as insane as Dallas coach Tom Landry alternating Craig Morton and Roger Staubach in the Cowboys game in Chicago in 1971 or Michigan coach Lloyd Carr starting Tom Brady in 1999, playing Drew Henson in the second quarter, then deciding at halftime who would start the third quarter. At least then it was Landry and Carr calling the shots. Caldwell was just a figurehead coach taking his orders from Polian. Manning had everybody walking on eggshells. He was an intimidating presence. He had become accustomed to getting his way, and quite frankly, that was often a good thing. If Peyton wanted it, Peyton got it. But he was not a doctor and he couldn't clear himself to play. The first step was proving he could throw.

It was the understanding in the front office that Manning

would go out after practice and throw for a little bit in front of the coaches and Polian. Nothing too complicated, nothing very organized. He was supposed to bring a receiver or two to run short routes. But it turned out to be as scripted as some of the predraft workouts. Caldwell, offensive coordinator Ron Turner, and quarterbacks coach Clyde Christensen were all there. Manning recruited running back Joseph Addai and Clark and others to catch passes. Christensen called the plays. Manning made thirty throws. It was run at game tempo, a seven-on-seven-type drill, only without defenders. Manning maxed out at 20 yards, the ball wobbled, and he was tired at the end. Polian was furious the audition took place. He had no idea it was going to be such a formal affair.

"Obviously, by that time, everything has pretty much hit the fan," Clark said. "If us running routes is going to help Peyton with his rehab, then darn it, I'm going to run routes for him. He's my quarterback. It's a no-brainer. But then you got the politics behind all of it. You hear this person is not happy. As a player, well, if I can help him with his rehab, I'm going to. At the end of the day, isn't that what we all want? Everybody getting better and getting healthy? I don't think anyone was really thinking clearly at that time. It was ugly. The bottom line is, it's the first time facing an injury that stopped Peyton from playing."

This had become Manning's show. It was perceived that Manning was now coach, general manager, and franchise quarterback, and with Irsay away at a league meeting when the audition took place, he was basically the owner, too. Polian's legacy in Indianapolis was drafting Manning and having the success of going to two Super Bowls, being in the playoffs almost every year, and having an incredible seven-season streak from 2003 to 2009 when the Colts won at least twelve regular-season games. He didn't want to confront Manning, especially if it became public.

Manning was not ready to play. It was not worth the risk. The

Colts needed to just say no. The episode caused friction in the organization. Polian denies he was upset with Manning for scripting a workout more involved than he had been led to expect. But the feeling around the Colts at the time was that he felt betrayed by his quarterback. "I wasn't ticked at him," Polian insisted. "I was ticked at the medical people for not letting me know."

Irsay was upset that Polian had not taken control. Manning was upset, knowing his days with the Colts were coming to an end. He did not play in the Houston game. He never got on the field that season. He never would again for the Colts.

Polian, the Colts vice chairman; his son Chris, the general manager; Caldwell, the head coach; and his coaching staff were fired once the season ended. Irsay hired Ryan Grigson from the Eagles in early January as the new general manager, and Grigson hired Ravens defensive coordinator Chuck Pagano as the new head coach two weeks later. By the time the football world descended upon Indianapolis for Super Bowl XLVI between the New York Giants and New England Patriots, Irsay had his new management team in place. If Manning had not had four neck procedures in a two-year period, the Colts possibly could have been the first team to play the Super Bowl on their home field. But even before Manning's neck became a major issue, there were signs that the Colts were taking a step backward. They had lost at home in the wild-card round to the New York Jets in 2010, one year after beating Rex Ryan's team at home in the AFC championship game to advance to Manning's second Super Bowl.

Manning was the unofficial Super Bowl ambassador. He took care of many of the logistical concerns for his brother Eli, who was playing the game in Peyton's home stadium. On the other side was Tom Brady, Peyton Manning's good friend and most intense rival. Manning did not have split loyalties. Four years earlier, he'd been watching from a private box at University of Phoenix Stadium in Glendale, Arizona, as Eli drove the Giants down the field to beat Brady and the Patriots in Super Bowl XLII. Peyton stood clapping for a long time when Eli threw the winning touchdown pass to Plaxico Burress with thirty-five seconds remaining to end New England's undefeated season. He might have been the most excited person in the stadium. It was a touching scene after the game when Peyton and Eli stood by Eli's locker and dissected the throws that won the game. Peyton was proud of the little brother he used to pick on.

Just two days before the Giants-Patriots rematch, ESPN reported that Peyton Manning had been medically cleared to play by two doctors, including Robert Watkins, the surgeon who'd performed the spinal fusion operation. It was now an issue of the nerves regenerating in his right arm to allow him to get the necessary velocity on his throws.

Archie Manning had gone through his own doubts whether the fourth surgery had ended Peyton's career, but "I never doubted Peyton in his will," he said.

On a visit to the home where he grew up in New Orleans, Manning sat at the foot of Archie and Olivia's bed, just as he had done during the college recruiting process. Instead of being seventeen years old, he was thirty-five. "I knew he wasn't going to go against a neurosurgeon who said, 'Peyton, you don't need to be out on a football field,'" Archie said. "I knew he wasn't going to test that."

He looked his parents in the eye. They had been with him every step of the way in his football career. His wife, Ashley, had given birth to twins in May 2011, giving Peyton a new perspective. "I'm going to do what the doctors tell me to do, so take that out of your worries. But in the meantime, I'm going to try as hard as I can to get well and play," Peyton said.

Archie sometimes thought, *After four neck surgeries, Peyton, this isn't worth it.*

The previous June, during the lockout and after one of his neck surgeries, Manning went to Denver to work out at the facilities of the Colorado Rockies. His college buddy Todd Helton was the Rockies first baseman. The plan was for Manning to throw short passes to Helton, but the football hit the ground before it had even traveled 10 yards. Helton thought Manning was joking. He was not. This was serious.

Once he was cleared by his doctors, around the time of the Super Bowl, Manning put the football part of his rehabilitation in the hands of David Cutcliffe, his offensive coordinator at Tennessee, Eli's head coach at Ole Miss, and now the head coach at Duke. Manning became a regular in Durham, North Carolina. Gradually, the arm strength was coming back, and he was starting to get some zip on the ball. He never had an Elway fastball, and he would never throw the way he did before the neck surgeries, but with his football smarts, he knew there were other ways to get it done.

It just wasn't going to be in Indianapolis.

Jimmy Irsay boarded his private Gulfstream jet in Tampa for the quick ride across the peninsula to Miami–Opa Locka Executive Airport. Peyton Manning's limousine driver took him right onto the tarmac; he got out of the car and walked toward Irsay's airplane. The owner of the Indianapolis Colts was standing at the top of the steps to greet him.

It was just the two of them and the pilot and the flight attendant on March 6, 2012, for the two-and-a-half-hour flight to

Indianapolis. Manning had missed the entire 2011 season but still collected the $26.4 million due on his contract. He stayed around the team for much of the year, but was helpless to prevent the Colts' worst season since 1991.

Even before the flight, they both knew Irsay had no choice. He had to cut Manning. Two days after they stepped on the plane, the Colts either had to pick up Manning's $28 million option for 2012, triggering his $7.4 million base salary, or they had to release the most important and popular player in the history of the franchise since Johnny Unitas and by far the most popular player since the team moved to Indianapolis in 1984. Did it make sense to pay $35.4 million to a quarterback who was going to be blowing out thirty-six candles on his birthday cake in two weeks and coming off major neck surgery at a time when Irsay was in rebuilding mode with major salary-cap problems but also with Andrew Luck, the newer and healthier version of Manning, in the draft? The answer had been provided in Jacksonville more than two months earlier with 2:24 remaining in the final game of the season. Jaguars running back Maurice Jones-Drew stretched out and picked up 5 yards on a third and 4 to clinch the 19–13 victory for Jacksonville. The loss was the Colts' fourteenth in sixteen games, and they earned the first pick in the draft in a tiebreaker over the Rams. It ended the Manning Era. The Colts had pulled off their mission statement: Suck for Luck.

"I walked out of the locker room in Jacksonville and tears were rolling down my face," Irsay said. "No one wants to be the person to say the party's over. It sucks."

Luck was Manning with a stronger arm and greater mobility. He was smart, obsessive about preparation, had perfect mechanics, never made anybody worry about post-midnight calls from the police, and was a great leader who held teammates accountable. The Colts had sure sucked enough for Luck, and it was just their luck that after making the playoffs nine years in a row and in eleven of the thirteen years Manning was healthy, the best quarterback prospect since Manning was available for them in the draft. It was like 1998, when the Colts had the first pick by going 3–13 and Manning, the best QB prospect since Elway in '83, was in the draft. The Colts didn't want to "Suck for RG3." They never considered Robert Griffin III but went all-in on Luck. He took them to the playoffs three times in his first three years, including an AFC championship–game loss to Tom Brady after the 2014 season, the Deflategate game.

In his heart, Irsay didn't want to let Manning go. He's an emotional man and has had his own off-the-field personal issues dealing with painkillers that eventually led to his getting arrested for driving while intoxicated. He had a strong bond with Manning and wished it could end differently. He never wanted Manning to play for another team. Lucas Oil Stadium opened in 2008 next to the old RCA Dome, where the Colts used to play; it was "the house that Peyton built." The $450 million retractable-roof facility was funded by a public-private partnership: Irsay put in $100 million, and public money accounted for the rest. The emergence of the Colts brand in Indianapolis once Manning arrived was a major reason the stadium was built, and with it, Indianapolis was awarded Super Bowl XLVI, which brought 116,000 visitors to the city and $364 million to the local economy. Irsay was a good owner. His father, Robert, was not. He traded away the rights to Elway in 1983 and the next year moved the Colts from Baltimore to Indianapolis in the middle of the night, robbing the city of a team that it loved so much.

"'The house that Peyton built' is appropriate. It sounds good, and it's worthy," Irsay said. "He's that sort of figure. He had that kind of influence and presence. He just meant so much to me, the team, city, and state. He's just beloved. I can't say enough about what he means to the franchise and to me."

Manning, who has an off-season home in Miami, boarded the

plane for the conversation he and Irsay didn't want to have but
knew was inevitable. The flight attendant remained in the front
of the plane with the pilot. No food was served. This was a serious business meeting. Irsay asked Manning to look at it from his
perspective. Irsay then looked at it from Manning's perspective.
The Colts were going to draft Luck. In the days before the salary
cap, it would have been just a matter of whether Irsay wanted to
spend the cash on Manning and then also pay big money to Luck
to learn sitting behind Manning for a year or two. That was the
protocol, but no longer. It just couldn't work. Quarterbacks taken
first overall are expected to start from the first game of their rookie
year and not be tutored by a veteran making over $30 million. Fi-
nances virtually dictate it works that way.

"You could have physically and literally had Andrew and Peyton on the same team, but what you would have done to both players would have been a catastrophe," Irsay said. "It would have been
so bad for the National Football League, so bad for Andrew Luck,
so bad for Peyton Manning. Peyton would have gone on with a
team that was with the likes of the replacement team in 1987 and
would have been 2–6 and they would be calling for Andrew Luck
to come in. I love history, and I love one guy staying with one team
and retiring with one team. Circumstances came that made that
impossible."

The salary cap changed the NFL world. If Irsay kept Manning, he wouldn't be able to construct a team around him. The
new collective bargaining agreement that followed the 2011 lockout established a rookie wage scale. Luck's deal would come in at
$22 million over four years. Getting Manning off the books would
allow Irsay to replenish the roster for Luck.

Still, this was Peyton Manning. You can't cut Peyton Manning. But you have to draft Andrew Luck. Manning didn't want
to retire. Luck didn't want to sit on the bench. This was not going
to be pretty.

You can't have them both, and Manning was not about to take a big pay cut. There was also the health factor—no guarantee Manning would come back at 100 percent or even close. The long incision on the back of his neck was a chilling reminder of what he had endured. He still had a long way to go in his rehabilitation to build back his arm strength.

Polian said if he hadn't been fired, his plan was to keep Manning and draft Luck, clearly not what Irsay had in mind. "The money was not an issue," Polian said. "Keep the guy in the wings. The guy in Green Bay, Aaron Rodgers, stayed in the wings for three years. What better way to have success for the long term than to have Peyton and Andrew Luck ready to succeed him."

Tony Dungy had been gone from the Colts for three years, but if he had still been there, he would have backed Polian's plan. "I thought that is what they were going to do," he said. "You have to draft Andrew Luck. I don't think Peyton would have resisted that, and it would have been the best thing for the franchise in the long run. That's what I would have recommended."

The disconnect between Irsay and Polian on so many issues about Manning led to Polian's getting fired. "It was the most sensitive time of my professional career," Irsay said. "History needs to be recorded."

As the private plane began making its way from Miami to Indianapolis, Irsay updated Manning on where the Colts doctors stood. Irsay revealed confidential salary-cap information to Manning to illustrate the bind the Colts were in. If Manning was paid his $28 million bonus, he could be playing in front of an offensive line of minimum-salary free agents. "There is no way you can construct a fucking football team with what was left," Irsay said. "Absolutely, positively, no way. It was a Rubik's Cube that couldn't be solved. He knew it. I knew it."

Manning and Irsay looked each other in the eye at thirty thousand feet. Manning would never ask Irsay not to draft Luck. He

knew the Colts had to do it. Irsay talks about the "horseshoes"—
that's how he affectionately refers to his franchise—and how he
was the caretaker of the horseshoes. He had to make the right
football and business decision.

"We just had a heart-to-heart," Irsay said. "We concluded in
finality, face-to-face, man-to-man, it wasn't solvable. The best interest of the franchise and for Peyton was to part ways, very unfortunately, because neither of us wanted it. Peyton said it: It wasn't
Jim's decision. It wasn't my decision. It was circumstances."

The plane carrying Manning and Irsay was somewhere over
Kentucky when they conceded that parting was unavoidable.
Manning's contract would be terminated, and he would immediately become a free agent. Tears came to Irsay's eyes "when we
realized we were starting to close the book," he said. "There was a
pause. We both knew we were upon a moment."

Irsay never said to Manning, "I'm letting you go." He couldn't
get the words out of his mouth. It was understood. Five weeks
earlier, the city of Indianapolis was the center of the NFL universe
with Super Bowl XLVI in town. Now that word had spread that
Irsay and Manning were on their way back home for a much less
joyous occasion, all the attention would be on Indianapolis once
again. As the private jet began its descent, they agreed to hold a
news conference the next day. Irsay's plane pulled into its hangar
and was met by a large media contingent. Irsay recalled that Peyton said, "All right, well, maybe I should just say a quick blurb, or
you should."

They were already in Irsay's car. He had offered to drive
Manning home. They opened the window and told the report-
ers, "We'll talk to you tomorrow." Irsay and Manning lived five
minutes apart in Carmel, twenty-three miles outside Indianapolis.
Irsay pulled into Manning's driveway. They both got out of the car.
They hugged in the dark. They said good night and went about
preparing remarks for the press conference.

It had been building to this moment for months. Irsay and Manning had talked about the future when Irsay hosted a party at the Super Bowl. They had a good relationship, going back to the first meeting at the Surf Club at Bal Harbour, Florida, a few weeks before the draft in 1998. On the morning of the farewell press conference, they first met in Irsay's office. "It was very intense," Irsay said. "This was as sensitive as it can get. Peyton casts such a mythic figure. I know I'm no match for that figure, but I have to do my job. So, I mean, it's hard. Peyton was really good. He stood true to really what we both knew. I think, in the end, he will always be reaching for that extra yard and that first down, and in the end, I'm the one who has to turn the lights off in the stadium."

Irsay was behind the podium with Manning to his right as the press conference ended an incredible era in Colts history. "Well, we're here to announce the conclusion of Peyton's playing career with the Colts," Irsay said. "We're here very much as well to honor all the incredible memories and incredible things that he's done for the franchise, for the city, for the state."

Irsay sat down and Manning pulled a piece of paper from his suit pocket. He had jotted down some notes. "I've been a Colt for almost all my adult life," he said. "But I guess in life and in sports, we all know that nothing lasts forever. Times change, circumstances change, and that's the reality of playing in the NFL."

The rivalry with Brady, Colts vs. Patriots, was over. Just twelve days later, a new phase began when Manning signed with the Denver Broncos. Manning vs. Brady would pick up where it had left off.

The parting with the Colts in early March allowed Manning to listen to recruiting pitches and offers for the first time since he was a high school senior. This time, the recruiting bothered him. It didn't feel right. But this is life in the NFL. Namath played for the

Rams. Montana finished with the Chiefs. Emmitt Smith spent two years with the Cardinals. Jerry Rice bounced from the Raiders to the Seahawks to training camp with the Broncos before he was willing to admit that his time to call it quits had come. Manning never had to take another snap to be considered a top-five quarterback of all time, but as long as he had the blessing of his doctors, he didn't want his career to end on the sidelines.

Elway, the Broncos general manager, took the early lead in the Manning sweepstakes. He put himself in Manning's situation and knew how he would want to be recruited. He went to the laid-back approach. "If I have somebody selling that hard, they are trying to hide something," Elway said. "That's why I said we're going to show what we are, what we are about, what we have to offer, and then let him go make his own decision. Knowing him and the type of guy he is, he's not going to want to get harassed or pushed or sold."

Elway had been around Manning in Hawaii and Florida, playing golf with Brady and Dan Marino. That was an impressive football foursome. When Manning was ready to embark on his recruiting trip, Elway and Denver coach John Fox were in Stillwater, Oklahoma, scouting Oklahoma State quarterback Brandon Weeden. Elway sent the private plane that took them to Stillwater on to Miami to pick up Manning and then stop back in Stillwater to pick up Elway and Fox and other Broncos staff and return to Denver. Too many people were on the plane for Elway to start talking business with Manning during the flight.

Elway waited for the private dinner he set up in the Palmer Room at the swank Cherry Hills Country Club in Englewood outside Denver to outline why the Broncos were the right fit for him. Fox also had a seat at the table. He's easygoing, a fun guy to be around, and he had pulled off a football miracle by making the playoffs and winning a playoff game the year before with Tim

Tebow. Elway invited former safety John Lynch, who had played the final four years of his career with the Broncos and was tight with Manning. They had become close friends at the Pro Bowl.

Early in the process, Manning called Seattle coach Pete Carroll to express interest in playing for the Seahawks. Carroll never heard back from Manning to set up a visit, but with the football world aware that Manning was now in Denver, Carroll and Seahawks general manager John Schneider arrived unannounced at an airport in Englewood. Word got back to Manning that Carroll and Schneider were in town and would like to meet him on their private plane or accompany him on his next flight, to Phoenix, where he was going to confer with the Cardinals. Manning declined the invitation and Carroll and Schneider left town without seeing him. Six weeks later, the Seahawks drafted Wisconsin quarterback Russell Wilson in the third round, seventy-four spots after the Colts selected Luck. In his second season, Wilson's Seahawks beat Manning's Broncos 43–8 in Super Bowl XLVIII at MetLife Stadium in East Rutherford, New Jersey. In his third season, Wilson lost to Brady and the Patriots 28–24 in Super Bowl XLIX in Glendale.

Manning met with the Cardinals; then as a favor to Marino, his idol, he met with the Dolphins in Indianapolis. He later worked out for the 49ers and Broncos at Duke and met with the Titans and worked out for them in Tennessee. The Jets made one of the first calls to Manning, but he had no desire to play in the same city as Eli. The Jets had had their best chance in 1997, but Bill Parcells wouldn't tell Manning he'd take him if he skipped his senior year at Tennessee. Playing in New York would have been a challenge for Manning, anyway. He reads everything and is sensitive to criticism. He would not have enjoyed the back pages of the New York tabloids.

There were three finalists for Manning: Denver, Tennessee, and San Francisco.

"I really thought it was going to come down to us and Tennessee," Elway said. "Obviously, with the connections he had in Tennessee, I was a little leery of those."

Manning called Elway on a Monday morning to reveal that he had picked Denver. Fox started dancing around the office after Elway gave him the thumbs-up.

Manning's decision to sign with the Broncos kept his rivalry with Brady alive. As long as the Broncos finished first in the AFC West and the Patriots finished first in the AFC East, they were guaranteed to play each other in the years when the AFC East was not scheduled to play the AFC West. Brady vs. Manning would still be an annual event. They hadn't played against each other in 2011 because Manning was injured. They hadn't met in the playoffs since the 2006 AFC championship game.

The first matchup between Brady and Manning's Broncos was in Foxboro, a house of horrors for Manning when he played for the Colts. The game was in early October on a nice 54-degree fall day in New England. Brady threw a touchdown pass to Wes Welker late in the first quarter, and Manning matched that with a 1-yard throw to Joel Dreessen in the first minute of the second quarter. The Patriots then scored 24 consecutive points before Manning made the final score respectable with touchdown passes late in the third quarter and midway through the fourth.

The 31–21 victory raised Brady's lifetime lead over Manning to 9–4. They appeared headed for a showdown in the AFC championship game when the Broncos finished the 2012 season with the number-one seed and the Patriots were number two. But the Ravens took care of both Manning and Brady in the playoffs. Fox called five consecutive runs by Ronnie Hillman, without letting Manning throw the ball once, when the Broncos were trying to eat up the clock and protect a 35–28 lead in the closing minutes. Denver had to punt the ball to the Ravens. Incredibly, the Ravens tied the game on a 70-yard prayer from Joe Flacco to Jacoby Jones with thirty-one seconds remaining.

After a touchback on the kickoff, the Broncos took over at their 20 with two time-outs and still thirty-one seconds on the clock. How many times in his career had Manning directed last-minute drives to win games? All Denver needed was a field goal. Fox had Manning take a knee instead, sending the game into overtime. Manning was then picked off at his own 45-yard line with fifty-one seconds left in the first overtime, setting up Justin Tucker's 47-yard field goal at 1:42 in the second extra period.

It was a devastating loss, one of the toughest of Manning's career. It was just 13 degrees with a wind chill of 2, and Manning looked uncomfortable in the second half. The focus after the game was on the Broncos' blown coverage on Jones's catch rather than Manning's interception or Fox's lack of faith in Manning's ability to pick up a first down at the end of regulation or win it after Baltimore's shocking touchdown.

"When you take a year off from football, you come back for all the enjoyable moments," Manning told the *Denver Post* outside the Broncos locker room after the game. "When you're not playing, you miss out on all the highs, but you also miss these disappointments. But I would rather be in the arena to be excited or be disappointed than not have a chance at all. That's football. That's why everybody plays it. You have to be able to take the good with the bad."

If misery loves company, then Manning could commiserate with Brady the next week. The Patriots suddenly were hosting the AFC title game against the Ravens instead of going to Denver. Not that it did them any good. For the second time in four years, Baltimore went into New England in January and eliminated the Patriots.

Brady vs. Manning in the playoffs would have to wait another year.

They met twice in the 2013 season as Manning was on his way to setting an NFL record with fifty-five touchdown passes. The first meeting was a brutally cold Sunday night in New England on Thanksgiving weekend. The temperature was 22 degrees with a wind chill of 6. The wind was swirling at 22 miles per hour. This was Brady weather.

It turned out to be a strange game. The Broncos went up 7–0 five minutes in when Wesley Woodyard forced a fumble by Patriots running back Stevan Ridley, which linebacker Von Miller scooped up and returned 60 yards for a touchdown. On the Patriots' next series, Miller forced a fumble by Brady, which defensive tackle Terrance "Pot Roast" Knighton picked up and ran 13 yards to the New England 10. Knowshon Moreno ran for 8 yards and then scored from the 2. It was 14–0 and Manning had nothing to do with either touchdown. That was not a good sign for the Patriots. It was 17–0 after one quarter and 24–0 at the half after Manning completed a 10-yard touchdown pass to Jacob Tamme.

Brady came out in the second half and threw three touchdown passes; New England scored 31 straight points to take a 31–24 lead with 7:37 left. The Broncos sent the game into overtime when Manning threw an 11-yard touchdown to Demaryius Thomas with 3:06 remaining.

Four years earlier, Belichick had made the strangest decision of his career when he elected to go for it on fourth and 2 from his own 28 with 2:08 left while holding a 34–28 lead in Indianapolis, rather than give the ball back to Manning. He thought there was a better chance of converting the first down than of stopping Manning, who had led two 79-yard touchdown drives in the fourth quarter.

He called a time-out before fourth down and kept Brady and the offense on the field. It blew up in Belichick's face when Brady's completion to Kevin Faulk was just short of a first down. Manning needed only four plays to get the Colts into the end zone for the winning touchdown on an easy 1-yarder to Reggie Wayne.

On this cold and windy night in New England, Belichick elected to put the ball in Manning's hands to start overtime. He took the wind. The NFL had changed the overtime rules for the playoffs in 2010 and then for the regular season in 2012. No longer could a team win the toss, move down the field, and kick a field goal to win it. The only way the game could end without both teams having at least one possession was if the receiving team in overtime returned the kickoff for a touchdown or moved down the field for a touchdown.

Detroit Lions coach Marty Mornhinweg had been ridiculed when he elected to kick off and take the wind in overtime in a game in Chicago in 2002. The Bears kicked a field goal on their first possession, and the Lions never touched the ball. Mornhinweg was fired after the season with a 5–27 record in two years.

Belichick, whose lack of confidence in his defense had cost the Patriots the game in 2009, this time trusted his defensive players not to give up a touchdown to Manning that would end the game on the first possession. They rewarded his faith. Manning had the ball twice in overtime: he moved the Broncos to their own 42 and the New England 42 before punting. The first two times Brady had it, he was able to get the ball only to the Patriots 37 and then the Patriots 43. After the second series stalled, New England punted, Broncos returner Tony Carter muffed the catch, and Nate Ebner recovered for the Patriots at the Denver 13.

Brady did two kneel-downs to position the ball in the middle of the field, and the game reached the two-minute warning. Then Stephen Gostkowski ended it with a 31-yard field goal. It was the thirty-eighth game of Brady's career with at least three touchdowns and no interceptions. He was second to Manning, who had forty-two.

This was just the prelude to the number-two Patriots playing at the number-one Broncos in the conference title game. Manning's offense had broken the NFL record for points set by Brady and the Patriots in their undefeated season of 2007. After Brady broke Manning's TD record by one when he threw fifty in '07, Manning took the record back and put it so far out of reach that he dared Brady to try to top it. In the season opener, Manning threw seven touchdowns against the Super Bowl champion Rams, tying the NFL record. That year, 2013, he threw for a record 5,477 yards, along with his Ruthian fifty-five TD passes.

The Patriots overwhelmed the Colts in the divisional round, and the Broncos struggled but survived against San Diego. When he was asked after the game if an off-season exam on his neck was weighing on his mind, Manning got laughs when he said, "What's weighing on my mind is how soon I can get a Bud Light in my mouth after this win. Priority number one."

On a gorgeous day in Denver in the championship game, there was no stopping Manning. He picked apart Belichick's defense for 400 yards and two touchdowns. Brady was shorthanded without tight end Rob Gronkowski, who had suffered a torn ACL in December, so he had no firepower to keep up with Manning. After he missed Julian Edelman on what would have been a 56-yard touchdown late in the first quarter, the Patriots had nothing going. Brady threw for 277 yards and one touchdown, but New England never threatened to win the game. This Brady-Manning showdown was a dud. Denver led 23–3 early in the fourth quarter on the way to a 26–16 victory.

Manning stood on the podium at midfield as the confetti landed on his head in the celebration after the game. "Empire State of Mind," an acknowledgment that the Super Bowl in two weeks would be in the New York area, blasted out of Mile High Stadium's sound system. It had been seven years and four neck surgeries between confetti showers for Manning, and it felt very nice.

"You realize you still want to win one more game," he said. "Being in my sixteenth season, going to my third Super Bowl, I know how hard it is to get there. It is extremely difficult."

It's too bad the season couldn't end right then. The Broncos never had a chance against Seattle. Center Manny Ramirez's first snap went flying over Manning's right shoulder as he walked toward the line of scrimmage out of the shotgun shouting instructions to his teammates over the loud pro-Seattle crowd. Seattle recovered for a safety just twelve seconds into the game, the quickest score in Super Bowl history, and the 43–8 rout was on. Manning threw two interceptions, the first one setting up Seattle's first touchdown to make it 15–0, and the second returned 69 yards for a touchdown by Super Bowl MVP Malcolm Smith. That return gave Seattle a 22–0 lead in the second quarter. The Broncos played the game in slow motion; the Seahawks were playing at warp speed. Manning was under constant pressure and was throwing a lot of ducks. He had happy feet. The Seattle defense seemed insulted anytime the Broncos ran a play that picked up yardage. Manning did complete a Super Bowl record 34 passes, but it was an empty number.

It wasn't the most lopsided loss of Manning's playoff career. Back in 2002, his fifth year in the NFL, the Colts lost to the Jets 41–0. He was gracious after that game, even asking if a reporter needed more time with him as he walked to the team bus that was waiting for him in the parking lot.

The Super Bowl showed his testy side. The NFL sets up a huge interview room for each Super Bowl team, and Manning was sitting at his podium about ten minutes into his press conference when a reporter for the *New York Daily News* asked him if he was embarrassed. Manning didn't appreciate the question, even though that's the description many of his teammates had already used.

"It's not embarrassing at all," he snapped. "I never use that word. There is a lot of professional football players in that locker room who put a lot of hard work and effort into it, to being here and play in that game. The word *embarrassing* is an insulting word, to tell you the truth."

Manning-Brady XVI, the sweet sixteen of their incredible rivalry, was in Foxboro in 2014 for the third straight time in the regular season. Manning threw for 438 yards with two touchdowns and two interceptions but had a harsh analysis of how he played in the 43–21 loss.

He said he told somebody right after the game that he stunk.

"I never heard you say you stink before," the friend said.

"I don't usually stink, but I stunk today," Manning said.

On a cold and windy day, Manning and Brady combined to throw 110 passes. Manning was 34 of 57. Brady was 33 of 53 for 333 yards with four touchdowns and an interception. It was New England's fifth straight victory after getting ambushed in Kansas City in the fourth game of the year, when for the first time in his career, critics were suggesting Brady was done. It was just noise, as the Patriots like to call outside distractions. "We're on to Cincinnati," Belichick said repeatedly in the days after the loss to the Chiefs, referring to the Patriots' next game.

The victory over Manning eventually earned the Patriots home-field advantage in the AFC playoffs.

"It's a team sport," Brady said after beating the Broncos. "At the end of the day, one person can't do it alone. I've been part of some great teams. I've been very privileged to play with great players and teammates that really work their butts off for each other. That's why you string together five wins in a row like we've done."

Brady-Manning XVII seemed inevitable as the playoffs approached. But Manning suffered a quad injury in Denver's four-teenth game, in San Diego, which clearly compromised his ability to move around in the pocket. Worse, his decreased leg strength made it difficult for him to get much on his throws.

He played poorly in a 24–13 loss at home to the Colts in the divisional round of the playoffs. After the game, Manning was noncommittal about returning for his eighteenth season in 2015, but after reporting to Elway in a meeting one month after the season that he was mentally and physically ready to play, he accepted a $4 million pay cut from his $19 million salary in early March and then passed a team physical to officially signal that he was coming back.

Brady and the Patriots overcame two 14-point deficits to the Ravens in the divisional round and then survived Flacco's Hail Mary attempt into the end zone to eliminate Baltimore 35–31. New England overwhelmed the Colts in the AFC championship game 45–7 and then beat the Seahawks in the Super Bowl 28–24, defeating the two teams that had defeated Manning and the Broncos in the postseason the last two seasons.

Manning's decision to pick the Broncos worked. Elway made it his mission to surround him with enough good players to give him a chance to get that second Super Bowl victory. It was a career-altering decision not only for Manning but for the coaches, executives, and teams he had rejected in March 2012.

After the 2012 season, the Jets fired general manager Mike Tannenbaum, who gave quarterback Mark Sanchez a lucrative contract extension as a make-up call for courting Manning. Rex Ryan was fired as coach two years later. The Cardinals fired coach Ken Whisenhunt and general manager Rod Graves after the 2012 season; the Titans did the same to coach Mike Munchak and senior executive vice president and chief operating officer Mike Reinfeldt. Dolphins GM Jeff Ireland was fired after the 2013 season, and 49ers coach Jim Harbaugh was pushed out after the 2014 season.

Elway and Fox had a falling-out after the 2014 season, Manning's third in Denver. The Broncos had underachieved, and Elway made Fox just another casualty of the Manning sweepstakes.

8

DREW, MEET WALLY

The New York Yankees were struggling in early June of 1925 when first baseman Wally Pipp reported for work at Yankee Stadium for a game against the Washington Senators with a severe headache.

The Yankees were just 15–26, and Pipp, who had knocked in 110 runs the previous season, had not been productive at the plate in his eleventh season with the Bronx Bombers. Miller Huggins, the Yankees manager, was looking to shake up the lineup to get the team untracked. The way the story goes, the Yankees trainers gave Pipp two aspirin on June 2, and Huggins gave him a seat on the bench. "Wally, take the day off," Huggins said. "We'll try that kid Gehrig at first today and get you back in there tomorrow."

Pipp never started another game for the Yankees. He was beaned in batting practice one month later, was hospitalized for seven days, and wasn't used much the rest of the season. He was playing in Cincinnati the next year. Lou Gehrig became known as the Iron Horse. He had pinch-hit the previous day for shortstop Pee-Wee Wanninger and then went 3 for 5 starting for Pipp. Huggins decided to keep the kid in the lineup, and by the time

Gehrig benched himself on May 2, 1939, he had played in a record 2,130 consecutive games.

The story of Wally Pipp is why so many of today's players in all sports are reluctant to come out of the lineup when they are banged up or even just to take a day off so they can catch their breath. They don't want to be "Wally-Pipped," the most famous victim of the next-man-up approach.

Drew Bledsoe was Wally-Pipped by Tom Brady. Bledsoe is the Wally Pipp of the NFL.

"I had a little better career than Wally," Bledsoe said.

Pipp was no slouch, though. He played in three World Series for the Yankees and in his career had 90 home runs and 1,004 RBI. He twice led the American League in home runs and led in RBI the season before he lost his job in New York. Gehrig went on to be the greatest first baseman in baseball history, and Pipp supposedly said, "I took the two most expensive aspirin in history."

Drew Bledsoe played fourteen years in the NFL after Bill Parcells picked him over Rick Mirer with the first overall selection in the 1993 draft. He signed a six-year, $14.4 million contract that was replaced two years later by a seven-year, $42 million contract that included a record $11.5 million signing bonus. His parents were both schoolteachers, and Bledsoe found it incomprehensible that "in my first year playing football, I made two hundred years' worth of my dad's salary."

He loved telling the story of calling the automated number for his bank to hear his account balance. "My first signing bonus check went to the same bank account I had all the way through college," he said. "It had the computer voice, and all the way through college I would dial it up and it would say, 'Your balance is negative $8.32.' Then I called it up right after I signed and the same voice said, 'Your balance is $1.3 million.' I thought it was really funny. It was unbelievable. Then my brother called it up. He couldn't believe it either."

Bledsoe threw 251 touchdowns in his career, started in a Super Bowl loss to the Packers, was a backup to Brady in a Super Bowl victory over the Rams, and built a nice reputation in New England for being active in charitable affairs. In 2011, he was voted into the Patriots Hall of Fame. He played nine years with the Patriots, three with the Bills, then reunited with Parcells with the Cowboys for two years. Parcells benched him for Tony Romo at halftime of the sixth game of the 2006 season, and Bledsoe never got back on the field. He retired at the end of the season. He started off his career as though he was going to be the next Dan Marino and ended up losing his job to a sixth-round draft choice in New England and an undrafted free agent in Dallas.

Of course, Bledsoe didn't get Wally-Pipped because of a headache. It was because of the sheared blood vessel from a vicious hit by Jets linebacker Mo Lewis in the second game of the 2001 season, from which he nearly died in the ambulance on the way to the hospital. That gave Brady his chance to start the next game, and other than the fifteen games he missed in 2008 after tearing his ACL in the season opener, he started every game through the 2014 season, including six Super Bowls, a record for a quarterback.

The Patriots had lost their first two games in 2001 with Bledsoe starting, and the feeling in the Patriots organization was that Bill Belichick was getting antsy to make a quarterback change even before Bledsoe was injured. He strongly considered opening the season with Brady but eventually backed off. Bledsoe was a proud player and was not short on self-esteem, so he believes had he not been injured, he would have retained his job as the Patriots franchise quarterback, and Brady would have had a much more difficult path to being known as one of the all-time greats.

"I think Tom would have certainly played a long time in the NFL and would have eventually worked his way into a starting job, but it may not have been with the Patriots, is the honest answer," Bledsoe said. "He demonstrated through two preseasons and through practice that he could play the game. Had I not gotten hurt, he probably would have worked his way into a starting job somewhere. As everybody knows, if you're a starting quarterback for the wrong organization, it doesn't matter what you do. The way it worked, he ended up being the starter for a great organization, one of the all-time great organizations, that won eleven games [in 2008] even without him. He ultimately would have been, in my opinion, a good starting quarterback. But if it had been for one of the bottom-tier teams, it would be probably a different conversation as far as where he fits with quarterbacks."

It was Bledsoe's team when he reported for his eighth training camp in the summer of 2000. Belichick, in his first year as the Patriots head coach, had veteran John Friesz and Michael Bishop, a seventh-round pick in 1999, lined up as the backups. Brady was clearly the highest-rated player on the Patriots draft board when they were picking late in the sixth round a few months earlier, and they had to take him, even though quarterback was not a need position. Bledsoe didn't think much of it. Brady was the third quarterback the Patriots had drafted since taking Bledsoe in 1993. Bishop and seventh-round pick Jay Walker in 1994 were never more than potential backup material. There was no reason for Bledsoe to believe that Belichick had drafted Brady to compete with him or take his job.

"At that point, quarterbacks had come and gone as backup quarterbacks," Bledsoe said. "Okay, he's another kid coming in."

Bledsoe immediately liked Brady. His wife really liked him. They had Brady over to the house a few times for dinner. Brady played with Bledsoe's little kids. "He was just somebody very easy to like and get along with," Bledsoe said. "No, he never babysat the kids. He drove a yellow Jeep, so I wouldn't leave him alone with our kids."

Bledsoe called his financial adviser, who took on only clients he believed in and not just because of their net worth. Bledsoe told his adviser, "I've got a kid here, I'm not sure if he's ever going to be anything, but he's just a good person and you would enjoy the relationship because he's a good guy. He'll probably never be a starter in the NFL, but he will be around ten years."

After two training camps, Bledsoe had formed an impression of Brady: Good. Not great. He threw the ball to the right place, he made the right read, and he did a nice job running the scout team. Great kid. "It wasn't a situation where I thought, *Oh no, this guy is going to beat me out and take my job.* That's never what it felt like," Bledsoe said. "He was tall, super skinny, arm was decent, threw a nice ball, but nothing super special."

Bledsoe is five and a half years older than Brady and thought of him as another little brother. He was happy to help Brady get better. Having a capable backup quarterback would only benefit Bledsoe and the team if he was out for a week or two. That way the Patriots offense wouldn't shut down without him.

Then Bledsoe suffered the sheared blood vessel, and the Patriots started to play well as he recuperated. The offensive line was getting healthy. It wasn't as if Brady was playing lights-out, but other than a loss at Denver at the end of October when he threw four interceptions, he was playing under control. Belichick was easing him in and not asking him to win games on his own. He was a game manager. When Bledsoe was cleared by doctors to return to action in mid-November, the Patriots were 5–4, and Belichick never gave Bledsoe a chance to win his job back. He had been Wally-Pipped.

Bledsoe's injury presented Belichick with an excuse to start Brady. He was never in Bledsoe's corner. "I don't know," Bledsoe said. "That's one I don't really need to comment on."

When Bledsoe went down, Brady hadn't built up enough collateral in the locker room for his teammates to believe he was capable of turning things around. The season was about to slip away.

"We just lost our $100 million quarterback and supposed face of the franchise," linebacker Tedy Bruschi said. "Yes, I was very down on the season. I was frustrated with the whole situation, being 0–2 after we were 5–11 the year before. I didn't know the severity of Bledsoe's injury at the time. I remember being frustrated with him. Just tired of losing at that point. Brady coming in was really an unknown commodity."

Belichick hadn't yet adopted his "Do your job" mantra, which became the rallying cry of the 2014 Super Bowl team, but Bruschi knew the Patriots had to play shutdown defense and hope offensive coordinator Charlie Weis could develop Brady. The players didn't know if Brady had just third-string talent. They certainly didn't think he was going to become Joe Montana. He didn't play very well in his first start against the Colts, but Bruschi realized a difference. Brady got rid of the ball. Bledsoe was a classic dropback passer; he was six five, 238 pounds, and he just stood there and planted his feet, and defenders would often just fall off him. But he took a lot of sacks and threw too many interceptions.

"The offense just had a different pace with Tom," Bruschi said. "That was refreshing to see."

The Patriots started to win with Brady. They knew Belichick was going to be faced with a difficult decision when Bledsoe was healthy. It had the potential to tear apart the team. Bledsoe had a lot of friends in the locker room and in the media. Brady was building relationships and trust. They were friends with each other. Bruschi felt Belichick couldn't go wrong. If he put Bledsoe back in, he would play well because the team had improved in the two months he was out. If he stuck with Brady, they would just keep trying to build on the momentum they were developing.

"There were pro-Bledsoe guys, there were pro-Brady guys,"

said Damien Woody, the starting center on Brady's first Super Bowl team. "I was pro-win."

Bruschi was close to Bledsoe, and Brady was just a young player, but he had no idea what Belichick was going to decide and then had no problem when he announced he was keeping Brady as the starter after Bledsoe was cleared to play. "It took balls for that decision," Bruschi said. "It was a gutsy decision. We all knew what balls it took by Bill, but we knew with either one we would have been fine."

Even after the Patriots went on to win the Super Bowl, Bruschi wasn't convinced about Brady. "We scored a defensive touchdown in the Super Bowl. We won the AFC championship and scored two special-teams touchdowns," he said. "Of course, the quarterbacks get all the credit. The kid was a good role player at that time. And Drew was the one who threw the touchdown in the championship game."

After the 2001 season, the Bills negotiated for one month with the Patriots about making a trade for Bledsoe. On the final day of the 2002 draft, less than three months after Brady's winning drive in the Super Bowl, Bledsoe was sent to Buffalo for a first-round draft pick in 2003. Trades within the division are rare, especially for a thirty-year-old three-time Pro Bowl quarterback who held all the important franchise passing records. It showed how little regard Belichick had for Bledsoe that he wasn't afraid to face him twice a year and was not concerned that he was strengthening a division opponent.

Bruschi believes that even if Bledsoe hadn't been injured, Belichick would have found a way to make the quarterback change. "There's probably no way Brady would have been denied," he said. "Knowing what I know about that kid and the work he would have put in, eventually Drew would be throwing two or three interceptions in a game and eventually Bill would have put in Tom because Drew was having a bad game. Tom would have buckled up his helmet before he went out there and said to himself, *I'm never giving this job back.* And I believe that. Then he'd play the last nine minutes of a game and drive the team down for two touchdowns and a field goal. You know Boston—all the talk would have started, and then Bill probably would have done it then."

Brady's idol, Joe Montana, lost his job to Steve Young with the 49ers when he was injured. He was also Wally-Pipped.

Montana suffered a bruised sternum and broke the little finger on his throwing hand after taking a crunching blind-side hit from defensive end Leonard Marshall late in the 1990 NFC championship game. Young tried to finish off the Giants, but a fumble by Roger Craig set up New York's winning field goal, preventing the 49ers from trying to win their third straight Super Bowl, something no team has ever done. If the 49ers had defeated the Giants, Montana would not have recovered in time to start the Super Bowl the next week against Buffalo. He was back healthy the next summer, but in a training camp practice, he suffered a slightly torn tendon near his right elbow when he was attempting to throw a pass downfield. Montana had been plagued by elbow problems since 1981, his third year in the NFL. Young was now the starting quarterback, as Montana hoped time would heal his elbow. He threw four times in one week in October to test the elbow, but there was too much pain, and he needed surgery to reattach the tendon. He missed the rest of the season and didn't return until making a farewell appearance in the second half of the final game of the 1992 season at Candlestick Park. The 49ers traded him to Kansas City after the season, and he played two years there before retiring.

Brady is so competitive that even before Bledsoe was injured he was telling friends he was going to beat him out. In the offseason between Brady's first and second years, Patriots personnel boss Scott Pioli was working late on a Friday night preparing for the draft. As he pulled out of his parking spot outside Foxboro Stadium, he saw the lights on in the practice bubble. He couldn't imagine why. It was after nine p.m. "I'm a little bit kooky like that," Pioli said. "I'm the guy who turns off all the lights in the office on the way out. It's just how I was raised."

He drove around to the front entrance to the bubble. He saw a yellow Jeep parked outside. He immediately knew Brady was inside. Pioli watched from a distance. Brady was by himself. He had elastic bands around his ankles doing footwork drills, drop-back drills with the football in his hands, and throwing into a net. Pioli and Brady had gotten to know each other in the weight room.

"Tommy and I became real close," Pioli said. "Far closer than probably I should have been. We were always sharing music and stuff. He loved music, but he had bad taste."

"Hey, kid, what are you doing here?" Pioli shouted across the bubble.

Brady was startled.

"I'm just getting a little extra work in," Brady said.

"Tommy, it's Friday night," "Pioli said.

"Yeah, I know, but I got nothing to do," Brady said.

Pioli said he thought to himself, *Here's this guy, he hadn't become Tom Brady yet, he was Tommy Brady, slappy, number-four quarterback of the New England Patriots. But he's still this brutally handsome guy and it's a Friday night, and he's there working out. That's good.*

They talked about family. They talked about the draft. Pioli turned to leave and Brady called after him. "Do me a favor."

"What's that?" Pioli asked.

"Don't tell anyone you saw me here tonight. This is between you and me, all right?"

"Yeah. Why?" Pioli said.

"It's Friday. Seriously, I would appreciate it if you didn't tell anyone," Brady said.

He used to sneak into the team facility and hide out watching tape. "I just fell in love with the guy because he became such a hard worker," Pioli said.

Now that he was starting, there was no way he was going to give Belichick a chance to even think about taking the job away from him. No longer was Brady the kid brother to Bledsoe.

Brady always said Bledsoe was very supportive, but as Bledsoe was in the final stages of his recuperation, some people around the team felt that he was actually disruptive in comments he was making about the Patriots being his team, that he was still the guy, and how he couldn't wait to get back on the field.

Montana despised Young almost from the day Bill Walsh traded to get him from the Bucs in 1987. He considered him a threat. Montana felt Young was working hard behind the scenes to take his job. Bledsoe and Brady were friends, but now Brady had Bledsoe's job and Bledsoe wanted it back.

"It did put a strain on my relationship with Tommy even though I still fully respected him and how hard he worked and what he was trying to do," Bledsoe said. "It certainly was not the same. There is no question about that."

Brady was riding this huge wave as the Patriots won the last six games of the regular season. Bledsoe knew that unless Brady was injured, he had no chance to get back on the field. He could either pout or do all he could to help Brady. "It was just the competition," Brady said. "It wasn't ever anything personal about Drew."

Bledsoe remained stuck to the bench until the second quarter of the AFC championship game in Pittsburgh. Brady first came up limping after a hit by Steelers linebacker Jason Gildon, and then Lee Flowers knocked him out of the game when he rolled into the back of his left ankle as he was completing a 28-yard pass to Troy Brown. Bledsoe entered with 1:40 remaining in the half and the Patriots on the Steelers 40. He had not played since September 23, but Weis didn't ease him back in. He called four straight pass plays, and Bledsoe completed all four, the last one an 11-yard touchdown pass in the corner of the end zone to David Patton. It took Bledsoe 126 days to get back on the field and then just forty-two seconds to get the Patriots into the end zone to take a 14–3 halftime lead on their way to a 24–17 victory. Bledsoe played the rest of the game and completed 10 of 21 passes for 102 yards. He was the most expensive backup in NFL history, but without him the Patriots would not have made it to the Super Bowl. On the podium after the game, as he raised the AFC championship trophy, tears were rolling down Bledsoe's cheeks. He had nearly died back in September. Now when his team needed him most, he was there for them.

The bye week between the conference championship games and the Super Bowl in New Orleans was eliminated when the NFL postponed the games scheduled for the weekend after the September 11 terrorist attacks and placed them at the end of the regular season. The condensed time frame added to the uncertainty as to whether Brady's ankle would allow him to play. The Patriots arrived in New Orleans with the first quarterback controversy in Super Bowl history.

"I want to play," Bledsoe said during Super Bowl week. "I want to play as bad as I ever wanted anything. It's the Super Bowl. It's what you play for. Obviously, I would love to be in there. I'd love to be playing in this game, but ultimately that's Bill's decision. Whoever plays has got to win."

Brady was 11–3 in the regular season and 2–0 in the playoffs, including the Pittsburgh game when he handed Bledsoe a 7–3 lead and Bledsoe won in relief. Bledsoe had been just 7–19 in his last 26 starts.

"Tom has gotten us here—let's get that straight," Bruschi said at the time. "Drew won the game the other day. What do you do? I don't know. That's why I'm not the head coach."

Belichick picked Brady, who had recovered from his ankle

injury. He had already alienated Bledsoe. He was not about to
alienate Brady. Contributing to the victory in Pittsburgh made it
easier for Bledsoe to handle the disappointment of not starting the
Super Bowl. He was amazed how much better the offensive line
had become in his absence. He had time to throw the ball. "That
was a cool sensation. That's not how it had been before," Bledsoe
said. "It was throw the ball, take a hit. Throw the ball, take a hit.
I actually was really having fun with it."

Bledsoe knew about the electricity of playing in a Super Bowl.
He knew about playing a Super Bowl in New Orleans. He'd been
the Patriots' quarterback when they'd lost to Green Bay in the
Superdome five years earlier. He prepared for the Rams as if he
was going to start, especially with Brady not having much time
to recuperate from the sprained ankle. In the tunnel before the
Patriots became the first Super Bowl team to run out as a group
rather than have their offense or defense introduced, Bledsoe was
pounding on Brady's shoulder pads and screaming encouragement
to him.

"The one thing I learned from the previous Super Bowl experience is no matter what happens, losing that game feels awful;
it's worse than never being there," Bledsoe said. "I just knew that
regardless of what happened in that game that we needed to win
the game. Tom needed to play well to do that. The simple truth is
if I didn't like and respect the guy, it would've been much harder
to be supportive. He has always been such a good person, it makes
it easier to cheer for him even though he stole my damn job."

Bledsoe stood on the Super Bowl sidelines helping Brady as
much as he could. He's never said the Patriots would have had the
same success that year or in the years that followed if he'd been
the quarterback. "I have no idea whether that is true or not," he
said. "That is the honest, honest truth. That's not being politically
correct. One thing that did happen that's very real is when your

starting quarterback that just signed a big contract goes down, and he was supposed to be your guy and your leader, everybody feels they have to increase their role and they have to support this guy and bring along this young guy. Then, on top of that, Tom played very well."

It took years for the relationship between Brady and Bledsoe to heal and get back to where it had been. They are very good friends again. They text all the time. Their families have spent time together. Bledsoe was coaching high school football for his sons in 2014 in Bend, Oregon, and called on Brady to provide motivational help before a big game. "I asked him to do me a quick favor, and he put together a little video for our high school before we faced our crosstown rivals," Bledsoe said.

Bledsoe's sons have always been great supporters of Brady, and he was happy to make the tape. "I love Drew," Brady said. "Drew has been like a big brother to me. Whenever he calls, I'm there to answer the phone, and whatever he asks, I'll always do anything for him. It's nice that our relationship has come to the point where it is now. We're great friends. We love being together and talking about things. He's still a real great mentor for me."

Bledsoe is proud of what Brady has done on the field and the man he has become off the field. "If you went back and introduced me to the kid that got drafted late out of Michigan and told me that he was going on to this level of success, I would have told you that you were full of crap," Bledsoe said. "Just like everybody else would've."

Brady and Manning could walk into any locker room and within fifteen minutes assume a leadership role.

Going into the 2002 season, Bledsoe was in Buffalo, and Brady had established himself, so he was able to assert his leadership skills. He began trash-talking on the field and in practice. "He's not afraid to use profanity," Bruschi said. Brady and linebacker Mike Vrabel incessantly trash-talked each other in practice. Vrabel had a way of getting under Brady's skin. Before one practice, Bruschi bet Brady twenty dollars he would pick him off. He did. Brady was so competitive he couldn't bring himself to hand Bruschi the twenty. "I don't think he had it in him to control himself enough to give me twenty bucks to my face," Bruschi said. "The twenty dollars was in my locker. That's all I needed to see."

Brady was smart enough to become friends with his offensive linemen. When Phil Simms played for the Giants, his best friend was left tackle Brad Benson. It was Benson who had to keep Dexter Manley of the Redskins and Harvey Martin of the Cowboys out of his face.

Brady quickly became one of the guys during his second year and impressed the linemen with his ability to drink beer and show no effect. In the summer, the hangout was Parente's, down the street from training camp at Bryant College. During the season, they would head to a place on Route 1 near Foxboro Stadium.

"Brady can pound the drinks now," Woody said. "I was never the biggest beer drinker, but guys like Joe Andruzzi, Matt Light— those guys could pour it down. We'd go to this establishment and eat and have a couple of drinks. One time Brady came in, and the dude, when I say pound it down, he was just pounding it down. Wow. I never knew he could put them away like that. I had new appreciation for him. This guy right there, he's all right. He wasn't the superstar. He was ascending. We had some great times."

Brady's beer drinking from his younger days in the NFL is still legendary. "He was always one of the guys. No one on the team could beat him chugging a beer," Bruschi said. "Linemen couldn't beat the kid. I remember seeing it for the first time and thinking, *Holy smokes, are you serious?* He was crushing guys."

Manning has a forceful personality and commands respect.

Brady is a nice guy, and players naturally gravitate toward him, regardless of whether they are the long snapper, like Lonie Paxton, who was part of Brady's Kentucky Derby crew, or Darrelle Revis, already a superstar when he arrived in New England for one season in 2014 and helped Brady win a Super Bowl.

John Fox had a routine of giving Manning each Wednesday off from practice in 2013 to rest two sprained ankles. Manning was sitting with his ankles submerged in the cold tub in the Broncos training room watching an opponent's tape on his iPad. Fox was running the practice when his cell phone buzzed. Manning had texted him a selfie. He was in the cold tub wearing his helmet and listening to the coach-quarterback communication from practice. "It was a joke, but still, I don't know how many players I've been around who would have thought about that," Fox said.

Wes Welker is one of five players who have caught passes from both Manning and Brady in the NFL. Tight end Jermaine Wiggins, wide receivers Torrance Small and Austin Collie, and fullback Dan Klecko are the others. Welker had the best years of his career with Brady before he left as a free agent in 2013 following a contract dispute with Belichick. He switched sides in the rivalry and joined Manning in Denver. Brady was upset when Welker left. He was among his best friends and he was his favorite target. Belichick usually doesn't make big personnel mistakes, and he didn't with Welker. Julian Edelman, a former college quarterback at Kent State, assumed Welker's role in the slot and became a more explosive player and a Super Bowl hero in the victory over the Seahawks when he caught the winning touchdown pass with just over two minutes remaining in the game.

As a receiver, if you have to leave Brady, it's not necessarily a bad thing to join up with Manning. Welker wasn't as productive in Denver, and concussion problems slowed him down, but he is the most accomplished receiver to play with both quarterbacks. He has put up Hall of Fame numbers, although he never was able to get a Super Bowl ring with either Brady or Manning. He lost two Super Bowls with Brady and one with Manning.

"There's a lot of similarities as far as making sure everybody is on the same page," Welker said. "The accountability, not only in meetings, but also on the field and in walk-throughs. They are second to none with their decision making. That's a key part of their success."

Kicker Adam Vinatieri had to win over his Colts teammates when he jumped from the Patriots in 2006. He won three rings with Brady with two Super Bowl–winning kicks, and in his first year in Indianapolis, he won his fourth ring. He has a special bond with Manning and Brady.

"When you win a championship, your football team is a fraternity of brothers," Vinatieri said. "It's not your biological family, but it may as well be. There is just as much family feel to a football team as there is to your real family. I got great relationships with those guys, and it's a bond that will never disappear. When you go onto a football field and you're fighting together, especially when you can hoist a Lombardi Trophy, it's something that never goes away."

Brady and Manning are not afraid to show their combustible side on the sidelines in full view of television cameras. Brady got into a heated argument with offensive coordinator Bill O'Brien after throwing a bad interception in a 2011 game against the Redskins. Brady was sitting on the bench and O'Brien was standing over him. O'Brien ripped off his headset and was gesturing wildly. Backup quarterback Brian Hoyer and then Belichick had to push O'Brien away.

The Patriots won 34–27.

Manning's best friend with the Colts was center Jeff Saturday. But that didn't prevent Manning from unloading on him during a 2005 game against the Rams. Manning threw the ball three straight times in the red zone, and the Colts had to settle for a field goal.

"We need to run the ball down there," Saturday shouted to Manning.

Manning got up from his seat on the bench, quickly walked over to Saturday, and screamed, "Hey, quit calling the fucking plays, all right?"

A few minutes later, as Manning sat on the bench next to tight end Dallas Clark and wide receiver Brandon Stokley stood next to him, he broke the news that he was miked up for the game.

"Miked up?" Stokley said. "Shut up."

Manning knew his argument with Saturday would get plenty of airtime.

"It's better than *Desperate Housewives*," he told Clark and Stokley.

The Colts won 45–28.

In Tony Dungy's second-to-last year with the Colts, in 2007, the team drafted Ohio State wide receiver Anthony Gonzalez in the first round. Stokley, a Manning favorite, had been injured, and the plan was for Gonzalez to be the new slot receiver. Ohio State was on trimester, and by NFL rules, Gonzalez was not allowed to participate in minicamps and other off-season workouts until finals were over. Manning was concerned that Gonzalez would not have enough time to learn the Colts offense to make a contribution early in his rookie year. So he got in his car and drove 175 miles to Ohio State.

"Two days a week, Peyton was driving from Indianapolis to Columbus, three hours each way, to throw balls to him for an hour and a half. He would prep him with everything and drive back," Dungy said. "He never spoke about it and nobody knew about it."

Manning had a simple message for Gonzalez. "We need you, so I'm going to get you ready," he said.

Gonzalez caught 37 passes as a rookie and 57 his second year, but injuries shortened his career.

Manning expects everyone to have the same commitment. If you wanted to play with Manning, you had to keep up with him. "You got to be able to function and you can't make mistakes," Dungy said. "As far as driving guys and pushing them, if you were going to play in that offense, you had to keep up that pace. They might say, 'Gee, I wish he'd relax. I wish he would calm down.'"

Dungy suffered an unspeakable tragedy in 2005 when his oldest son, James, committed suicide while at school in a Tampa suburb. After taking time away from the team, Dungy was back in his office when Manning walked in. "Coach, we're here for you," Manning said.

Dungy will never forget the look on Manning's face. "We always talk about family a lot," he said. "What's going on with Eli? I had known Archie for so long. James was there a lot with the Colts. I could tell Peyton was shaken. He's so close with his dad and so close with his brothers, he understood."

Manning spoke to his teammates about being there for Dungy emotionally.

Brady conducted a bedside vigil for Charlie Weis, his offensive coordinator in New England, in June of 2002 after Weis slipped into a coma and nearly died following complications from gastric bypass surgery. "To our family, Tom Brady is a hell of a lot more than a football player," Weis said.

9

THE COACH IN THE GRAY HOODIE

Tom Brady meets Bill Belichick at least every Tuesday and Saturday during the season to prepare for the next game. They talk about plays he likes, go over the game plan, discuss corrections that need to be made from the previous game.

That's around forty meetings per year multiplied by a lot of years to equal hundreds and hundreds of hours, just the two of them in Belichick's office. They will sometimes meet five or six times in a week, adding even more hours to their weekly interaction. They are the most successful coach-quarterback combination in NFL history. They've won four Super Bowls together, tying Chuck Noll and Terry Bradshaw and one more than Bill Walsh and Joe Montana. They won 160 regular-season games together through the 2014 season, and that is number one in the NFL since the 1970 merger. Don Shula and Dan Marino are next with 116. They've also been together longer than any coach and quarterback in NFL history.

Nobody knows Brady better than Belichick. But nobody really knows Belichick, not even Brady.

"When it's outside of football, he's a totally different person," Brady said. "As soon as he's in football mode, it's like hitting a switch."

The nonfootball Belichick might be a lot of fun. He might be the life of the party. He might be different from the tortured football genius whom the public sees on the sidelines and in his press conferences. To experience that part of his personality, "it has to be in a nonfootball environment," Brady said.

Surely in all their years together, Brady has been exposed to that side of his coach. "Me? Very rarely, very rarely," he said.

They must have gone out for a pizza and a couple of beers after a long evening meeting before they went home. "I don't think we ever have," Brady said. "We're around each other so much, whenever we have time, nothing ever comes of it."

Belichick once showed up at a team Halloween costume party organized by Randy Moss. But he and Brady keep their distance away from the field.

The NFL has become a game of coaches and quarterbacks. Elite coaches paired with elite quarterbacks win Super Bowls. They need to think alike. Brady is as serious about football as Belichick. They are both heading to the Pro Football Hall of Fame, and there's a good chance one would not have been in position to make it without the other. Belichick coached the Browns into the playoffs just once in five years in Cleveland with Bernie Kosar and then Vinny Testaverde as his quarterback. He was going nowhere in one year plus two games with Drew Bledsoe in New England. Brady came in and went 11–3 the rest of the regular season and then won two playoff games and the Super Bowl.

Tom Brady saved Bill Belichick's job.

Bill Belichick saved Tom Brady's career.

Belichick rescued Brady and threw him a lifeline in the sixth round of the 2000 draft. John Elway was going to be great regardless of where he played. It was the same with Peyton Manning. They were going to play and be given every opportunity to succeed.

If Brady had been picked by the Browns, a quarterback grave-yard, he would not have been the same player. What if the Giants had taken the advice of their longtime scout Ray "Whitey" Walsh, who loved Brady? Maybe he would have beaten out Kerry Collins, and then the Giants never would have made the draft-day trade four years later to get Eli Manning. Or maybe he never would have gotten off the bench but just bounced from team to team.

Brady might have succeeded with his hometown 49ers, but they drafted quarterbacks Gio Carmazzi before him and Tim Rattay after him. Steve Young had been forced to retire after the 1999 season because of multiple concussions. Steve Mariucci was the 49ers coach; he had done an excellent job with Young and before that Brett Favre in Green Bay. Walsh was back with the 49ers, running the team from the front office. He was also the best quarterback coach in history. But the 49ers didn't want Brady. Jeff Garcia, coming across the border from the Canadian Football League, took over the job in San Francisco that Brady craved.

He wound up in the perfect situation in New England. The owner loved Drew Bledsoe. The coach didn't. Bledsoe was Bill Parcells's draft pick. Brady was Belichick's. Belichick learned from Parcells to "go by what I see"—production, not reputation, is the ultimate criterion. Belichick takes it a step further in minicamp: no jersey numbers. Offense in blue, defense in gray. That promotes team-building by forcing the players to learn each other by name and not just by number. And when coaches watch the tapes of the practices, they have to learn the players by their movements, not their number.

"I love coaching Tom," Belichick said. "I've been fortunate to have him his whole career. We spend a considerable amount of time together. I think that's important, to have that relationship between the head coach and the quarterback so at least we're on the same page with what we're trying to do. He has great feedback. Nobody works harder or prepares better than Tom does. He's about as good as it gets in that category."

A coach and a quarterback don't have to be best friends, but it helps if they have each other's back. Jimmy Johnson and Troy Aikman had a contentious relationship after Johnson took over in Dallas in 1989 and used the first pick in the draft on Aikman. Just over two months later, Johnson used the first overall pick in the supplemental draft to take Steve Walsh, his quarterback at the University of Miami. Johnson's plan was to immediately trade Walsh and receive more in return than he invested. Walsh was a smart player with an average arm. Aikman was a smart player with a gun. But when Johnson was not able to get a package he liked, he kept Walsh for the entire 1989 season. Aikman was the better quarterback and was clearly the long-term answer for the Cowboys, but Walsh was the quarterback for the Cowboys' lone victory in their 1–15 season, in Washington when Aikman was injured. Early in the 1990 season, Johnson traded Walsh to the Saints for draft picks in the first, second, and third rounds.

The time with Aikman and Walsh together created a cold war between Johnson and Aikman. The quarterback considered asking for a trade. If the Cowboys were going to succeed, Aikman and Johnson needed to be thinking as one. There had to be trust. Johnson was fond of fish and had seven tanks in his house in Valley Ranch, in the same development as the Cowboys headquarters. He discovered that Aikman liked fish, too, and offered to help him set up his saltwater fish tank. Johnson went over to Aikman's house, and they bonded over sea clowns. No joke.

"The relationship was a struggle initially, and there was some conflict," Aikman told the *Dallas Morning News* in 1994. "But I think the reason for that, number one, was because we were losing and we were both frustrated. I think it also took me some time to understand him, and I think now he understands my will to win and the commitment I have to the team. I think Jimmy and I probably have as strong a relationship as any head coach and quarterback in the league. There are still things that I don't necessarily agree with, and I'm sure there are things I do that he probably doesn't like. But that will always happen with two people who are as competitive as we are. We have a relationship now where, if there is a concern, we can sit down and talk about how to resolve the situation."

A few weeks after Aikman expressed warm feelings for Johnson, the Cowboys won the second of their back-to-back Super Bowls. Three months later, the friction between Johnson and Cowboys owner Jerry Jones became unbearable, and Jones paid Johnson $2 million to leave. Aikman was distraught. He had totally bought into Johnson's program of discipline and accountability and was miserable when Jones hired Barry Switzer. Aikman had played for Switzer at Oklahoma before breaking his leg and transferring to UCLA. Aikman had no use for Switzer and his lackadaisical approach to running an NFL team, especially a young team loaded with talent coming off two titles. Switzer won a Super Bowl with Johnson's players in his second year in Dallas, but he and Aikman never developed a strong working relationship.

Dan Reeves and John Elway battled for the ten years Elway played for him. Reeves was so distrusting of Elway that he fired offensive coordinator Mike Shanahan because he felt they were plotting behind his back and changing the game plan.

When Reeves was fired by Denver owner Pat Bowlen after the 1992 season, Elway said playing for Reeves the previous three years had been hell. "Just tell him it wasn't exactly heaven for me, either," Reeves said. "One of these days, I hope he grows up. Maybe he'll mature sometime."

Parcells created so much tension in Giants practice that

quarterback Phil Simms would be mentally fatigued by the time he arrived home. He got nervous before seven-on-seven drills. Parcells picked on him because he knew Simms was thick-skinned, and making him accountable meant making the whole team accountable. Brett Favre would drive Mike Holmgren out of his mind with stupid mistakes; the coach was so fed up, he once considered benching Favre for Mark Brunell. During the 1994 season, Holmgren went as far as polling his coaches about who should start. Enough hands went up for Brunell that Holmgren thought hard about making the change. Holmgren decided to stick with Favre, but when he met with him the next day in his office, he never told him he'd considered benching him. Favre was too carefree to be motivated by the fear of losing his job.

The relationship between Belichick and Brady was never adversarial. Brady cares so much and approaches each practice as if he has to persuade Belichick not to bench him. That has allowed Belichick to give Brady a little bit of the Parcells-Simms treatment. He knows he can yell at him and Brady can take it. The greater message is being delivered to the team. If the coach can yell at the four-time Super Bowl winner, you'd better watch your ass. You're next.

"He knows me as well as anybody. I know what he expects of me," Brady said. "We don't probably talk as much as people may think. He trusts me to do my job and lets me do my job. There's times where I get to express certain things to him, and I think he has a lot of trust in the things that I say and confidence in the things that I say."

Belichick was asked at Super Bowl XLIX in Phoenix about his relationship with Brady. He guards anything regarding his personal life more closely than his game plans. "Tom and I have been together for fifteen years, so I would say our relationship covers a lot of ground," he said. "We played golf together for three days at Pebble Beach."

During a break in the 2014 pro-am tournament at Pebble Beach, Brady told Jim Nantz and Nick Faldo of CBS that he enjoyed the opportunity to play golf with his coach. "He doesn't yell at me out here like he does during the weeks of practice," Brady said. "We haven't had too many chances to do things like this, so this is a really special week for me to be with him."

Peyton Manning was also at Pebble Beach in February 2014, a few days after the Broncos were crushed in the Super Bowl by the Seahawks and a little more than two weeks after he'd played so well beating the Patriots in the AFC championship game. Belichick calls Manning the best quarterback he ever faced, so spending time with Belichick and Brady was good for Manning's state of mind after the Super Bowl loss. "I have great respect for the way they play, the way they approach the game," Manning said. "They're both very similar that way. They are football junkies, if you will. I think that's a compliment. I consider myself that as well, and I think all football players should be, so yeah, I've enjoyed those times."

Manning and Belichick would have been a great combination, too, and chances are, Manning would have more than one Super Bowl ring if he'd played for Belichick and the Patriots.

Tom Brady has never spoken much about Spygate, the scandal that resulted when the NFL, acting on a tip from Jets coach Eric Mangini, a former Belichick assistant, caught a member of Belichick's video crew videotaping the defensive play calls from the Jets sideline during the 2007 season opener at Giants Stadium. It was against league rules, a point driven home by a memo from the league office the previous September. Belichick, who claimed he simply misinterpreted the rule, was fined the maximum, $500,000, by Roger Goodell, who also fined the organization $250,000 and took away a first-round draft pick. Goodell considered suspending

Belichick but ultimately decided the fine and the loss of the draft pick were sufficient punishment.

The scandal cast doubt on the integrity of the league and created headlines for months. Goodell said it had to be assumed that Belichick had been taping defensive signals against NFL rules ever since he had been a head coach.

Belichick is such a control freak, he accounts for every minute of the day. If spying wasn't helping him, why would he do it? The idea was to match the coded defensive signals with the play call and then try to use the information to the Patriots' advantage the next time they played that team. It was a time-consuming process. Stealing signals was not against NFL rules, but using video equipment to assist in the process broke the rules.

Once things settled down in New England after Goodell punished Belichick, there was a quiet moment between Patriots owner Robert Kraft and Belichick. Kraft was incensed that his organization and brand had been tarnished, but he never considered firing Belichick. Instead, he asked him, on a scale of one to a hundred, how much the tapes had helped the Patriots.

"One," Belichick said.

"Then you're a real schmuck," Kraft said.

Brady had already won three Super Bowls by the time Belichick was punished, raising the issue of whether their Vince Lombardi Trophies were tainted and deserved an asterisk. Simply because he was the quarterback who would have benefited from knowing what defense was called before the snap, Brady's accomplishments were also questioned.

Did they beat the Colts in those playoff games because Brady was being told in his radio helmet before it was turned off with fifteen seconds left on the play clock whether the Colts were in a man-to-man or a zone or were disguising a blitz? Was he able to move the ball right down the field in the last minute of their Super

Bowl victory against the Rams because the Patriots had played Saint Louis during the regular season and Belichick was able to decode the Rams defensive signals and tell Brady what was coming during the final drive?

Brady is driving through Boston traffic now on his way home from Gillette Stadium many years after the scandal. The question about Spygate doesn't make him drive off the road, but it's clearly a topic that ticks him off. "I haven't thought about that in a long time," he said. "Even when we went through it, I didn't think about it."

How much did the espionage help him? He barely waited to hear the end of the question. "Not one bit. Not one bit," he said. "I'm the quarterback. I go up under center. I'm the one that makes every decision on the field. I didn't benefit from anything other than you go out there and try to do the best you can. You evaluate what the other team is doing and you make a quick decision. I don't think any of that ended up factoring into anything we ever did."

The Patriots played with a chip on their shoulder the rest of the season, winning fifteen straight games after the spying stopped to finish off the first 16–0 regular season since the NFL expanded from fourteen to sixteen games in 1978. They barely missed completing their perfect season when the Giants came from behind to beat them in the last minute of Super Bowl XLII.

"Our team being 18–0 before we lost to the Giants really spoke for itself," Brady said. "But none of that had any influence on me in any game we ever played, you know. It was a whole lot of nothing from my standpoint."

If Brady has one major regret in his career, it's not winning the Super Bowl with that 2007 team. "To me, that was the greatest team that ever played in the NFL," he said. "We won so many games against the toughest competition that year by big margins."

Dungy seemed to relish the idea that Spygate creates doubt about the Patriots dynasty. "Really, a sad day for the NFL," he said at the time. "It's another case of the ninety-nine percent good things that are happening being overshadowed by one percent bad. Again, people aren't talking about our product; they're talking about a negative incident."

Now he's sitting at a hotel coffee shop in midtown Manhattan, but Dungy's feelings haven't changed. He retired from coaching after the 2008 season and joined NBC for its *Football Night in America* studio show preceding *Sunday Night Football*. He believes Belichick's comments to Kraft that signal stealing may have helped the Patriots by only one on a scale of a hundred, but says that was enough to give the Patriots an advantage.

"A 'one' when it's close in a championship game—if you can get one signal, or one time you know a blitz is coming, that's all you need," he said. "Sure, it helps. One play can be the difference between losing a playoff game and going to the Super Bowl."

He said the Patriots always requested extra sideline passes for cameramen. Dungy never knew exactly what was going on, but knew he had to take precautions. Days before the Colts played in Foxboro in the 2003 AFC championship game, word got to him about Belichick's spying. He said that Dave Moore, a tight end who played for him in Tampa, had played that season in Buffalo with former Patriots quarterback Drew Bledsoe and Bledsoe had tipped him off. "He said when they were getting ready to play the Patriots, Bledsoe told their coaches, 'Here is what you have to do. Here is what is going on. You got to change the signals,'" Dungy said. "He said, 'They are taping your signals, so you better change your defensive signals.' It's not like they are the only guys who ever broke any rules. Everybody is trying to get an edge. So you have precautions. You're always worried about that kind of stuff. The league is always one step behind. To me, there's a difference between bending the rules and taking every advantage you can get and breaking the rules."

Dungy never discussed his feelings with Belichick. "No, no," he said.

The anti-Belichick group—and there's a waiting list to get in—points out that in the first seven seasons after the spying ring was disassembled, he didn't win the Super Bowl. To them that proves the cheating paid off. The much smaller pro-Belichick group, which is still accepting applications for membership, says the Patriots won seventeen straight games in 2007 after the cameras were put in storage and Goodell had the tapes destroyed and still made it to three Super Bowls, winning one, in the first eight years after Spygate.

Belichick is a polarizing figure, and some view Brady as part of the Belichick evil empire. The Deflategate fiasco only cemented that feeling.

The Patriots were 9–0 in 2007 after beating the Colts when it became a realistic possibility that they would not lose a game the rest of the season. Don Shula, the coach of the 1972 Dolphins, who were 14–0 and then won three playoff games for the only perfect season in history, told the *New York Daily News* that Belichick's accomplishments that season deserved an asterisk.

"The Spygate thing has diminished what they've accomplished. You would have to have that attached to your accomplishments. They've got it," he said. "Belichick was fined $500,000, the team was fined $250,000, and they lost a first-round draft choice. That tells you the seriousness or significance of what they found. I guess you got the same thing as putting an asterisk by Barry Bonds's home-run record. I guess it will be noted that the Patriots were fined and a number-one draft choice was taken away during that year of accomplishment. The sad thing is, Tom Brady looks so good, it doesn't look like he needs any help."

Belichick and Brady would later become embroiled in the Deflategate controversy before Super Bowl XLIX, when the NFL investigated claims that the Patriots removed air pressure from many of the twelve footballs they supplied for their offense in the AFC championship game against the Colts, which New England won 45–7. Belichick denied any knowledge of the deflations. Brady claimed he would never do anything to break the rules. In the two weeks between the conference championship game and the Super Bowl, the Deflategate story overshadowed the game. On the Thursday before the Patriots left for Phoenix, Brady held a press conference to answer questions about the deflated footballs. He was bombarded with questions. "I didn't alter the ball in any way," he said.

Belichick's history of cheating made the Patriots an easy target. As he was giving an impassioned defense of his team in the deflated-football scandal, Belichick spoke in more detail about Spygate than he had when the incident occurred. He said the signals were "in front of eighty thousand people, okay? So we filmed him taking signals out in front of eighty thousand people, like there were a lot other teams doing at the same time, too. Forget about that. If we were wrong, then we've been disciplined for that."

Brady's image took a big hit as the Super Bowl approached. Many not residing in Patriots Nation viewed him as the mastermind behind deflating the balls. The pendulum started to swing a bit back in Brady's favor, however, after he threw two touchdown passes to overcome a 10-point deficit in the fourth quarter to beat Seattle. Fans related to Brady jumping up and down like a five-year-old after safety Malcolm Butler's end-zone interception in the final seconds of the Super Bowl clinched the title. The postgame pictures of Brady with his wife and two of his children on the field warmed up a country overrun with freezing temperatures.

A new controversy briefly took over for Deflategate: Why

hadn't Seattle coach Pete Carroll just given the ball to the unstoppable Marshawn Lynch at the goal line instead of having Russell Wilson throw a risky pass? Brady came so close to losing his third straight Super Bowl, which could have changed the narrative of his career.

Tom Brady Sr. waits in the family area outside the locker room or in the tunnel for his son after games. There have been times when Belichick emerges first but never has Brady Sr. approached him to talk about the game or how his son played. "Are you nuts?" he said, laughing.

Brady Sr. hears a lot about Tom's relationship with Belichick. He agrees with Tom's assessment. "Tommy has said to me different times, Belichick has a perfect soldier with me," Brady Sr. said. "Tommy is the perfect foil for Belichick. When Randy Moss comes in and sees Tommy getting chewed out and not coming back at it and accepting it, the other fifty-two guys fall in line. That is absolutely the ideal military regimen he inherited from his father at Navy. That's exactly what he wants. If you have somebody who doesn't fall in line, like a Wes Welker, you are out the door. Tommy is absolutely the perfect quarterback for Bill Belichick because he understands what Belichick is doing and he has enough pride to know that no matter what Belichick might say to diminish his efforts, it's not going to impact who he is and what he knows he can do."

One Wednesday afternoon in November, it was cold and miserable outside, an early taste of the New England winter. The Patriots were in the middle of another very successful season, but this practice was not crisp. Brady was not sharp. He beat himself up on the way home as usual. He does that even if he practices well but misses one pass that he thinks he should have made. Every second of practice is taped, and the next day at the team meeting, the first play Belichick showed was a bad pass by Brady.

Brady's father said Tom described what Belichick said: "Brady, if you throw a fucking pass like this, it's going to be picked off and run back for a touchdown. You're supposed to be an All-Pro."

Brady had already won three Super Bowls, which made him the perfect target for Belichick. He could have taken the Patriots indoors to practice in their field house, but he liked to make things as difficult as possible in practice, especially with an outdoor game coming up. There was no use practicing in a controlled environment if the ball was going to be wet or cold on game day.

Brady Sr. is astounded at the lack of compliments Belichick has publicly thrown his son's way. It's not the Belichick way. It's not the Patriots way. "They couldn't care less. They are not trying to shine his star," he said. "If Belichick had fifty-three guys named Joe, he would love it."

Manning has been celebrated for his individual accomplishments. When he threw the pass that broke Favre's all-time touchdown record in 2014 with the 509th of his career, it was all the Broncos could do to stop themselves from wheeling a podium out to the middle of the field and having Manning give a speech. They did celebrate with a video presentation on the scoreboard. When Brady surpassed fifty thousand yards for his career, all his father could remember Belichick saying was, "We're not into individual statistics, but I do have to recognize fifty thousand yards."

None of this bothers Brady, because all he wants to do is win. Never once, in a quiet moment, has Belichick initiated a conversation with Brady about all they have accomplished together. Not once has he reflected on winning all those Super Bowls and what a great combination they've been. "Never. Nope," Brady said. 'He's not a look-forward or look-to-the-past kind of guy."

Belichick was sitting at his podium on media day in downtown

Phoenix at Super Bowl XLIX. It's the one place every coach in the NFL wants to be on the last Tuesday in January. They are up there for an hour, and all kinds of questions are asked. Some coaches enjoy it. Belichick showed up in his flip-flops and a sweatshirt with the sleeves cut off, and looked like he was about to get a root canal. Some of the questions are pure Xs and Os. Belichick gives nothing up. Some are about injuries. If a player has a sprained ankle, the Patriots describe it as a leg injury and won't give up top-secret information, such as which leg. Don't even bother asking Belichick about his personal life, other than the fact that he enjoys having his son Stephen on his staff, which allows him to teach him the business and spend more time with him.

Ask him about what he and Brady have accomplished together and he frowns. "We're just focused on this game," he said. "We're not really worried about any of the past games or anything in the future."

The Patriots had twenty rookies on the team in 2000. Brady became the leader of the group. He was invaluable on the scout team. Belichick noticed. When quarterbacks coach Dick Rehbein died during training camp in 2001, Belichick and offensive coordinator Charlie Weis alternated coaching the quarterbacks. That was the start of the daily relationship Belichick had with Brady. "I feel like Tom and I do have a good relationship, and I have a lot of respect for Tom," he said. "No other quarterback I'd rather have quarterbacking our team than Tom Brady. I guess that's the best way I could sum it up."

Belichick provided a little bit of insight into their relationship in an interview with Bill Cowher on CBS in 2013. Brady is so prepared when he meets Belichick that the coach must match his intensity. Even on a Tuesday. "Tom's one of the toughest players that I've ever had to coach because when you walk into the meeting with Tom, he's already seen every game, like the Colts, that the

Colts have played defensively," Belichick told Cowher. "So, you can't go in there unprepared, you can't go in there saying, 'Well, I don't know if they're going to do this.' He'll say, 'Did you see the Tennessee game? That's what they did.' So you got to be as well prepared as he is. That's a good thing, but it's also a hard thing. You can't throw the curveball by him. You better know what you're talking about. He does."

Matt Cassel, the former Brady backup, said Belichick is consistent in his approach to his players. "He wants everybody to feel a little bit uncomfortable," he said.

Belichick and Jimmy Johnson are good friends. Belichick makes a trip down to Johnson's home in the Florida Keys every off-season to spend time fishing and talking football. Johnson didn't treat all players the same. His rules were different, based on importance to the team. He cut fringe linebacker John Roper for falling asleep in a meeting, but he said if he caught Aikman snoozing, he'd whisper in his ear, "Come on, Troy, wake up."

Belichick never has to be concerned about making an example of Brady sleeping in a meeting. Brady likes to be in bed by nine p.m. during the season. He gets his rest. "Bill has such respect for Tom. He knows that Tom knows what he's doing," Cassel said. "Did he yell at Tom? Hell, yes. It kept everybody accountable."

Brady has been coached hard by Belichick, and that's all he's ever known in the NFL. Manning started off with Jim Mora Sr., in Indianapolis, an old-school coach who helped revive Manning's hometown Saints in New Orleans. Mora was hired by the Colts the same year Indianapolis drafted Manning. The Colts were just 3–13 in 1998, then 13–3 in 1999, the best single-season improvement in NFL history, but after a bye in the first round of the playoffs, they lost at home to the Titans. They were struggling again in 2000, and after a 40–21 loss to the 49ers in which Manning threw four interceptions, one returned for a touchdown and the three others setting up seventeen points, the Colts were 4–6. That prompted the famous Mora rant. After he said his team's performance was disgraceful and sucked, he was asked about the Colts' chances to make the playoffs.

"What's that? Playoffs? Don't talk about . . . playoffs! You kidding me? Playoffs? I just hope we can win a game."

Mora was fired after the 2001 season and replaced by Dungy, a mild-mannered man who believed coaches should be home having dinner with their families as often as possible and never sleep in the office or watch tape until two in the morning. Manning was much more high-strung than his coach. It's the coach who usually has trouble putting things in perspective. "He's really a creature of habit and he came to appreciate my consistency," Dungy said. "He was always trying to improve things, reinvent the wheel. That was the hard part for me—to rein him back in."

When Dungy retired after the 2008 season, Polian replaced him with Jim Caldwell, the Colts offensive coordinator. His personality was similar to Dungy's. In their first year together, Manning and Caldwell made it to the Super Bowl against the Saints, back in Miami, where the Colts had defeated the Bears in a downpour four years earlier. This time, the weather was nice.

Manning had once worn a bag on his head at a Saints game as a kid at the urging of his big brother, Cooper, when Archie was the quarterback. Peyton grew up around the Saints. But now the Colts were trailing New Orleans and moving into position for the tying touchdown in the Super Bowl. They had a third and 5 at the New Orleans 31 with 3:24 left. Manning dropped back and looked for Reggie Wayne cutting from left to right. Manning could complete that pass in his sleep. Unfortunately, Wayne cut off his pattern and cornerback Tracy Porter jumped the route and picked off Manning. He returned it 74 yards for a touchdown to clinch the game. The criticism Manning heard before he won the

Super Bowl had returned. He was too classy to assign blame on the interception. It wasn't his fault.

Manning would play only one more playoff game for the Colts, a wild-card loss to the Jets at home the following season. He sat out the 2011 season and went to Denver to play for John Fox, another player-friendly coach. They made it to the Super Bowl their second year together but were blown out by the Seahawks. Fox had a mutual parting with the Broncos after his third season. Gary Kubiak took over, the fifth head coach of Manning's career.

Brady has played for just one, arguably the best of all time.

"It's hard to imagine them not together," Fox said. "I'm not knocking Bill or anybody, but you show me a great coach, I'll show you great players. You could almost say great quarterbacks. Don Shula is the winningest coach ever in professional football. His quarterbacks were Unitas, Griese, and Marino. I'm not slighting Don Shula, but I think he would probably mention that."

The dynamic between Brady and Belichick is much different from the one between Manning and his coaches. Belichick is the producer and director, and although Brady is the star of the show, he's executing Belichick's script. Manning began calling plays at the line of scrimmage early in his career, and as he played for different coaches and different teams, they all adopted Manning's way of doing business. Therefore he has continued operating at peak efficiency as he has transitioned into the later years of his career. Brady appreciates Belichick's attention to every little detail and returns his compliment by saying there's no other coach he would rather play for in his career. "He's a no-nonsense coach," he said. "I think why he's been able to endure is because he has the respect of all the older players, because you believe that what he's telling you and teaching you is the right way to do it. How he prepares our team every week is phenomenal. He's always got his foot on the gas pedal."

He has eased up only four times since he arrived in New England—in the hours after the Patriots have won their four Super Bowls. He's full of hugs on the field, showing the genuine affection he really feels for his players, who have sacrificed so much since the first day of training camp. Belichick drives them, but he also knows how to take care of his players' bodies over the course of the long season. When the Lombardi Trophy was brought onto the field in New Orleans, Houston, Jacksonville, and Phoenix, and Belichick was there to accept it, he's been able to take a deep breath and relax. Even smile.

Brady's father knows why the relationship between Belichick and his son is "100 percent professional." One day Belichick is going to have to cut him or trade him or convince him to retire, and as long as he doesn't establish personal relationships, his feelings won't get in the way of business decisions. "To my knowledge, he and Tommy have never been to dinner, never been to lunch," he said. "That's perfectly fine with Tommy, because he's got a whole bunch of great friends. He doesn't need to be personal friends with the coach. He's got more personal friends than he needs. He just needs to have a coach have the organization going in the right direction."

Patriots owner Robert Kraft had four sons with his wife, Myra, the love of his life, who passed away in the summer of 2011. "I always thought my wife was going to outlive me by thirty years, except for that lousy ovarian cancer," Kraft said. "Having my own sons and the players really saved me."

Kraft gets teary-eyed talking about Myra. They met in Boston when he was twenty and she was nineteen. He was attending Columbia University in New York. She was at Brandeis University in Waltham, Massachusetts. He spotted her in a coffee shop, then tracked her down at the Brandeis library the next day, and they started dating. They were married in June 1963, one week after he graduated from college. They were married forty-eight years when she passed away at the age of sixty-eight.

On a quiet morning before the start of the 2014 season, Kraft is having breakfast at the Palm Court at the iconic Plaza Hotel at the corner of Fifth Avenue and Central Park South in New York City. He owns an apartment at the Plaza and stays there on frequent business trips to Manhattan. He is dressed casually in a sport shirt, jeans, and sneakers. In a few months, he will be in a business suit lifting another Lombardi Trophy.

Kraft has been close to many of his players since he purchased the Patriots in 1994. He's been particularly close to Bledsoe, Richard Seymour, Jerod Mayo, and Vince Wilfork but none closer than to Brady. Kraft is a strong supporter of Israel, where he has many business and philanthropic interests. He's brought Seymour and Benjamin Watson on trips to Israel and watched as they were baptized in the Sea of Galilee. "It's just something that turns me on, being able to give them that experience," Kraft said.

Kraft considers his players part of his family. He has a genuine affection for Brady, his wife, Gisele, and their kids. Kraft and Brady text each other and are not afraid to express their feelings. "Mr. Kraft and I have had a very special relationship over the last fifteen years," Brady said. "He has been a part of so many decisions in my life, and I am always grateful for his thoughts on things I am going through and have gone through. I have been very lucky to have someone that has the wisdom and experience to see the big picture of my life."

When the weather gets warm and Brady and his family travel to Cape Cod, they have spent time with Kraft. He hosts an annual pre-training-camp party for his players and their wives and children at his home on the Cape, and when linebacker Brandon

Spikes was celebrating his birthday, Kraft took him out to dinner afterward. He is accommodating and accessible to all his players, but Brady is special to him.

"He is genuine, caring, and sensitive," Kraft said. "He's almost too caring and sensitive. Then he can flick the switch and be a killer on the field. When my wife died, Tommy and a group of players, led by him, were so supportive, they were like my children. They really made a difference in my life. They looked out for me, they were inviting me places. Tommy is like a fifth son. He and his wife, there is no other couple like them in America. Even the movie stars. And they are both so nice. There isn't a mother or father in America who would meet Tom Brady and wouldn't want him to marry their daughter."

Kraft invited Brady to join him on one of his trips to Israel before he met Bundchen. "He knew that spirituality was very important to me," Kraft said. "Every year my wife and I would take a group of people, mainly gentiles who had never been to the Holy Land. Going with Tommy, seeing how he took everything in, being with him at the Wall . . . I explained to him the history of how people put notes in. He put a note in."

In Kraft's office, there is a picture of Brady and him at the Wall. "I know that he and Gi are into spirituality," he said. "This might not be our last trip."

Kraft took Brady to Jerusalem and Bethlehem. "I remember him buying Bibles for his family," he said.

"We spent a memorable holiday together with Mr. Kraft and Mrs. Kraft in Israel," Brady said. "We connected on so many levels spiritually and emotionally and had some experiences I will never forget. I was still a young man but couldn't keep up with RKK's pace. He never slowed down. I won't ever forget it."

Kraft is from Brookline, a Boston suburb, and had been a season ticket holder since 1971, the year Foxboro Stadium opened.

He later bought the stadium and leased it to the Patriots. Before he purchased the team for $172 million, he was offered $75 million by Patriots owner James Orthwein to buy his way out of the lease. Orthwein was planning to move the team to his native Saint Louis, which lost the Cardinals to Arizona in 1988, but Kraft would not let him break the lease. He bought the team from Orthwein instead.

The Pats had been a moribund franchise. The only two things it had going for it were Bill Parcells, a future Hall of Fame coach, and quarterback Drew Bledsoe, both of whom arrived in 1993.

Parcells and Kraft were eventually involved in a power struggle, a fight the owner is always going to win. Kraft was not happy that Parcells would commit to coaching the team only one year at a time. Parcells made Kraft feel like an outsider. Parcells was not happy that Kraft took away his power over the draft. That led to their parting following the Patriots' loss to the Packers in the Super Bowl. The worst-kept secret in the NFL was that Parcells was on his way to the Jets. He didn't even travel on the team plane home from New Orleans. Kraft then hired Pete Carroll, at the time the defensive coordinator of the 49ers, who had been fired as the Jets coach after just one season in 1994.

Carroll inherited a team loaded with the young talent Parcells drafted, and even though he made the playoffs in his first two seasons, each year the team's record regressed, and Kraft fired him after the 1999 season. Carroll developed into an outstanding head coach, winning two national championships at Southern Cal and then leading the Seahawks to the Super Bowl title in 2013 and back to the Super Bowl in 2014, where they lost to Kraft's Patriots. Kraft replaced Carroll with Belichick, giving him three of the highest-profile head coaches of this generation.

In the first twenty-one years of Kraft's ownership, the Patriots went to seven Super Bowls and won four. That's more appearances and victories than any other team in the NFL during that period;

no other team was even close. The Steelers were next with four Super Bowl appearances. The Steelers, Giants, Broncos, Packers, and Ravens were next with two Super Bowl victories. Six of the Patriots' appearances and all four of their victories came in the Belichick-Brady era.

"I've had two quarterbacks start the year," Kraft said of his first two decades as the Patriots' owner. "It's part of a way to do business. You stick with people."

Brady helped out the Patriots when he signed a new deal before the 2013 season. He received a $30 million signing bonus and made a total of $33 million over the next two years. Starting with the 2015 season, his salaries total $27 million for the next three years. The average of $9 million per year is not even half his market value. Brady did that to ease the burden on the Patriots salary cap, allowing them to remain competitive and put a championship-caliber team around him. Brady was in a better position than anybody in the NFL to give his team a hometown discount. His wife made nearly $50 million in a recent twelve-month period.

"Would the other player do that? The other person?" Kraft said, referring to Peyton Manning. "I don't know. Think about it: we sat and redid his contract so he could remain with the Patriots for his career."

Manning was due to make $19 million in 2015. After he limped to the finish line with a leg injury and the Broncos lost their only playoff game in 2014, the Broncos asked Manning to take a pay cut to $15 million, which he agreed to do. But he was still making nearly double Brady's $8 million for 2015. Brady's average salary of $9 million was just seventeenth among quarterbacks.

"Tommy does a lot of good, quiet, special things that make a difference, especially with sick children," Kraft said. "I've been a party to it. He's idolized. Peyton is special. He's very, very special. But as a human being, I don't think there is anyone who could be better than Brady. I've met a lot of people. He's off the charts."

Manning also has a big heart. A high school football player from Long Island tragically died after suffering a severe head injury following a collision during a game in 2014. In the eulogy, it was mentioned that Manning was his favorite player. The Broncos were informed by a woman who attended the funeral, and two hours later Manning signed a personal note of condolence on one of his jerseys and it was sent overnight to the family.

Brady and Manning are very giving of their time to charity. In 1999 Manning established the PeyBack Foundation, which assists disadvantaged youth with programs providing leadership and growth opportunities for children at risk. It has provided more than $10 million in grants and programs in Colorado, Indiana, Louisiana, and Tennessee. Manning contributes financially as well. Brady has been involved almost his entire career with the Best Buddies Challenge, which benefits people with intellectual and developmental disabilities. Brady takes part in a flag football game every year as part of the weekend and hosts a big dinner on Cape Cod.

The Manning Passing Academy at Nicholls State University in Thibodaux, Louisiana, is one of the most popular football camps in the country. Peyton, Eli, Archie, and Cooper are there, and the four-day camp has become so big that it sells out its 1,200 spots way in advance. Campers get the chance to learn from the Mannings. Campers have included Russell Wilson, Andrew Luck, and Harry Kraft.

Young Harry was named for Robert Kraft's father. Harry's father is Jonathan Kraft, the Patriots president, who is Robert's oldest son. Prior to his senior year in high school, Harry attended the Manning Passing Academy for the fourth time; it's owned, of course, by the family of Tom Brady's number-one rival, Peyton, and his brother Eli, who beat the Patriots twice in the Super Bowl. The first time Jonathan signed Harry up for camp, in 2011, he didn't tell Archie or any of the Mannings in advance. Jonathan arrived in a limousine. That's how they knew the Patriots family had come to Thibodaux.

Harry's grandfather Robert flew in from a conference in Sun Valley, Idaho, in 2014 to observe. His father was also there to watch as the temperature neared 100 degrees. Harry was an excellent high school quarterback with a strong arm, but he was only five nine. Although he was a little taller than his grandfather and father, he inherited their genes for height, which meant an NFL career was not likely. He was recruited by Dartmouth as a quarterback and committed to play at the Ivy League school starting in the fall of 2015. Dartmouth's coach is Buddy Teevens, who got a close-up view of Harry at the camp. He's run the Manning Passing Academy since its inception in 1996, when he was coach at Tulane.

"Harry is super sweet and smart," Archie said.

He then laughs, knowing he's about to say something funny. "I don't think he's ever going to play for the Patriots," he said, "but he's probably going to own them."

Archie keeps an eye on the youngest Kraft at his camp. "We love Harry," Archie said. "People get the wrong idea about our camp. We have 1,200 kids. You're not going to have 1,200 blue-chip players. Our goal is to enhance the high school experience; it's not just trying to get you to be a college player or a pro player. Harry's a typical camper, and he's a good little player. He has a good time and he enjoys all the things we do. It really makes me feel good that they make the effort to come all the way to Thibodaux."

Robert Kraft spends time sitting with Archie in his golf cart. One is the patriarch of the First Family of quarterbacks. The other owns the most successful team in the NFL, whose only two losses in the Super Bowl were inflicted by last-minute drives by Archie's youngest son.

"They have been gracious to Harry," Kraft said. "The Manning family has represented the best in excellence. They're a great family and great people, and they've achieved at a high level and kept a sense of humility about them."

When the Krafts and Mannings are together, they represent twelve of the first forty-nine Super Bowl games and seven championships. It would have been more, but the old man of the Manning family played on lousy teams.

10

BOYS WILL BE BOYS

It was the last day of training camp, and Peyton Manning and Dallas Clark left their dorm room on the basement floor where the Colts veterans reside at Anderson University, about forty-five miles northeast of Indianapolis. They had nothing but mischief on their minds as they walked up one flight of steps.

They commandeered a fifty-five-gallon garbage can and went into the bathroom, put it under a showerhead, and filled it with water. Lots of water. Too much water. The usual protocol for the prank was to fill the can about halfway. Manning never does anything halfway. He and Clark were dragging a garbage can filled nearly to the top.

By the end of training camp, players are tired of being away from home; they are sick of institutional food, bored with endless meetings, worn out by practice, and certainly fed up with looking at each other and being yelled at by coaches. They are a family, or more precisely, frat brothers. They need to find ways to entertain themselves.

"Don't put that much water in," Clark warned Manning.

He didn't listen.

They leaned the can against a dorm-room door with a couple of rookie offensive players inside whose main priority was making the team and not doing anything to piss off Manning.

Manning and Clark pounded on the door and took off. What happened next?

"They opened the door and it just oozed," Clark said.

The dynamic duo went back to their room in the basement pleased they had once again flooded some poor rookies' room. Then they noticed something was terribly wrong. Their ceiling was leaking. The room they had just dumped the water in was directly above theirs, creating an unintended shower. "I think we went too far with this," Clark said. "Man, someone is going to have to clean this up."

The practical joke was the signal that they had survived another training camp. "We're adults, right?" Clark said. "Why are we acting like kids? There is no excuse. But it's one of those things that happen when you're in that environment and around the guys."

Manning and Brady take their jobs on Sunday very seriously. The part of their personality that is reserved for just their teammates is their ability to stoop to childish levels the rest of the week. Brady and Manning are two of the most accomplished practical jokers the NFL has seen in a long time. That's saying something, too, because Brett Favre was one of the best. He used to throw stink bombs in the locker room to make it smell like the residual effect of eating a plate of baked beans.

In the middle of the Green Bay winter, when the weather was appropriate for polar bears, Favre would remove the car keys from a teammate's locker before practice, hand them off to one of the locker-room workers, and request that he move the car to the opposite side of Lambeau Field while they were out on the field and then return the keys to the locker. Of course, when practice was over and the players had showered and dressed and it was pitch black in the dead of another endless Green Bay winter night, the player would hustle out to his car not far from the locker-room exit, but his car would no longer be in the parking spot he'd left it in that morning. Favre was thirty-five years old going on fifteen.

Brady has the impeccable image and the supermodel wife. Jay Feely, his college buddy and longtime NFL kicker, says Brady is so secure in who he is that he often signs off on texts to him by saying, "Love you." Manning is known as an avid letter writer. Not e-mails. Handwritten letters. He will write to players he admired when they retire.

Brady and Manning have the highest character, but it has never been a good idea to mess with either one of them. Part of Manning's standard routine is to change the language on a team-mate's cell phone to Chinese. "That was pretty clever," Clark said. Eli is also known to be quite skilled at changing the settings on cell phones. It must be in their genes. Matt Cassel learned the hard way that being close friends with Brady doesn't earn one an exemption when he feels like screwing around. He became Brady's favorite target.

Brady sat close to the door of the Patriots quarterbacks meeting room. Cassel would come in and swing the door open, nearly nailing him. "Dude, you're going to hit me, you're going to kill me," Brady yelled.

One day, Cassel was coming into the meeting room with a plate of food. Brady was in his usual spot. "So he put his chair close up to the door knowing that I was going to come in," Cassel said. "I spilled my food all over the place."

Cassel couldn't just leave it at that. He had to get even. He found Brady's Nike shoes in his locker and filled them with shaving cream. Naturally, when Brady came in to get dressed after a post-practice shower, he put his sneakers on and his feet were buried. Brady retaliated by throwing a protein shake on Cassel. Brady was willing to call a truce, but first he wanted Cassel to address him with reverence. "He wanted me to call him Daddy," Cassel said. "There is no way I'm calling him Daddy."

Cassel threatened to get back at Brady. "I can call it off," Brady said.

Cassel didn't have a clue what he was talking about. He thought maybe Brady was going to do something to his helmet. It was much worse and much funnier.

"I didn't care at that point," Cassel said.

Yes he did.

"Of course, I come in from practice and there's three of my tires sitting there in front of my locker," Cassel said. "I'm like, 'Son of a bitch!' He hid one of them in the training room. I couldn't get the tires on my car after practice, so I had to get a ride home."

Brady is telling his version of the events and can't stop laughing. Just about everything about his time with Cassel makes him laugh. "He was a fun guy. We were like little brothers together for the years we played together. We had an exchange the previous day. He threw something on me, I threw something on him, he threw something on my car, I threw something on his car. So it just went back and forth," Brady said. "So finally when we went out to practice, I took all four tires off his car, and we left three of them right by his locker and hid his other tire until the next day."

The visual is humorous: Brady with a tire jack in his hands looking over his shoulder to see if Cassel was coming. "God, no," Patriots center Dan Koppen said. "He made a phone call and magically it happened."

Brady again was ready to call a truce. He had one of the locker-room guys put the tires back on Cassel's car. "The offensive linemen thought it was funnier than hell," Cassel said.

Koppen and tackle Matt Light came up with a plan to ostensibly help Cassel get even but it was truly designed because there was so much fun going on and they wanted in. Koppen and Brady are close friends. Brady invited Koppen to be in the audience at 30 Rockefeller Center when he hosted *Saturday Night Live* in 2005 after the Patriots won their third Super Bowl in four years. They socialize and go to dinner with their wives. Their friendship didn't end when Koppen was no longer with the Patriots after the 2011 season. "I think success hit him so hard and early that he didn't know how to handle a lot of that," Koppen said. "He's gotten a lot more comfortable in his skin as he's gotten older. There's some places he stays away from. He can't go to dinner at Chili's on Wednesday night. That doesn't happen. When he goes out, it's probably special. He probably stays in more than he goes out."

One night during the 2007 undefeated season, there was a big get-together for special-team ace Larry Izzo's birthday. "Thankfully, the place was rented out and the public was not in there," Koppen said.

Thankfully because it was a karaoke party, and Brady is just a normal guy who is not afraid to make a fool of himself with his friends. He grabbed the microphone. "I don't remember what he sang, but he sings awful," Koppen said. "He's got an awful singing voice. When he's out in a secured environment, with guys on the team and their wives, he's more laid-back and can have a lot of fun."

Koppen's close relationship with Brady didn't prevent him from messing up his car. He was comfortable pranking him, especially when he was going to blame it on Cassel anyway. The first step was getting into Brady's car. "Stole the keys," Koppen said.

To prepare for the occasion, Koppen went shopping the day before and purchased several extra-large bags of Styrofoam packaging peanuts. Koppen and Light opened the sunroof of Brady's car and poured in peanuts until it was full.

It wouldn't have been any fun if Koppen and Light couldn't observe Brady's reaction. They knew that on the day of the attack

Belichick was holding an indoor walk-through practice on the club level of the stadium. There's a huge window overlooking the players' parking lot. Koppen and Light walked over to get a bird's-eye view of their work. They liked what they saw. They liked it a lot.

"Hey, Tom, come over here and check this out," Koppen said. "Look what Cassel did to you now." Brady came over and looked down. He saw his car overflowing with peanuts. At least they weren't real peanuts in the shell. Koppen thought he was framing Cassel, but Brady was onto him.

"Dan has been hit in the head too many times," Brady said.

By the time practice was over, Brady's car was vacuumed and cleaned out.

"That was kind of a letdown," Koppen said. "We wanted him to go out there and just open the door and all the peanuts fall out."

Brady didn't retaliate. "I wanted them to get the last laugh," he said.

He had gotten a taste of life in the NFL as a rookie when Bledsoe put confetti in the air-conditioning vents in his yellow Jeep. He turned the fan on high. Brady put the key in the ignition and his car suddenly looked like Times Square on New Year's Eve, or as he would soon find out, it was like standing on the podium at midfield after winning the Super Bowl. "He blasted the AC," Brady said. "The whole car got showered with confetti."

Bledsoe was sitting in his car next to Brady enjoying the show. "He thought it was the funniest thing in the world," Brady said.

After the episode with shaving cream and the protein shake and Cassel's tires and Brady's peanut-filled car, word spread around the locker room and right up to Belichick's office. He was not happy. According to Cassel, the coach came into the locker room, rounded up Brady, who was already a three-time Super Bowl winner and two-time Super Bowl MVP, and brought him together with Cassel, a backup trying to make living. He sat them down. Cassel says Belichick was red-hot and told them, "You two assholes are starting World War III. We're going to get somebody hurt. Can we stop this shit?"

It stopped. Brady having Cassel's tires removed made him the winner. "The old adage is, You never mess with anybody that has more money than you," Cassel said.

Brady is proud of his practical joke prowess. "I have my moments," he said. "People don't expect it from me. The guys I've been around a long time know I like to joke around and have fun as much as anyone. It's a little challenging now as an older player. There's so many young guys on our team. You try to find a way to connect. It's hard to be humorous all the time. Sometimes they don't get it. You have to pick the right spot."

Manning and Clark weren't one-hit wonders in Colts training camp, and packaging peanuts weren't limited to Foxboro. They got hold of a few bags. Then they got the keys to the car of one of the assistant coaches who was new to the team. They moved his car to the center of the quad at Anderson University. All the coaches and players had to walk through the quad on the way to breakfast. They also used the sunroof as their port of entry and filled up the car. They went one step further than Koppen and Light. They purchased plastic wrap, using roll after roll and completely enclosing the car.

"It was just sitting right in the middle of this park," Clark said.

Manning was the ideas person. He left most of the dirty work on this job to Clark and Austin Collie. They discussed potential punishment before they executed their plan. "You could look at it as, 'Oh, I'm with Peyton, they won't do anything,' or 'Wait a minute, they wouldn't do anything to Peyton, but they would do something to me,'" Clark said.

Collie feared the second scenario. "He was freaking out," Clark said.

He thought he was going to be cut. He survived. So did Manning and Clark.

If you are going to be a practical joker, then it's useless to complain when the tables are turned.

Koppen finished his career in Denver in Manning's first year with the Broncos in 2012. He has a unique claim to fame. Not only have Manning and Brady both stuffed their hands under his rear end to take the snap from center, but he successfully pulled off practical jokes on both of them that they probably won't mention when they give their speeches after induction into the Pro Football Hall of Fame.

Brady was victim number one. It starts as he's positioning his hands under Koppen's backside as he calls the play at the line of scrimmage in practice.

"All the ladies were jealous because he's touching my ass," Koppen said. "But he came back and said that there were only two butts he would want to touch, his wife's and mine. That made me feel good."

The next step was Koppen passing gas on Brady's hands as he was about to snap him the ball. He feels that's what cemented their friendship. "I think it becomes really special when you're able to fart on him and do all that stuff," he said. "That takes it to a whole new level."

He farted on Brady's hands in practice?

"He did," Brady said, as if he were providing confirmation in testimony in a courtroom. "You get used to it. And sometimes Dan would be chewing tobacco and he would spit on the ball. So when he'd snap it up to me, I would get a handful of his little dip spit. Oh, it was the nastiest thing. He would just laugh, ha, ha, ha. He obviously got the biggest kick out of it. I didn't get the biggest kick out of it all the time. It was funny, like, the first two times, and after that, I said, I don't want to be touching that anymore."

Koppen arrived in New England as a fifth-round pick in 2003.

Brady was already a Super Bowl MVP. How long did it take Koppen to feel secure and comfortable enough to fart on Brady?

"That's a legitimate question," Koppen said. "I think a couple of years."

Brady just didn't stand under center and let Koppen get away with the flatulence. "He will usually come back with hitting you in the nuts the next play," Koppen said. "There is give-and-take."

In a game, it was serious business. No farting. "Maybe accidentally," Koppen said. "In the game, Tom didn't care. The practice ones are the special ones where you actually plan it out. You just save one. You see if you can save one during the team drills. I would tell the guy next to me I was going to fart on Tom the next play."

When Koppen joined Manning, he went from one of the all-time greats to another of the all-time greats. "Pretty good," he said. "Peyton is fun to be around. He's got great stories. He's a great guy to sit down and have a cup of coffee with or have dinner with and just listen."

Koppen was comfortable with Brady. In Denver, he took over as the starter when J. D. Walton was injured early in the season. He quickly developed a rapport with Manning, who could be tough on teammates, but Koppen expected a lot, too. "If they got worn out by Peyton, they were in the wrong business or they were on the wrong team," Koppen said. "Yeah, he was hard on people, he asked a lot of questions, he demanded a lot from his teammates. That's what it takes to win sometimes, especially when people are getting to know each other. I want to know what you are going to do in this situation. All right, this guy blitzes, who has him? So it never really bothered me."

Koppen traveled west to Denver and packed his sense of humor. "I don't think I farted on Peyton," he said. "I only had a year with him, so we never got that far."

One day in practice, however, Koppen did victimize Manning.

Football jersey tops are extremely long, even on these awfully big guys. On cue, as they broke the huddle, Koppen and the Broncos linemen pulled their jerseys out and dropped their pants. The shirts covered their asses, so it was hard to tell their pants were down. "Peyton got under there. He was so focused, he didn't realize it," Koppen said. "Everyone was bare-assed. He got up under there for a little bit. It got a little weird after a while. Does he realize that I'm bare-butt right now?"

Apparently not. "That's an old rival center-quarterback exchange," Manning said. "So, yeah, that's a good one."

Manning has been on the giving end a lot more than he's been on the receiving end. "I don't have a ranking," he said. "I don't have a list."

He does enjoy the camaraderie of his teammates. "In the locker room I think it's important, you spend a lot of time, you are grinding, it's May and we're going from six forty-five in the morning until two o'clock and we haven't had a chance to breathe yet. It's been meetings, treatment, lifting, practice, all that," he said. "So when you have a chance in the locker room to keep things loose, keep the team close together, laughing is a good thing, especially when you are in what I call a grinding profession. That's where that comes from."

The Patriots of Belichick are considered to be about as amusing as a computer infected with a virus. Perception isn't necessarily reality in the NFL. The Cowboys of Tom Landry were supposed to reflect their stone-faced coach. One visit inside their locker room in the 1980s told a vastly different story. They were a loose, trash-talking, fun-loving team. Now, when Landry briskly walked through the room, the players would pretend to be sitting at their lockers studying the playbook. As soon as Landry exited, the clowning resumed. The stories about the Belichick era are similar. The players don't show much of their personality to the public— they answer questions as if reading from a manual prepared by

Belichick—but when the cameras and notepads are out of sight, they love to joke around.

Somehow a pig's head ended up in their locker room, donated by guard Joe Andruzzi. It was moved from locker to locker and then into the coaching room, where it took up residence in the stall of Belichick's trusted assistant Dante Scarnecchia. A live duck was next to make an appearance. "Nate Solder took it home and kept it as a pet for a while," Koppen said.

Belichick was never the target. "Bill's kind of the sacred cow in the group," he said. "No one really goes after him that much."

No cows, sacred or otherwise, have been brought into the locker room for show-and-tell.

Brady marveled at the creativity of the offensive linemen led by Light and Koppen. During practice when the scout team was running plays to give the first-team defense a look at the upcoming opponent, the starting offensive linemen would jog around the perimeter of the field to stay in shape. The Patriots tape their practices with all twenty-two overhead cameras, much like game day, to give the coaches and players a full view. It's a common teaching tool.

"When the scout teams' plays were being filmed, the offensive linemen would run with their pants down," Brady said. "No one would see it because everyone was just watching the practice."

The players then gathered to watch the tape of practice in the team meeting room, and the streaking was there on the screen for all to enjoy. "It was so funny," Brady said. "It takes a lot of personality to do that."

Peyton Manning takes even being funny seriously. When he hosted *Saturday Night Live* in 2007 shortly after the Colts beat the Bears in the Super Bowl, he studied as though it was a championship game and was so good that he was invited back when *SNL* held its fortieth-anniversary show in 2015. He and Derek Jeter playfully argued onstage over who was the best athlete to ever host the show. Manning is so entertaining on television that he was among the celebrities invited to participate in the Top Ten list on David Letterman's final show.

Manning's United Way skit on *SNL* was hilarious. He was in a park in New York playing football with kids. He called the plays and fired the football (they were Nerf balls) at the children, hitting one boy in the back of his head. He was so disgusted that the pass was not caught, he sent the kid to take a time-out in a Porta-Potty and yelled at him to close the door. "Get your head out of your ass!" Manning screamed at the kid. "You suck!"

He then tried to teach the kids how to break into a car on a city street. When a police siren sounded, he yelled, "Cops! Cops! Every man for himself!" The segment ended with this suggestion from United Way: "Spend time with your kids. So Peyton Manning doesn't."

He attacked the script as if it was the playbook for a championship game against Brady. "He was the only guy I've ever known to host the show to have a binder with tabs. That preparation certainly came through on Saturday," former *SNL* cast member Seth Meyers said on *Mike and Mike* on ESPN Radio.

Brady enjoyed his turn to host two years before Manning. "He's the coolest person any of us will ever meet," Meyers said. "But he's really nice."

Manning could have owned New York if he had left Tennessee in 1997 and been drafted first overall by the Jets or had signed with them when he became a free agent in 2012. His brother Eli is laid-back, and he has cashed in by playing in the biggest market in the country. Peyton is so glib and so personable, he might even have been in the running to replace his pal Letterman as host of *The Late Show* when Letterman retired in 2015 if he had been around New York full-time.

Brady was funny on *SNL,* but Manning is a natural in front of the camera. Brady opened his *SNL* monologue with a bit where he sings and dances—a very liberal interpretation of what constitutes singing and dancing. The audience was larger than when he was singing karaoke at Izzo's birthday party.

"I won the Tour de France, and I did it with no pants," Brady croons. "So when I rode by, you saw my sweet behind."

In one skit about sexual harassment in the workplace, Brady fondles one of Amy Poehler's breasts after asking her out to lunch and then arranges a date with Tina Fey when he approaches her in the office dressed in a sport shirt, tie, and underwear.

Brady's parents were in the audience for the show. "He never lets us know he's nervous under any circumstances," Brady Sr. said. "We were nervous because I've never heard him sing before. Oh my god, where did that come from? The opening was pretty darn good. He acted when he was in grammar school when all the kids do school plays, but I've never seen him have any propensity toward acting."

Archie Manning wasn't nervous before Peyton played in his first Super Bowl. "The Colts deserved to play in that Super Bowl," he said. "I didn't have anxiety. I had pride."

But as he sat in the audience for *SNL* at 30 Rockefeller Plaza with Olivia, Eli, and Cooper in studio 8H at NBC headquarters in midtown Manhattan, he was shaking. It was Peyton's thirty-first birthday, and at the end of the show, Eli and Cooper wheeled out a birthday cake during the closing credits. Eli won the Super Bowl the following year, and *SNL* executive producer Lorne Michaels asked him to host. But after Peyton received rave reviews, Eli knew the timing wasn't right to try to one-up his big brother. He has an understated sense of humor and is the best practical joker in the Giants locker room, but following Peyton so quickly was a no-win situation. "Eli is not dumb," Archie said. "He told Lorne, 'Get me the next time.'"

When Eli won his second Super Bowl, beating Brady again following the 2011 season, Michaels called, and this time Eli accepted. Archie wasn't as nervous about Eli hosting, for two reasons. He had already been through it with Peyton, and Eli is so calm he often doesn't register a pulse.

"When Peyton told me he was going to do *Saturday Night Live*—and I don't ever question Peyton—I don't think he really wanted to do it," Archie said. He was getting pressured by his high school friends. "I knew all through the years, there was a certain group of guys telling him, 'Peyton, if you ever get a chance to do *SNL*, you damn well better do it,'" Archie said. "So he was not going to say no."

Peyton brought the news to his parents that he was going to hit the big stage in New York.

"We're going to go, aren't we?" Olivia asked.

"I don't know if I want to be there, Liv. This is not what he does," Archie said.

Peyton had been rehearsing in New York all week. Meyers, who also wrote for the show, and the rest of the writers met every Tuesday night for dinner in the back room at Lattanzi, a classic New York restaurant in the famed Theater District. The creative brains of the show would brainstorm late into the night writing and rewriting. They came up with some clever skits for Manning.

Archie and Olivia left on a flight Friday from New Orleans to New York. They arrived in the evening and were relaxing in their midtown hotel when Archie's cell phone rang.

"Get over here," Peyton said.

"Where?" Archie asked.

"NBC," Peyton said.

Archie walked over to Fiftieth Street, was let through by security, and was brought to the greenroom. Peyton was sitting by himself watching an Elvis Presley concert that the King of Rock 'n' Roll had performed in Las Vegas. The writers had put together a skit in which Peyton was going to play Elvis. Peyton was studying his moves intently.

"I don't seem good enough as Elvis," Peyton told Archie. He watched more tape.

"How is the week?" Archie asked.

"It's good," Peyton said.

He asked Peyton to turn off the video. "I got anxiety about you doing this. How is it going to be? What's it going to be like?" Archie said.

Peyton didn't hesitate. "We're going to kick their ass!"

He was talking about the entire cast. He wasn't talking about himself. He was talking about the *SNL* team. Manning is always about the team and competition. It made Archie relax.

Peyton kicked ass. It helped that the Elvis skit was left in rehearsal. The *SNL* producers had called an audible. Manning could relate.

Brady had a blast doing *SNL,* but he has been more a fixture modeling in print ads, which take advantage of his good looks. Manning's memorable commercials for MasterCard, Papa John's Pizza, and Nationwide Insurance have made him one of television's most popular pitchmen. Brady models for UGGs. He also made a very funny cameo appearance in the movie *Ted 2* and has appeared in *Entourage,* both on television and in the movie.

Manning and Brady came across as very likable on *SNL*. "It was so fun to do that when I finished it, I was almost disappointed that I'll never have a chance to experience that again," Brady said. "It was such a unique thing that I was bummed when it was over. Even if I ever happen to do this again, it will never be like the first one, because I had no expectations going in. You can just go, 'Holy shit!' It was awesome. It was a great experience."

Brady knew Manning would do well when it was his turn. "It was so out of the box for both of us. He was pretty awesome, I got to say it," he said. "He's got a great sense of humor about him. He's very witty, a very funny guy. He's got more of a slapstick humor than I do."

Manning had no problem poking fun at himself when the script called for him to tell a story about visiting eighty-five-year-old Joe O'Malley in a veterans' hospital in Boston.

He said O'Malley asked him, "Peyton, what do Tom Brady and the circus have in common?"

"What's that, Joe?" Manning asked.

"They both have two more rings than you do," O'Malley said.

By the end of the 2014 season, Brady had one more ring than a three-ring circus. Manning was still stuck at one.

Eric Decker played two years with Manning in Denver. They became close friends, and along with tight end Jacob Tamme, who also played with Manning in Indianapolis, the three would ride together to games at Mile High Stadium from the Inverness Hotel and Conference Center in Englewood, the team hotel for home games. Manning was behind the wheel and Tamme was in charge of the music, even though Decker is married to country singer Jessie James. The Broncos issued only one parking pass per family, so the players would ride together and the wives would meet them at the game. "We figured it was really good team-building time to just really calm the nerves," Decker said. "Tamme was the DJ and was riding shotgun. He was older than me. I allowed him to sit in the front. I think it was a roundtable discussion of what mixes to play, but Tamme controlled it."

Manning's preference was the Coffee House channel on SiriusXM. The twenty-five-mile drive north from Englewood to Denver is how Decker really got to know Manning. "Everyone looks at him as this iconic football player," Decker said. "He's a family man, a good person who likes to have fun. He's a jokester. I don't know if people know that. He's a lighthearted fun guy. He's a guy's guy."

Manning knows the name of everybody in the building. When a new player arrives, he's the first to introduce himself or play golf with him. "You know that he has your back, which is great," Decker said.

In April 2013, Peyton and Eli invited their receivers to Duke for a passing camp. Peyton throws to the Broncos. Eli throws to the Giants. The players all pay their own way to get to Durham, North Carolina, and then Peyton and Eli take care of the rest. Victor Cruz, Hakeem Nicks, and Louis Murphy from the Giants and Decker, Demaryius Thomas, and Wes Welker from the Broncos were there.

On the last night, the entire group went to dinner at a steak house between Chapel Hill and Raleigh. There was a wine cellar downstairs. Before dinner, Peyton approached all the receivers except for Decker and told them he was going to be handing each an envelope. "Decker is getting pranked," he told them.

Five of the envelopes would have a blank sheet of paper. Decker's would be different. At the appropriate time, Manning handed out the envelopes. Decker looked inside. It was on Duke stationery. Under the letterhead DUKE FOOTBALL was Decker's name and the Broncos address.

To the right was the heading INVOICE. It was an itemized bill:

On-field instruction from Duke Coaching Staff ($500 per session) $2,500

Laundry service from Duke Football Equipment Staff ($20 per session) $100

Taping, treatment, etc. from Duke Football Athletic Training Staff ($50 per session) $200

Facility Fee (use of Pascal Field House, Brooks Building and
    Yoh Center) $300
Airport Shuttle FREE
Total payment due in 30 days
Please include the invoice number on your check
Make all checks payable to Duke University Football
Subtotal $3,000
Tax Rate 7.25%
Tax $217.50
Other $—
TOTAL Due: $3,217.50

No way, Decker thought to himself. He didn't even notice that
Manning's math was off. He swallowed hard. He looked at Manning, who just shrugged. "I didn't want to say anything and be
rude," Decker said.

He looked around the table as the rest of the players opened
their envelope. Thomas was sitting next him. He was shaking his
head, commiserating with Decker about the unexpected expense
they had all incurred.

"I know. I know," Thomas said.

Decker was soon to be married, and he was still working on
his rookie contract. He was making $1.323 million for the upcom-
ing season, but it was a year before he cashed in as a free agent
when he signed a five-year, $36.25 million deal with the Jets.

Manning let Decker squirm for a little bit so they all could
enjoy the moment. Then he called it off.

"It probably lasted five minutes," Decker said. "But it felt like
an eternity."

He didn't immediately retaliate. "We still have a relationship,"
he said. "So I am sure down the road I will get the chance."

Colts coach Tony Dungy commanded such respect that Manning never dared mess with him. Manning did once tell a player

that Dungy had gotten word he was out late the night before and was very upset. "I had guys coming to my office to apologize," Dungy said. "I would say, 'What are you talking about?'"

Six games into the 2001 season, Colts star running back Edgerrin James tore his ACL and missed the rest of the season. In the off-season, the Colts had signed Dominic Rhodes, an undrafted rookie free agent from Midwestern State. Rhodes would rush for 113 yards and a touchdown that would give Indianapolis the lead for good in their Super Bowl victory five years later against the Bears. Dungy needed Rhodes to be a quick learner as a rookie, and he stepped up.

On his way to rushing for 1,104 yards his first year, Rhodes passed 1,000 yards—the first undrafted rookie ever to hit that milestone—as he gained 141 yards in the final game of the season, a home game against the Broncos. He needed only 37 yards going in, and Dungy was going to make sure he got them. "The funniest thing I heard Peyton do was tell Dominic, when he gets to 1,000, they're going to stop the game and give him the game ball," Dungy said. "They know how many yards he needs."

Rhodes had a 4-yard run midway through the second quarter and he was up to 1,001 yards. "Dominic doesn't come to the huddle," Dungy said. "He's waiting for the ball. Finally, they get him in the huddle and get the next play going. He's like, 'Where's my game ball? How come they didn't stop the game? Where's my announcement?' Guys were rolling."

Brady had a lot to live up to in New England when he took over for Bledsoe, who not only was popular in the locker room, but pulled off the most legendary practical joke in Patriots history. The removal of Cassel's tires was the equivalent of just getting to the Super Bowl. Bledsoe earned the Lombardi Trophy.

The Patriots landed back at Boston's Logan Airport at four in the morning after playing on the West Coast. There was seven inches of new snow on the ground. The usual routine was, the players rode the team bus for the half-hour trip back to the stadium, where they'd parked their cars. The players were not looking forward to cleaning off the snow and driving home in the middle of the night. Patriots guard Todd Rucci and backup quarterback Scott Zolak were appalled when they found out that Bledsoe was big-timing them by having a car service waiting for him at the airport to take him home. His plan was to have his wife drive him to work the next day. Rucci had other ideas.

Bledsoe and Rucci had been going back and forth embarrassing each other. Rucci once made a collage of nearly naked women and taped the pictures on the passenger side of Bledsoe's Chevy Suburban from the headlights to the taillights. He knew from where Bledsoe was parked he wouldn't see the passenger side as he got in the car. Fans were waiting as usual for players to come out after practice to sign autographs as they drove out of the secured players' parking lot. "They weren't going to wait for Todd Rucci and fat linemen to get autographs," Rucci said. "They were going to wait for Drew Bledsoe."

The fans were allowed to line up and approach the players as they pulled out. They were only allowed on one side of the car. The passenger side. Bledsoe had no idea how Rucci had decorated his car.

Bledsoe headed home from the airport as the Patriots arrived in the snow, and Rucci and Zolak headed right to Bledsoe's car in the parking lot at Foxboro Stadium. They borrowed a couple of shovels from the stadium's maintenance office and spent two hours burying the car. "We make his car into a snowball. We got every available piece of snow within twenty feet piled up, and I made the point to get underneath the car to pack the wheel wells so there was absolutely no airspace whatsoever around his car," Rucci said. "The great thing is, Mother Nature cooperated with us and it started freezing rain a few hours later. His car was literally frozen."

Bledsoe showed up the next day and at first had a hard time even locating his car. It was buried. "He had trouble getting into his car for days," Rucci said. "It was great."

It took one month, but Bledsoe got even. On Christmas Eve day, before practice, Bledsoe stole the keys to Rucci's condominium in Franklin, a Boston suburb, and hired a moving company where friends worked. "I came back home around four p.m., and I found my dog and an autographed picture of Drew Bledsoe on the living-room floor saying, 'Merry Christmas,'" Rucci said.

That's all he could find. The couch was gone. The silverware was out of the drawers. The bed was gone. The pictures were off the walls. It's a good thing he was single at the time. "I don't think my dog was inconvenienced," Rucci said. "He got his bed and bowl."

It was as if no human lived in the apartment. Rucci walked down to the basement and found all his furniture and life's belongings. "At that point, I figured, *Okay, this is a good one, it was a great one, you got me.* I found everything in the basement. I'm trying to get my king-size mattress up a flight of condominium stairs, which is very tight," Rucci said. "It was hot, I'm sweating. I could not do it. I was so irate. I just spent the night in a hotel up the road and completely pissed off he got me so well. It was great, absolutely great."

Rucci knew the owners of the moving company. The apartment was back in order after Christmas. But on Christmas night, Rucci was invited for dinner at the Bledsoes and spent the night. "I couldn't even look him in the eye," Rucci said. "With the unlimited funds a quarterback has, he can play above the rim a lot easier than I can."

Bledsoe wasn't done. He put classified ads in the local paper for each of the two cars Rucci owned. He priced them reasonably. He listed Rucci's home phone number. By the time Rucci returned home from practice, he had seventy-three messages on his answering machine. "It was well deserved what I did to him," he said. "It was pretty well deserved what happened to me."

No hard feelings. Bledsoe was later the best man at Rucci's wedding, and their families spend every July 4 weekend together at Bledsoe's vacation home in Whitefish, Montana. They sit around the campfire and tell their kids stories of how they used to torture each other.

The stories also got passed down to the next generation in the locker room. Bledsoe set the bar awfully high at New England. Brady has tried not to lower it.

"We're in such an intimate environment with each other," Brady said. "You're at work from six in the morning until four in the afternoon. You're in close proximity to these guys for seven months of the year. It's blood, sweat, and tears in everything you're doing. There is a natural camaraderie and bond that probably few professions get to experience. When you're getting the crap knocked out of you and you look to the guy next to you, you got to believe that the guy has got your back. That is what makes football really special."

11

WHO YOU GOT? BRADY OR MANNING?

Rex Ryan had just beaten Peyton Manning and the Colts in the wild-card game in the 2010 playoffs in Indianapolis, and now it was on to Foxboro for a matchup with Tom Brady and the Patriots.

He had once famously declared after the Jets hired him that he didn't take the job to kiss Bill Belichick's rings. He should have added that he wasn't going to kiss Brady's ass, either.

The Jets upset the AFC South champion Colts on a Saturday night at Lucas Oil Stadium. The Patriots had a bye, and Belichick gave his players the weekend off. Brady came to New York, where he and his wife, Gisele, have an apartment, and on Saturday night they went to see *Lombardi*, a hot show on Broadway. It was not quite the same as Tony Romo spending the Cowboys' bye week after the 2007 regular season ended vacationing in Cabo San Lucas with then-girlfriend Jessica Simpson and catching grief for a lack of commitment when the Cowboys, the number-one seed, lost in the divisional round to the Giants. Brady is so committed to preparation, he probably had his Belichick playbook tucked inside his *Lombardi* playbill.

If the Colts beat the Jets, they would play in Pittsburgh and the Patriots would meet the winner of the Chiefs-Ravens game being played the next day. If the Jets won, the Patriots would play New York. Prior to the season, Brady declared, "I hate the Jets." The feeling was quite mutual.

Brady was in the Circle in the Square Theatre on Fiftieth Street and Broadway, checking his cell phone at the intermission for Jets-Colts updates. He and Gisele were back in their apartment in time to watch the second half. Even so, when word got back to Ryan that Brady was out on the town, in the Jets' town no less, rather than scouting the entire game on television, he embraced the opportunity to tweak Brady, and he hit him where it hurts.

"Peyton Manning would have been watching our game," Ryan said.

Just a few days earlier, in the run-up to the game with the Colts, Ryan praised Manning's study habits and threw it out there that Brady gets more help from Belichick than Manning receives from his coaches. Ryan loves to agitate Brady. That next weekend, the Jets beat the Patriots, the second most significant victory in team history, after Super Bowl III.

Ryan lasted six years with the Jets. The Patriots won the AFC East six times. Ryan was 3–9 against Brady in the regular season and 1–0 in the playoffs. Years later, he admitted that by trash-talking him, he was just trying to distract him.

"Of course I was," he said. "That's one of those deals—look, the dude is ridiculous. Tom Brady is ridiculous. He studies his fucking ass off and so does Peyton. They are 24/7. Damn near. Maybe they had a little time so they went to Broadway. So I said, 'Oh, I got them,' because I knew it would piss him off. This dude is fricking all football. He's got a life outside of football when the season is over. He's a football junkie. They probably kick his ass out of the building. I was tweaking his ass. I respect the shit out of those two guys. But at the same time, fuck, I got to beat those fuckers. I have to be at my very best to have a chance to beat them. I know they are that good."

Ryan thinks he is that good, too. Ask and he will tell you he and his twin brother, Rob, are the two best defensive minds in the NFL. He senses Brady and Manning don't like facing his defense as much as he doesn't like facing them.

"I don't know if it's the same feeling they get toward me, but I recognize there's like, 'Fuck you, Rex,'" he said. "They have a little bit of that in them to where it's like, 'Yeah, I made you prepare,' and that's why they can't wait to kick my ass. You know what I mean? I sense it because I see it in their faces."

Ryan was fired by the Jets after the 2014 season and hired by the Bills, and by remaining in the AFC East he doomed himself to still facing Brady twice a year. He is almost reverential talking about whom he fears more if he has to stop one in the last two minutes. "I fear nobody . . . maybe a little bit," he said, laughing. "I've been beaten by both of them in those situations. It's like, *Oh shit, this guy is going to do it to me again.* They are deadly. It's impossible to choose between the two. I just see them as Hall of Fame quarterbacks."

In games through the 2014 season, Brady is 11–5 against Manning. In their head-to-head battles, Brady has thrown 31 touchdowns and 13 interceptions. Manning has thrown 33 touchdowns and 22 interceptions. Brady is 160–47 in the regular season and has an NFL-record 21 playoff victories with 8 losses. Manning is 179–77 in the regular season and 11–13 in the playoffs. Manning is second in career regular-season victories. Brady is third. Brady's 77.3 percent regular-season winning percentage is by far the highest of all time. Brady has played with the better teams and the better coach. He has four Super Bowl rings. Manning has played with the better skill-position players. He has one ring.

"I hate comparisons, but I'm talking about style," said Ernie

Accorsi, the former general manager of the Colts, Browns, and Giants. "Brady is more like Montana. Peyton is more like Unitas."

Brady and Joe Montana each won four Super Bowls. Their styles are very similar. Manning has one Super Bowl championship. Johnny Unitas won two NFL championships and one Super Bowl. Manning wears number 18. Unitas wore number 19. Close your eyes when Manning played with the Colts and he looked just like Unitas on the field. They're the top four quarterbacks in NFL history.

When Unitas died in 2002, Manning wanted to honor him by wearing black high-top cleats, Unitas's trademark. The league threatened Manning with a $25,000 fine if he wore black shoes. The Colts as a team wore white. Manning didn't want to bring anything negative to Unitas's name, so he elected not to wear the black shoes.

Brady vs. Manning has been the best argument in the NFL for a long time. It's like asking: Coke or Pepsi? Vanilla or chocolate ice cream? Ginger or Mary Ann? It's a personal choice where you can't go wrong.

The pro-Brady faction has plenty to back up its argument. He's tied with Montana and Terry Bradshaw for the most Super Bowl victories of any quarterback. His six Super Bowl starts are a record for QBs. He won two Super Bowls with last-minute drives and another with just over two minutes remaining. He's been consistently excellent despite a changing cast of players around him, and other than the short time he played with Randy Moss—thirty-seven regular-season games and three playoff games—and the young tight end Rob Gronkowksi, he's never had the benefit of playing with a receiver or running back with Hall of Fame talent.

The pro-Manning faction has plenty of ammunition as well.

Most touchdown passes in a season and career. Most passing yards in a season. And he surely will finish with the most career passing yards and career wins. He's been fortunate to play with potential Hall of Fame receivers Marvin Harrison and Reggie Wayne in Indianapolis and a young star in Demaryius Thomas in Denver. He is a surgeon on the field, and considering the influence and power he holds, he is a basically a player-coach.

The anti-Brady argument: He has won his four Super Bowls by a combined thirteen points and never by more than four points. He could have lost any or all of those games. The first three titles came in the Spygate era. The fourth came two weeks after Deflategate.

The counterargument: His two Super Bowl losses were by three and four points. He is a couple of plays away from being 6–0. The impact of Belichick's spying was overblown. Deflategate was a farce.

The anti-Manning argument: He's won just one Super Bowl, lost two, he is under .500 in the playoffs, and his team was eliminated in its first playoff game in nine of the fourteen years he made the postseason. It's hard to justify or rationalize his lack of success in the playoffs. Even in his Super Bowl championship season, his playoff stats were unimpressive: three TDs and seven INTs.

The counterargument: It takes more than a great quarterback to win a championship. Neither of the Super Bowl losses were his fault.

Tim Hasselbeck, a former NFL backup, said prior to Brady's fourth Super Bowl title that he would rather have Manning. One day after Brady beat the Seahawks, Hasselbeck, an ESPN analyst, went on WEEI radio on Boston and reiterated his position.

"As somebody who played at the quarterback position in the NFL, at a time that both of those guys were playing, nobody's changed the game more than Peyton Manning or changed the

way that position is played more than Peyton Manning," he said.
"And from my experience as a quarterback in the NFL, that's a
fact. Also, what I said was when you look at wins and losses, especially in the postseason, there are so many other factors that
dictate who wins and loses the game. It's such a team environment, so . . . I just don't think it does the careers justice for any of
these quarterbacks to try to narrow it down to just what happens
in these postseason games."

He said Brady is better right now, but he says he would rather
have Manning's career. "Peyton Manning has won a Super Bowl;
he's achieved things that most quarterbacks aren't able to ever
achieve," he said. "He's going to own basically every passing record that exists. So you ask me whose career I would rather have,
based on that and how I explained to you he changed the game of
football from an offensive perspective, that was my answer."

The last two minutes of a game often tell the true greatness
of a quarterback. Right before Eli Manning drove the Giants to
the winning touchdown in the final minutes of Super Bowl XLII,
Accorsi turned to his son in the stands in Phoenix and said they
were about to find out if Manning was all he thought he could be.
Accorsi made the biggest trade in Giants history on draft day in
2004 to acquire Manning from the Chargers. Manning then went
right down the field and scored to beat New England. He did it
again in Super Bowl XLVI.

Seattle cornerback Richard Sherman faced Peyton Manning
and Brady in back-to-back Super Bowls. Even though the Seahawks destroyed Denver, he still holds Manning in high regard.
After Brady took a knee to end the game against the Seahawks,
Sherman walked over to Brady while he was still on the ground
and extended his hand. "You're a great player," Brady said.

"Those two, you really can't go wrong picking either one of
them," Sherman said. "They're such computers of this game. You
respect every quarterback because you know they work hard, they

study it. But those guys go out there and execute what they see. It's harder to do what you practice, to execute when everything is flying around, to know exactly where guys are going to be and hit them on a consistent level. Those two guys have been doing it for years. That's what you respect."

Sherman, a Stanford graduate, is one of the brightest players in the league, and going against Manning and Brady makes him study even more. "You know they're going to find the deficiencies, so you have to find them first," he said. "You have to self-scout, because you have to know when they are going to attack you and what they like to do, as well as scouting them. You probably have another six or seven hours of film on your hands if you're doing it right."

Former Giants defensive end Michael Strahan, inducted into the Pro Football Hall of Fame in 2014, was a big part of the defense that held Brady to just 14 points in the first Giants-Patriots meeting in the Super Bowl. He says he would fear Brady more than Manning with the game on the line in the last couple of minutes.

"I fear Tom Brady more than anybody," he said. "Tom Brady, I don't know, there is just something about Tom, not taking anything away from Peyton at all. I don't want to face him either. But there's just something about Tom. Maybe because we've seen him do it time and time again. Here's a guy who's won quite a few Super Bowls and been to multiple others. How can you not choose him?"

Montana cast his vote for Brady as well. "He has all the traits that make a great quarterback," he said. "No matter what happens the play before, he's going to fight until the end. That's the thing you got to have. They are both fun to watch. This is a tough one. I think the only reason you go with Tom is, he's proven more in the playoffs down the stretch. I'd take Tom."

Manning and Brady will be in the Hall of Fame as soon as

they are retired the required five years. Their legacies are secure. The gaping hole in Manning's résumé is the postseason, and it's why he loses points in the argument against Brady.

"I look at the critical moments in games. I look at the fourth quarter and two-minute ball games," said former Giants linebacker Antonio Pierce, an analyst with ESPN. "The next thing I look at is, how do they perform in the postseason? I would never put Eli as one of the greatest of all time in the regular season, but I'll put him up there in clutch moments and the postseason. He's that guy. Brady is that guy. Peyton has shown he's not that kind of guy in the postseason. For every comeback against the divisional foes that he's had in the regular season, it's a lot different when the lights are brighter and more cameras are on you in the postseason. To me, that is the one glaring difference between Tom and Peyton."

Manning's late-fourth-quarter interception returned for a touchdown in the Super Bowl loss to the Saints was more Wayne's fault than Manning's. Still, the record shows that the Colts were down 7 points and Manning couldn't get them into the end zone. In Brady's first two Super Bowl victories, he drove the Patriots for the winning field goal on the final drives against the Rams and Panthers, and in the first loss to the Giants threw a late TD pass to take the lead, but the New England defense couldn't stop the Giants. In the victory over the Seahawks, Brady threw the winning TD with 2:02 remaining.

Manning's reputation for not being able to win enough big games has followed him from Knoxville to Indianapolis to Denver.

"Completely unfair. Completely unfair," said former Colts president Bill Polian, who drafted Manning in Indianapolis. "We can have a long discussion about this, but the Super Bowl is one game. For the life of me, I can't see how you can take a guy's performance and just isolate it to the playoffs and forget the regular season."

Given the choice of the two, Polian said, "Obviously, I'm going to take my guy. They are without doubt the two preeminent quarterbacks of their time. There's nothing more to say, really, than that. They're both the greatest of their time. To have the good fortune to be associated with either of them is an incredible blessing."

Dungy takes the glass-half-full approach when he evaluates Manning's record in the postseason with the Colts. "I knew the flaws in our team," he said. "For those first few years, the Patriots were just better on defense than we were. They had better people and they probably had a better overall team, but we felt we could beat them if we played our game. I thought, for us, winning twelve or thirteen games every year was more of a tribute to Peyton than the fact that we weren't winning in the playoffs."

Dungy smiled. "Not many people look at it that way," he said. "When I got to the Colts, I'd never coached a team that won twelve games. Now we're winning twelve games every year."

Dungy and former Patriots safety Rodney Harrison work together on NBC's *Football Night in America* studio show on Sunday nights. They argue all the time about which quarterback they would take to win one game.

"I'm taking Peyton," Dungy said.

"Brady is the best closer. I'm taking him," Harrison said.

Dungy said he's been around Manning too many times when he's pulled games out. He was ready to take him out of the game in Dungy's return to Tampa in his second year with the Colts. Dungy really wanted this game. He had coached the Bucs from 1996 to 2001 but was fired after too many playoff failures. Jon Gruden won the Super Bowl in his first year with Dungy's players and now Dungy was back in town.

"This defense is one of the best defenses that has been put together of all time," Dungy told his players. He would know. He built it.

"We can beat these guys," he told them, "but we can't fall behind. You get behind with that noise, we don't have a chance."

It was a Monday night game. It had a playoff-game intensity
and atmosphere to it, but the Colts were letting Dungy down.
They were getting embarrassed. Manning had just thrown an interception that Ronde Barber returned 29 yards for a touchdown
with 5:09 left in the fourth quarter. Bucs 35, Colts 14.

"I was going to take Peyton out," Dungy said. "We needed to
make sure we didn't get anybody hurt."

He was ready to bench the starters. Offensive coordinator Tom
Moore convinced Dungy to give them one more series. The Colts
got a 90-yard kickoff return from Brad Pyatt.

"Okay, let's go," Dungy said to Moore.

He put Manning and the first-team offense back in.

Four plays later, James Mungro scored from the 3.

Bucs 35, Colts 21, with 3:37 left.

Indianapolis's Idrees Bashir recovered the onside kick, and on
the sixth play, Manning completed a 28-yard touchdown pass to
Marvin Harrison. Bucs 35, Colts 28, with 2:29 left.

The Bucs went three-and-out. Manning took over at his own
15 with 1:41 remaining. He put together a five-play 85-yard drive
with Ricky Williams scoring from the 1. Bucs 35, Colts 35, with
35 seconds left.

The Colts blocked Martín Gramática's 62-yard field goal attempt on the final play of regulation.

Tampa won the toss in overtime and moved to the Colts 41
and punted. Manning took over at his own 13 and moved into position for Mike Vanderjagt's 40-yard field goal. It was blocked, but
Tampa's Simeon Rice was penalized for leaping. Given a second
chance and 11 more yards, Vanderjagt hit a 29-yard field goal to
complete one of the great comebacks in NFL history.

"From then on, no matter what the score was, or how much we

were down, I always felt we would win," Dungy said. He says he has "so much respect for Tom," and how he's been able to change his style depending on the personnel around him. But he's still all-in on Peyton in the discussions with Harrison.

"The thing I always tell Rodney is, I can go back and show you Peyton Manning on the last drive beating the Patriots. Not all the time, but he did," Dungy said. "You can never show me Tom Brady on the last drive beating us. Anytime he had the ball and had to score to win, we won the game."

Polian and Dungy remain loyal to Manning, but Colts owner Jimmy Irsay burned some bridges in a 2013 interview with *USA Today*. It was Manning's second year in Denver, and Irsay felt that his departure and the arrival of Andrew Luck had worked out as planned for all concerned. But he lamented that Manning was able to secure only one ring in Indianapolis.

"We changed our model a little bit, because we wanted more than one of these," Irsay said, showing his ring. "Brady never had consistent numbers, but he has three of these. Pittsburgh had two, the Giants had two, Baltimore had two and we had one. That leaves you frustrated. You make the playoffs eleven times, and you're out in the first round seven out of eleven times. You have to love the Star Wars numbers from Peyton and Marvin and Reggie. Mostly, you love this." He again showed off his ring.

Days later, Irsay attempted to backtrack, saying he meant the Colts should have surrounded Manning with a better defense and special teams. Years later he said that if the Colts had won two Super Bowls, he would've said they should've won three.

"That was not a slap at Peyton at all. I know how competitive he is," Irsay said. "I know how all of us feel about not getting more than one. It's not a slap at anyone. It's just a fact. It's just something that we all wish we had the opportunity to have done. In the end, when you sit back and reflect on an era, it doesn't diminish all the incredible things that you've done. There was the championship and there wasn't the sort of bitter pill that Buffalo had to live with."

The 2010 Jets and the 2012 Ravens are the only teams to beat Manning and Brady back-to-back in the playoffs. Veteran safety Bernard Pollard was on the Baltimore team that beat the Broncos in double overtime in the divisional round and then dominated the Patriots the following week in the AFC championship game in Foxboro. Eliminating Brady and Manning one week apart was an impressive accomplishment.

"I don't really like either one of them. On the field, I dislike both of them," Pollard said. "A lot of people might hate me for this, but off the field I'm fans of both of them."

Brady is higher on the fear factor scale for a defense than Manning in Pollard's mind. "Ooh, that's tough, but I would rather see Peyton," he said. "Tom is a guy, he sees things, he understands things. They're both Hall of Famers. Beating the Broncos in the playoffs, that was fun, because we were able to outsmart Peyton. We didn't give up any big plays. Foxboro was a lot of fun, too. Brady is probably the most competitive guy I've ever played against. Between him and Philip Rivers. To beat that guy at home in the championship game, where we lost the year before, that was fun."

Pollard's place in Patriots history runs much deeper than helping the Ravens beat New England in the playoffs. As Brady was dropping back to pass halfway through the first quarter of the first game of the 2008 season against the Chiefs, he had his eyes fixed downfield. Pollard, then playing for Kansas City, was on the ground a few yards from Brady's legs. He lunged forward and hit Brady in his left knee.

Brady stayed down and then limped to the sidelines. It didn't take long for the diagnosis: torn ACL. Out for the season.

"Oh, man, I felt horrible," Pollard said. "Obviously, I heard everything when it popped. I felt it. I went to the sideline and the first thing I told [coach] Herm [Edwards] was, 'Hey, he's done.' I did not mean to do that. Man, I was kind of freaking out. As a player, we don't want to see that. You have some players who actually want to see guys get hurt like that. It was a crazy play."

Seven years earlier, in the second game of the season, Edwards had been the Jets coach when linebacker Mo Lewis crushed Drew Bledsoe as he neared the New York sideline. A sheared blood vessel in Bledsoe's chest nearly killed him. Brady took over and never gave the job back. Matt Cassel stepped in for Brady and led the Patriots to an 11–5 record, but they missed the playoffs. Cassel was traded after the season to the Chiefs, of all teams.

Pollard felt guilty about hurting Brady and some thought it was a dirty play. He indirectly sent get-well wishes to Brady but never apologized. "There was no reason to apologize," he said. "I didn't do anything wrong."

Former Ravens linebacker Ray Lewis created headlines when he told Sirius XM Radio "the only reason we know—I'm just being honest—who Tom Brady is, is because of the tuck rule," referring to the controversial fumble reversal in New England's victory over Oakland in the 2001 playoffs. "So now you've got to ask yourself: When did the legacy really start?"

He said the Patriots wouldn't have gone to the AFC championship without the tuck rule. "That's a fumble," Lewis said.

Brady didn't seem concerned. "Everyone has an opinion," he said. "I think Ray's a great player. He's a first-ballot Hall of Famer. I was fortunate enough to play against him."

Lewis looked foolish claiming Brady would be an unknown without the tuck rule and quickly came back to say his frustration was with the rule, which has since been removed, and he was not being critical of Brady. "I have immense respect for Tom Brady and everything he has achieved in this league," Lewis said. "He will go down as one of the all-time greats."

. . .

Phil Simms, the lead analyst for the NFL on CBS, meets with Brady and Manning before he does their games. One of them is very open. The other is guarded. Which is which?

"Now, who do you think?" Simms said. "I'll say, 'Peyton, what about so-and-so defense?' And then twenty minutes later, I'll say, 'Peyton, so what else is going on?' He just gets into it. I would say for both of them, being an analyst and being an ex-quarterback, going to talk to them, I would say I'm really conscious of being very prepared when I meet them."

Brady is not as talkative as Manning. As an extension of Belichick, he's not about to give away any secrets. "Not to say he holds back, but I think that's just part of their organization and how they are," Simms said. "It doesn't bother me. I get enough."

Manning was twenty-two when he came into the NFL, but Simms said his greatest attribute was, "He was a thirty-five-year-old man in his head. He was one of those kids that when he was ten years old, when the adults all sat around the table and the kids went and played, he probably sat at the table and wanted to hear what the adults were saying."

He is revered around the league. Players and coaches gravitate toward him. He's held court at the hotel at the Pro Bowl in Honolulu as players and coaches stop by for a chat. One year Simms was there to broadcast the game and sat down for what he intended to be a quick lunch by the pool on the Friday before the game. Manning soon joined him. They began talking and Belichick walked by. Manning invited him to sit down. Then it was Sean Payton. Then Shannon Sharpe. "About eight hours later, we are still there," Simms said. "He kept going down the line of people and had them sit down. It was hilarious."

Manning is not a trash-talker. Brady is one of the best. Sherman says he loves Brady's game and demeanor. "As a competitor, as a player in this league, love him. I relish competitors like that. You love his fire for his team to win games," he said.

Brady was once fined $10,000 for kicking Ravens safety Ed Reed in the thigh as Brady was sliding with his right leg up in a playoff game. He texted Reed to apologize. It's not often quarterbacks get fined for chippy play. Sherman got into some trash-talking with Brady during a regular-season game in Seattle in 2012. Brady told him to come to see him after the Patriots won the game. Seattle scored two fourth-quarter touchdowns to win it, and Sherman got in Brady's face. He then posted a picture of the postgame meeting with the caption "u mad bro?" Brady got even in the Super Bowl two years later, but he stayed away from Sherman's side of the field.

On a December night in 2010, Brady went too far with the New York Jets. After he threw a 1-yard touchdown pass to Aaron Hernandez on the first play of the fourth quarter, making it 38–3 on the way to a 45–3 victory, the Jets felt Brady was a little too excited about a meaningless touchdown. They thought he was pointing to their sideline after the score.

"Just Brady being Brady," Ryan said.

The next day, Ryan grabbed a football—which he claimed was a game ball—and marched his team to the side of the practice field and buried the ball. It's an old trick Belichick once pulled with the Patriots. Ryan was steamed about the 42-point loss.

"That's getting your ass kicked," he would say years later looking back on that game. "I don't expect the guy to feel sorry for me, but trying to rub my nose in it a little bit? That's why I said we are going to get them back. I told the team, 'We're going to get these fuckers back at their place in six weeks.'"

The Jets beat the Colts in the wild-card game, setting up the rematch in Foxboro. Ryan had his players so fired up early in the week, there was a fear they would peak in practice and have nothing left for the game. Five days before kickoff, cornerback Antonio Cromartie was standing by himself at his locker as the media-access period for the day had about ten minutes remaining. Ryan's "Brady being Brady" comment was still in Cromartie's head. His distaste for Brady produced one of the great responses in NFL history. All it took was one question from a columnist from the *New York Daily News:* What do you think of Tom Brady?

"An asshole. Fuck him," Cromartie said.

Brady's response was classic. "I've been called worse," he said. "I'm sure there's a long list of people that feel that way."

The Jets had the last word. They beat the Patriots 28–21, sacked Brady five times, and hit him hard many other times. The cover shot in *Sports Illustrated* pictured Jets linebacker Calvin Pace pummeling Brady. For years, that was prominently displayed on the wall in Ryan's office.

Brady vs. Manning has been great for the NFL. It's been great for Brady and Manning. They have pushed each other to the very top of the heap of the all-time best quarterbacks. They have needed each other and been there for each other. They are Magic and Bird, Wilt and Russell, Ali and Frazier, Palmer and Nicklaus, but even better.

They are great rivals. They are great friends.

"I have great respect for him," Manning said.

"It's nice to have a peer that you can really rely on, you know is completely trustworthy," Brady said.

Friends say Manning might own an NFL team one day. Brady is interested in running a franchise. It would be fitting if they can work together and finally stop trying to beat each other.

No introduction will be necessary.

ACKNOWLEDGMENTS

I had known Peyton Manning since the day before he was drafted, covered the first game of his career against his idol Dan Marino in 1998, and, with his brother Eli playing in New York, had seen him quite a bit over the years. He knew me by name. He knows everybody by name. I had been around Tom Brady as well, covering Jets-Patriots games and being at his Super Bowls, but didn't have much luck the first time we tried to meet face-to-face.

It was the summer of 2002, after his first Super Bowl victory. The Patriots set up a lunchtime interview for me to sit down with Brady at training camp at Bryant College in Smithfield, Rhode Island. He was on a tight schedule. Me too. I waited and waited and saw the window to interview him before practice closing and still no Brady. I knew this wasn't going to work.

His meetings ran right through his lunch break between two-a-day practices. I had other commitments and could not stick around until the afternoon practice was over, as the Patriots suggested, but drove back to New York. My phone rang around six p.m. "Hey, this is Tom Brady," he said. "Sorry about what happened today."

We had a long talk. I got what I needed for my column for the *New York Daily News,* and soon after, we had a head-nod relationship. When he saw me in big groups around him at training camp or at the Super Bowl, we would nod at each other. When I wrote the headline-grabbing story about Antonio Cromartie calling Brady an asshole before the Jets played the Patriots in the 2010 playoffs, I knew he wasn't really that way. But then again, I never played against him.

After Brady addressed the New England media at the opening of training camp in 2013, I walked over to speak to him alone. I told him about my book project and asked if we could get together. "No problem," he said. "Set it up with Stacey. Tell him we spoke about it."

Stacey James, the Patriots vice president of media and community relations, is one of the best in the business and a good friend. I left it up to James to let me know when Brady could work me into his schedule. We tried for late in camp but couldn't find a day. The Patriots bye week didn't work either. The next opening came in November.

James wanted me to have as much time with Brady as possible and came up with a plan. He knows Brady very well and was concerned that if we just sat down in a meeting room at the facility, when otherwise Brady would be on his way home to see his kids, he wouldn't be able to give me quality time. He suggested I ride with Brady from Foxboro to downtown Boston, where Brady was living at the time, and with usual Boston traffic, I would probably get close to an hour. I hesitated at first. Would he really be able to give thoughtful answers while he was driving? Yes, James said, he always does his conference calls with the visiting media as he's driving home.

So when Brady exited Gillette Stadium after a quarterbacks meeting into a brutally cold New England mid-November late afternoon and we walked together toward his car in the players' parking lot, my journey to tell the story of Brady vs. Manning was officially under way.

"Ready?" Brady asked as I met him leaving the Patriots facility. "My car is over there."

He told great stories, he was insightful and forthcoming, and the ride went way too fast. When we reached downtown and were stopped at a traffic light, he gave me his cell phone number and e-mail address for any follow-up questions. He asked me questions about the process of writing a book. He always looks you in the eye when he's speaking. Except when he's driving, of course.

The funniest part of the trip came when he dropped me off at a hotel so I could catch a taxi to take me back to my car at the stadium—it was a ninety-dollar ride, by the way. As we pulled up to the hotel, we shook hands as the valet attendant came to the driver's side, asking if Brady needed to have his car parked. He said, "No thanks," and drove away.

I asked the guy if he could help me get a cab. He had a startled look on his face. "Was that . . . ?" he asked.

"Yes."

The meeting with Manning the following June was more routine. Patrick Smyth, the Broncos' excellent vice president of media relations, told Manning that Brady had spoken to me, and he recommended that it would be a good idea to also have his voice in the book. I went to Denver and spent some time with Manning in the Broncos facility after practice. He was typical Manning. His answers had depth and substance. He was thoughtful. He had gotten over being mad at me for asking him minutes after the Super Bowl loss to the Seahawks if he was embarrassed. Oh well, I thought it was a good question.

I want to thank James and Smyth for setting up the most important interviews for the book. Those are what I call two-tape-recorder interviews. "Double fisted," Patriots owner Robert Kraft said when I placed two recorders at the breakfast table when I met him at the Plaza Hotel in Manhattan. There's always the chance my digital recorder will malfunction. The odds that two would fail me at the same time were minimal. The interviews with Brady and Manning would be irreplaceable. I took no chances. They both worked.

I want to thank Tom and Peyton for their cooperation.

Aaron Salkin, the Patriots director of media relations, provided me with key statistics from the Brady-Manning rivalry. He even offered to pick me up after Brady dropped me off at the Boston hotel and take me back to Foxboro and save me the ninety dollars. Of course, by the time he told me this, I was already in the taxi.

Kraft and Colts owner Jimmy Irsay were very gracious with their time. There was one awkward moment with Irsay. I did the interview with him on the phone at the time that he was having legal troubles, in June 2014. We agreed that our conversation would be confined to Manning and football and that I would not ask him about his recent arrest on misdemeanor charges of driving while intoxicated and four felony counts of possession of a controlled substance—prescription pills. I agreed to the ground rules.

Halfway through the interview, an ESPN alert popped up on my cell phone. The state of Indiana had just suspended Irsay's driver's license for one year. The reporter in me wanted to ask him about it. But I had given my word and stuck to it.

My travels took me to a breakfast meeting with Tony Dungy, a trip to Phil Simms's house, and a Starbucks in Rhode Island to meet Dan Koppen. I had several long talks with Archie Manning and Tom Brady Sr., the patriarchs of the families. They provided me with great family photos. I had lunch with Ernie Accorsi, a former NFL general manager and one of the foremost football historians. I met with Scott Pioli when he was working for NBC. I had a long talk with Drew Bledsoe.

I went to Ann Arbor to meet former Michigan coach Lloyd

Carr to ask him to explain how the greatest quarterback in NFL history had such a hard time getting on the field at The Big House. Thanks to Dave Ablauf, the associate athletic director for communications at Michigan, for getting me in touch with Carr. Bill Hofmeier of ESPN and Chris McCloskey of NBC worked hard to set up interviews with their football talent who had Manning-Brady connections. My buddy Drew Kaliski, the producer of *The NFL Today* on CBS, sent me the video of an excellent interview Bill Cowher did with Bill Belichick.

Of course, I want to thank Nate Roberson, my editor at Crown, for his guidance and patience. He was always encouraging and knew deadlines were just a suggestion. He made this book better.

I spent many hours writing at Old Stone Trattoria in Chappaqua, New York, and I appreciate the hospitality of Angelo, who owns the place, and Hector and Marta, who know me so well they didn't even have to ask what I would like to eat. As Peyton sang in the Nationwide commercial, "Chicken parm, you taste so good." It was the perfect place when I needed a change of venue. Risten Clarke, as part of a high school internship, provided valuable research.

My wife, Allison, my best friend, pushed me every step of the way, even when we went to Aruba for one week right after Brady won his fourth Super Bowl. She insisted I write a thousand words every evening after we came off the beach and before we went to dinner. That worked for one day. My oldest daughter, Michelle, a nutritionist, made sure I ate only healthy snacks during the writing process. I got hooked on Skinny Pop, the world's greatest popcorn. Michelle felt strongly both ways in the Brady-Manning comparison. My daughter Emily is incredibly knowledgeable about football, is an excellent writer, and did some editing for me. She cast her ballot, too, in the Brady-Manning debate. It's a secret. My son Andrew was my number-one assistant. He is also a huge Jets fan, and that means he's always hated the Patriots. He's smart, and being a sport management major at Brady's alma mater, he decided the book would be more compelling if the Patriots beat the Seahawks in Super Bowl XLIX. As much as it hurt this kid who bleeds green, he texted me the morning of the Super Bowl, "I'm rooting for Brady."

Finally, I want my parents to always know, even though I can no longer tell them in person, how much I appreciate the tremendous sacrifices they made to put me in the best position to succeed. I miss you both every day.

INDEX